More Advance Praise for *Managing Online Forums*

"Patrick O'Keefe has been building online communities for nearly ten years. He's got more expertise and experience than anyone else when it comes to leveraging the power of community. Read this book and you'll save time and frustration. Best of all, you'll get results."

—Zack Urlocker, Executive Vice President, MySQL

"This book is great advice for anyone managing an online community or thinking of creating one. *Managing Online Forums* is full of practical, specific advice from someone who has obviously had more than just a few tours of duty in the online trenches. O'Keefe covers all aspects of the job, providing many words of warning and wisdom along the way. This book should be required reading for all online community managers."

—April "CuppaJo" Burba, Community Manager, NCsoft

"More than a guide to growing your forum, this book is a true experience on how to build a real, lasting online community. Insightful, educational, and well-presented, Patrick doesn't hold anything back. I highly recommend this book for all those serious about starting and maintaining an online community."

—David Askaripour, Founder, Mind Petals Organization

"This is a fabulous read that I'm sure everyone will be posting and blogging about. The comprehensive templates for your user agreement, member contacts, and policies alone make it worth the price of the book. *Managing Online Forums* should be a reference manual for every administrator in the world of virtual communities."

—Cynthia Mosher, Webmaster and Administrator, *Mothering Magazine* and MotheringDotCommune Forums

"I found the book *Managing Online Forums* insightful, easy to read, and knowledgeable about forum sites. I would highly recommend it to anyone interested in learning more about Internet forum sites or running them. It's useful information and a great marketing tool for any product; a must read!"

—Debbie Hammond, CEO, ClockWork Entertainment

"Most people learn community management the hard way—by firsthand experience. With this book, you can learn how to take care of many situations before they arise. I wish I had had it when starting out years ago."

—Jeremy Rogers, coauthor, *Building Online Communities with phpBB 2*

"I've run online communities for many years, and *Managing Online Forums* opened my eyes to many things I could do better. It's required reading for novices and experienced administrators alike."

> —Jared W. Smith, coauthor, *Building Online Communities with Drupal, phpBB, and WordPress*

"*Managing Online Forums* is the best guide of its kind. The hands-on approach serves both the novice and the veteran administrator alike. It is an easy book to read, regardless of one's technical literacy, and deserves a spot on the bookshelf of any current or future community admin."

> —Jonathan Bailey, Webmaster and author, *Plagiarism Today*

"This was a brilliant read and I highly recommend *Managing Online Forums* for both new as well as veteran forum administrators. Patrick has distilled the essence of what it takes to run a vital community without getting mired in the technology or overly psychological. I have been successfully running the world's largest community for Scuba Diving for years and I still learned a lot! You can bet that I will be rereading this as well as having my entire staff read it. It deals with real-world scenarios, and it's obvious Patrick writes from his experiences as well as his heart."

> —Pete Murray, owner, ScubaBoard.com and InterMedia Publications, Inc.

"You can never know enough about managing a forum, from how to handle your staff, to ensuring the users are happy, to making money! Yes, the last chapter is about making money, but you can't do that without doing everything else first! This book is most definitely for everyone—seasoned or new—you will learn an awful lot. It is written in an easy, concise way that allows you to read from front to back or dip in and out for something specific. This is a great book that I will continue to dip into."

> —Sarah Large, Administrator, SitePoint Forum

"Patrick O'Keefe has run one of the most prominent Yankees fan sites online, and he knows of what he writes. *Managing Online Forums*—like his YanksBlog.com—is full of insight and information, well-written, and very deserving of a wide readership."

> —Matthew McGough, writer/legal consultant, *Law & Order,* and author, *Bat Boy: Coming of Age with the New York Yankees*

MANAGING
ONLINE FORUMS

MANAGING
ONLINE FORUMS

Everything You Need to Know to
Create and Run Successful
Community Discussion Boards

Patrick O'Keefe

AMACOM

American Management Association
New York • Atlanta • Brussels • Chicago • Mexico City • San Francisco
Shanghai • Tokyo • Toronto • Washington, D.C.

This publication is designed to provide accurate and authoritative information in regard to the subject matter covered. It is sold with the understanding that the publisher is not engaged in rendering legal, accounting, or other professional service. If legal advice or other expert assistance is required, the services of a competent professional person should be sought.

Various names used by companies to distinguish their software and other products can be claimed as trademarks. AMACOM uses such names throughout this book for editorial purposes only, with no intention of trademark violation. All such software or product names are in initial capital letters or ALL CAPITAL letters. Individual companies should be contacted for complete information regarding trademarks and registration. See page viii for a list of registered trademarks used in this book.

Library of Congress Cataloging-in-Publication Data

O'Keefe, Patrick, 1984-
    Managing online forums : everything you need to know to create and run successful community discussion boards / Patrick O'Keefe.
        p.   cm.
    Includes index.
    ISBN 978-0-8144-0197-2 (pbk.)
    1. Online social networks—Management.   2. Internet—Social aspects.   I. Title.
HM851.O547   2008
004.693—dc22

                                                                    2007052950

Printing number

10   9   8   7   6   5   4   3   2   1

This is for everyone who stood beside me

when it really mattered,

when tough decisions had to be made.

Like when I had to ban . . .

well, you know who.

Trademarked terms in this book:

Contents

Chapter 6. Banning Users and Dealing with Chaos   181

Foreword

Community is the cornerstone of our civilization. So it should come as no surprise that the World Wide Web has exploded into communities, large and small. While they may vary in every conceivable way, at their core, each one is just a gathering of people sitting around a campfire, telling each other stories. It was around just such a campfire that I met Patrick, and so it seems fitting that I'm here introducing his first book, which just so happens to be about managing your own community.

Building your own community can be one of the most enjoyable journeys you can take as a Webmaster. You are giving people a place to meet and connect, share their ideas and thoughts, and build relationships that grow out of common experiences. Building a community is about creating a fun, safe place that encourages expression and conversation.

As a professional programmer myself, I've always found the technical aspects of running a community pretty simple. But if you aren't a programmer then you and Patrick have a lot in common! He couldn't program his way out of a paper bag. So it's a good thing that you don't need to know how to program to run your own community. Inside the pages of this book, Patrick gives you great insight into all the skills you'll need to get up and running and manage your community. This includes managing users, an area where you are likely to spend most of your time and a subject I've learned a lot about from Patrick over the years.

Community without leadership is, at best, just a bunch of noise, and, at its worst, it can get downright scary. Anyone can be taught to lead, and Patrick does a fine job in this book of imparting what he's learned from both running his own communities and being on staff at others. But some people are natural leaders. It's something they are born with that inspires people to gravitate toward them. Patrick is one of those people.

Leading a community is about making choices. They won't all be the easy choices, but Patrick helps guide you to make the best choice you can and move on. Whether you are looking for ways to make money or handle a problem, this book will give you solid advice on just about everything you might run into.

Having been both member and staff at many of Patrick's forums and communities and someone who's run a good number of his own communities, I don't hesitate to tell you that Patrick has shared with you what usually takes years of experience to gain on your own. Whether you are new to community administration or a seasoned admin, you can learn a lot from his experience. I hope you enjoy the book as much as I did.

Chrispian H. Burks
Binary Publishing, Inc
http://www.binarypublishing.com

Acknowledgments

Thank you to everyone who has supported me. First and foremost, my family: Mom (Wanda), Dad (Patrick), my brothers (Sean and Trent), and my entire family, immediate and extended. In addition to everyone who has supported me, I dedicate this book to my grandfather, Pa (Patrick), and to Great Grandma Burt, both of whom passed away while I was working on it.

Thank you to everyone who has served as a staff member on my team. Great staff members are essential to great communities, and I've been blessed to have many kind, helpful, and dedicated people who have assisted me in achieving the goals that were set for the communities that I have managed. This includes Adam Polselli, Billy Sauls, Brandon Eley, Brandon Levan, Brian Walker, Bryan Downing, Chris Wodicka, Chrispian Burks, Daniel Carroll, Danielle Williams, Dimitri Seitz, Doug North, Greg Heinisch, Eric Miller, Frank Clemens, Heidi Wilmott, James Dasher, Jared Smith, Jeremy Rogers, Josh Ulfers, Joshua Pohlman, Justin Lieber, Kiel Spencer, Keith McLaughlin, Ken (Spike), Kevin McDaniel, Laurie Snow, Marc Philpott, Nate Spencer, Nick Hammond, Pat McQuinn, Paul Woodland, Quiff Boy, Ramona Iftode, Richard Fitzgerald, Ryan Zieno, Sam Unruh, Scott Stubblefield, Scott Shepard, Seamus Molloy, Shawn Morrison, Tammy McBeth, Tanner Smith, Thomas Rutter, Trey Jenke, Vincent Grouls, and Wayne Clarke, among others.

Thank you to all of the members who have openly supported and continue to support the communities that I manage. You are a big part of what makes it all worth it.

Thank you to Brandon Eley, Bryan Downing, Chrispian Burks, Jared Smith, and Stephan Segraves for the help, feedback, and encouragement and for sharing in my excitement. It has meant a lot to me. Thank you also to Chrispian for writing the foreword.

Thank you to everyone at AMACOM for your work, expertise, support, and patience. I've loved working with all of you and look forward to what's next. To the great team of editors that worked on this project, thank you for helping the book to reach it's full potential. Jacqueline Flynn, for believing in the subject and giving me a chance. Erika Spelman, for her constant attention and guidance. Ashley Hamilton and Christina Orem, for making a noticeable, dramatic impact in the quality of my writing. Jennifer Holder and Cathleen Ouderkirk, for their support and contributions. Thank you to Johnson Design for the jacket design.

Thank you to Studio B and the Salkind Literary Agency and to my awesome agent, Neil Salkind, for his excellence, knowledge, and dedication. Thank you to Jeremy Wright for introducing me to Neil when I had finally had enough of pitching it to publishers myself and decided to hire an agent (best decision ever!).

Thank you to Alex Belth, Andrew Tatum, Anthony Violante, April Burba, Cynthia Mosher, David Askaripour, David Williams, Debbie Hammond, James Fintel, James Varghese, Jared Smith, Jeremy Rogers, Jonathan Bailey, Keith Custodio, Kyle Hunt, Lee LeFever, Matthew McGough, Michael Singer, Pete Murray, Ray Angel, Reuben Regier, Ryan Leslie, Sarah Large, Tom Tollefson, and Zack Urlocker for their help and support.

Thank you to Ted Sindzinski for sharing his incredible knowledge with all of us. Thank you to Jonathan Bailey for reviewing portions of the book. Thank you to Sarah Large and Keith McLaughlin for allowing me to use examples from the communities that they manage.

Thank you to both Georgina Laidlaw for encouraging me to write and SitePoint for publishing my articles and giving me an outlet in which to grow.

Thank you to everyone who showed me what not to do—how not to act. Thank you for showing me what I did not want to become. Thank you to all of the idiots out there that I had to deal with. I learned a lot from you and I share it in this book with the hope that, when you bother the next person, he or she will be ready for you.

This book is the result of my experience with people. Lots of people. Virtually every staff member that I have ever had has changed me and improved me. The same can be said for many of the people who have visited my communities. It is in dealing with every one of these people that my beliefs, my theories, my strategies, and my mind have been formed and are now emptied onto these pages. There are many people who have encouraged me to write this book and who have given me confidence, feedback, and support. There are other people that have served as inspiration for me as well, such as administrators under whom I have served. Everyone who has and continues to support me: Thank you for your help, your support, your encouragement, and, perhaps most important, for your friendship.

Introduction: Is This Book for You?

I wrote this book for anyone who wants to run an online community—or already does. As the administrator, you are the person who has to lead the community, take it to the next level, make the tough decisions, take the heat, deal with the people, manage the staff, and keep the community running smoothly on all fronts.

This book targets those who are looking to maintain a professional, well-run operation. For the most part, I try to steer clear of technical issues, such as your particular administration-control panel, code editing, and custom programming. That's not what this book is for. I do discuss concepts and ideas that may require those things, but whether you have the knowledge or will have someone do it for you is up to you. Although I talk about an array of related subjects, this is a management book first and foremost.

I've been managing communities since 2000. Of course, I wish I knew then what I know now. That's what they all say, though. But that's what this book is: what I know now. And if you are just starting out, this book allows you to start off with what I know now, to get a head start. It will help you lay the groundwork for an excellent community and give you a solid base of knowledge to grow from and build upon.

If you're knee-deep in community management and have already created a successful community, this book can help you hone your skills and become a better administrator. The best always get better. They never stop learning or stop improving.

What you take from the book is up to you. At the very least, it will give you something to think about, opening up the opportunity for improvement.

Although this book is certainly about community forums, many of its principles and strategies can apply to other types of communities, including groups (such as MSN Groups, Yahoo! Groups, Google Groups, etc.), chat rooms, blogs (comment moderation), social networking sites, and more.

A book like this is never complete. There are so many things to talk about, and there will always be emerging issues. However, I believe that certain principles are enduring and I hope that my management philosophies, which I have used for years, will remain strong. This book will get you on your way to becoming a competent manager of communities, making it easier for you to tackle whatever tomorrow brings.

How This Book Is Organized

In order to get a general understanding of the content that lays ahead, let's take a look at how it's organized. There is definitely some overlap among sections, but I hope you will find that it's organized in a way that makes sense.

Chapter 1: Laying the Groundwork

Before you begin developing your community, there are some things that you should think about and decide so that you can know who or what your community is going to be. This chapter will help you pursue those goals in the best manner possible.

Chapter 2: Developing Your Community

Success starts from the ground up, including the initial decisions and development. This chapter talks about the physical and technical aspects of your community and walks you through some of the important things to give thought to before you open your doors. Or, if you've already launched, these are things you might want to consider adjusting in order to enhance your offering.

Chapter 3: Developing Guidelines

Guidelines are essential to any professionally managed, well-run community. Without guidelines, you are unable to maintain order. They tell people what your community is all about and what is expected of them. And, when it comes time to correct the actions of a member, they give you something to refer to.

Chapter 4: Promoting Your Community

The best online community in the world will be a bore if nobody knows—or cares—about it. In this chapter, I touch on some of the more popular means of bringing people to your community and letting them know that you exist.

Chapter 5: Managing Your Staff

Your staff members will play a vital role in the performance of your site. They make your life easier and they help you to accomplish the goals of the community. In order to do that, however, they need to know what to do and how to do it. It's important that your setup gives them this while encouraging them to work as a team and maintain an open line of communication with you so that issues that need attention get attention.

Chapter 6: Banning Users and Dealing with Chaos

Part of managing a community is dealing with spammers, idiots, and people who just can't seem to follow your guidelines. Of course, it gets worse—there are people out there who will actually want to do harm to your community. In this chapter, I talk about how to deal with them while keeping your community on topic and on point.

Chapter 7: Creating a Good Environment

This chapter features a number of suggestions about how to encourage a positive, friendly, productive atmosphere in your community.

Chapter 8: Keeping It Interesting

Here I talk about a selection of ideas and methods to bring people back to your community and keep them in tune with it. Sometimes, people will forget that you're there. Remind them.

Chapter 9: Making Money

Whether you want to pay your bills or, perhaps, become wealthy, chances are you are interested in generating some revenue from your site. In this chapter, I discuss many of the most popular ways to do so, including display advertising, paid memberships, and more.

Appendix A: Online Resources

Just as it sounds, this appendix highlights many related, useful online resources.

Appendix B: Blank General Templates

Although you should craft your own to fit your needs, here you'll find some general guideline and contact template examples that you can adjust as you see fit.

Appendix C: Glossary

This section of the book defines various terms for reference purposes.

Communities, Forums, and Boards

The definition of *community* in this book is "community forums." This is a book about managing online community forums. So, when I say *community*, it means the same as *forums* and vice versa.

Book Website

This book has a companion website, maintained by the author. Find it at http://www.managingonlineforums.com. This website features a blog with book-related news and updates, a sample community with physical examples of a few things I talk about in the book, reader testimonials and reviews, an errata, links to online resources mentioned in the book, and more.

After You've Read the Book

After you've had the opportunity to read the book and give it some thought, I'd love to hear your thoughts. If you found a mistake or a typo, I definitely want to hear from you as well. You can contact me directly via e-mail at patrick@ifroggy.com. If you have any questions about community management or would like some advice, I'll do my best to answer those as well.

CHAPTER 1

Laying the Groundwork

"The dictionary is the only place that success comes before work. Hard work is the price we must pay for success. I think you can accomplish anything if you're willing to pay the price."

—VINCE LOMBARDI

To start your community off right, you must have your mind in the right place. You should know what your community is, what you are trying to accomplish, what you'll need to do to accomplish it, and you need to ensure that you can provide the community with the stability that it needs to flourish long into the future. This chapter gives you an idea of what to expect and will help you to make some of those important, initial decisions.

Fundamental Decisions

Before launching your community, inevitably there are some decisions to make or, at least, some things that you should think about that will help determine your community's existence. Some of them will affect most everything that you do from this point forward, from decisions you make to any work that you do.

What Will Your Community Cover?

Although a general, discuss-basically-anything community is always an option, chances are that you want to focus on some specific subject or niche, even if it is fairly general.

Whether it's programming (or just a specific programming language), sports (or just football), writing (or just nonfiction), you'll need to determine what subject will be the focus of your community. You don't want to try to be everything to everyone. You want to do what you do—and do it well.

Whatever the subject, it is usually not important that you be an expert on it or even know it all that well—the most important thing is that you are committed to it and to your community.

For instance, I own KarateForums.com (an active martial arts discussion community) and PhotoshopForums.com (an active Photoshop help and discussion community). I've never done any martial arts, and when I started PhotoshopForums.com, I had never even used Photoshop (a kind user sent me a—yes, legal—copy of Photoshop Elements a bit later). Again, you don't need to know about the subject matter as long as you are committed to the idea. I started these communities for various reasons. Besides random revelations, I sensed a need, saw that a good domain name was available, and thought that I could do it better than anyone else—and not just talk about it but actually do it.

You can surround yourself with smart people (or people smarter than you) on your staff of whom you can ask questions relevant to the subject of your community, on those (perhaps rare) occasions where it will be needed. Don't get me wrong, being passionate about the subject of your community can be very helpful and may help ensure your passion for the community itself (and, as such, your long-term interest and enjoyment in your work, which is very important).

But, I'll say it again: Have passion for the community. If you have it, you can succeed. If you have passion for the subject, but no passion for the community or for running the community, you really don't have very much at all and you're in for a struggle.

Whom Do You Want to Attract?

Even a community that is for "everyone" really isn't for everyone because by nature, a community for everyone will turn certain people off. Make sense? What type of users are you after?

This doesn't have to be that specific. But visualizing it can help you to make decisions and plot a course. For instance, you can simply target anyone interested in having a baby—or you can target pregnant mothers under the age of twenty-five. You can target baseball fans—or fans of the New York Yankees. You can target computer users—or you can target users of a certain operating system. Does your community target a specific age group or gender? Are you looking for users who are experts in your subject matter? Or beginners? Attempting to bring them both together? Whomever you target, you'll want to develop your community with them in mind.

You will probably (and naturally) attract people outside of your targeted audience, and chances are that'll be perfectly OK with you. But having your primary audience or audiences in mind will help you to make appropriate decisions about your community.

What Will the Benefits of Your Community Be?

How will you attract people to your community? What will make them come? And stay? These can be few or many—tangible or intangible. You can help people or provide them with useful information, you can provide a friendly atmosphere or an exclusive atmosphere, you can give them direct access to your company—you can do a lot of things. The things that make you interesting, unique, different, and special—those will be your key benefits.

Assuming it exists, you can learn from your "competition." What are they doing well? What are they doing poorly that you can improve on? What are they missing that you can provide? How are they different from you? The limitations of your competition can be inspirational.

How Will You Support the Community Financially?

Before you jump headfirst into anything, you should think about the money it will take to support your community and keep it online. Sit down and figure out how much it will cost you to keep the community running at an optimal level for the foreseeable future, and plan for that figure to increase. Simply put: Will you be able to support it?

If you would like the community to pay for itself or even turn a profit (or a great profit), how are you going to do that? Advertising? Affiliate programs? Donations? Will you eventually embrace some sort of subscription model where people pay for enhanced options in your community? Chapter 9 will assist you in your efforts.

The bottom line is that you do not want to start your community only to realize in a few months that you are not comfortable with the amount of money that it takes to maintain it.

What Is Your Situation?

There are generally four different ways to assume charge of a community:

1. Create a brand-new stand-alone community.

2. Launch a brand-new community and content site at the same time.

3. Launch a brand-new community as an addition to an existing content site.

4. Purchase or take over an existing community.

You can approach all four situations similarly, of course, but there are some additional considerations that will require your attention in order to get the most out of your situation.

Create a Brand-New Stand-Alone Community

This is a community that stands on its own. You will not have the advantage of directly linking with an existing, established website (not your own, at least) that will be able to send you traffic. The primary (possibly only) draws are the forums themselves. This is, perhaps, the most challenging scenario of the four as far as getting going is concerned. But that shouldn't scare you—this is the way that many, many forums started off, including mine.

If you do have a high-quality product, it may be possible for you to partner with an active and established content site where you will become the site's community. For more details on this, check out chapter 4.

Launch a Brand-New Community and Content Site at the Same Time

Having an active content site to go right along with your community can definitely help to get your community going. Mainly, it will give you more to discuss, bring more people to the community, and keep them on your entire website (content and community) longer. This is if it is active. And it's important that it be. You'll want to have writers (or one active writer, at least) lined up before you launch to ensure that you will have a steady flow of content. In general, the more active it is, the better off that you will be.

You should integrate the content site and the community as much as you tastefully can. For example, let's say that you have some sort of articles site.

One simple way to integrate it with your community would be to display the five most recently published articles from your content site somewhere in your community. Give your authors special distinction in your community so that they will stand out from the crowd. Get as many of your authors as possible to participate in and (if applicable) answer questions in your community. On your content site, be sure to include a visible link to your community. On your index page (or every page, if it's reasonable), you could display the five or ten most recently active threads from your community. On all of your articles, be sure to include a "Discuss" link of sorts where users can access your forums in order to discuss the articles that they are viewing. Here are some ways that this link can be set up:

- If your system allows users from your content site to go right to your community (logged in or anonymous—logged in is probably the way to go and would make junk far less frequent) and reply to a special thread that was automatically created for an article, great. The first post in such a thread should be a link to the article. This helps people find out what others are talking about, allowing them to more easily contribute. This brings more attention to both sections of your site. Some content-management systems and/or community software may be able to make this happen. If not, this feature will likely require custom programming. If you can swing it, it's the ideal solution because the seamless integration encourages users to participate. SitePoint (http://www.sitepoint.com) has a setup like this.

- Start a thread (manually) in your community for each article that you publish and then hard-code a link to the thread in the article. Obviously, it's better to automate this process (as outlined above), otherwise it adds to the time required to maintain your site (and may create problems down the road if, for example, you change software and the URLs change). Regardless, it will definitely encourage people to participate.

- Create some sort of static link to your community's index page or a specific forum that relates to the article. For example, if your content management system (CMS) allows a specific discussion URL to be associated with all articles in a given category of your CMS, you could make it so that your individual discussion forums match your content categories (in one way or another). Further, you could make it so that all "Discuss" links for all articles in a given content category link to the forum most closely related to that category. For instance, you could have a baseball section on your content site and all of your baseball articles would then include a link to your community's baseball forum. Failing that, simply include a direct link to your community's index page. What can I say? It's better than nothing!

- If your content section has a really simple syndication (RSS) feed (or something of that nature), you could achieve half of the effect described in the first method by setting up what is commonly referred to as a "news-posting bot" to automatically post threads in your community from your feed(s). You could have a feed for each content category (if necessary) and have the bot post items from that feed into the most appropriate forum. Taking from the earlier example, you'd have an RSS feed that is just articles in your baseball section, and the bot would post those items in your baseball forum in your community. You can set it so that an excerpt of the article posts with a link to the full article—or you could just post a link to the full article.

  The point is that if you have an articles section and you have a community, you should integrate them in every way that makes sense. They can help each other. Obviously, some methods are more effective than others, but even if you go with the simplest form of integration, it's that much more exposure for your community—and your content site—and is definitely worth it.

Launch a Brand-New Community as an Addition to an Existing Content Site

This is where you have an already established (and hopefully reasonably successful, at least) content site and want to expand it by adding a community. If all goes as it should, it will enhance your content, keep your users at your site longer, give your site the opportunity to gather more of a following, and allow you to make more money.

The same ideas about content site and community integration apply here as well. Having an established content site gives you a leg up in that you will already have some loyal users and some traffic coming in. Once you integrate your community and your content site, users will find your community and potentially want to become members.

Regardless of your situation, it's definitely important that you maintain some sort of constant activity in your community so that you can keep the users that you will have at the beginning. It may just be you and these users talking things out for quite a while, but it is important that it stays active. Even if it is just you, your brother, and his friend talking, pretty much any activity is good activity.

Purchase or Take Over an Existing Community

This is where you've bought (or taken over) an existing community. This situation has its own challenges that require your attention.

Before buying a community, you should consider where it is, what your goals for it are and/or would be, and how far the community is from those goals. In doing so, you are trying to figure out how much work it will take to get it running properly, and this will help you to determine whether it is worth it, all things considered.

For example, my communities are based on a very firm foundation of respect and are family friendly where the subject matter allows them to be. If a community allows its users to get away with being disrespectful, vulgar, or otherwise inappropriate, it is probably not worth it for me to buy it because of the effort that it will take for me to turn it around. It will end up being a waste of my time and my money. I would never just let a community run as it has, if I know of a better way or I'm not comfortable with how it's running, simply so that I can make a buck.

You should care (and make it clear to your members that you care) about people more than numbers. When people learn that you bought the site, they will probably have doubts about your intentions, as they should, perhaps. They may think that you are in it just to take a profit and that you don't really care about the community itself. After all, you did just spend the money to buy it, so you need to make that money back and then some, probably. There is nothing wrong with money being a motivator, but it cannot be the only one. You must want to manage the community, want to work hard, and want to be successful.

So you need to put these thoughts to bed and reassure people that you are there to make the community as great as it can be. Introduce yourself, explain your background and your aim, speak openly, answer questions in a kind and respectful way, and make yourself available. Be upfront and honest. People will get behind you, get away from you, or be indifferent, but at least they will know you and have a better idea of what to expect. They may not like what you want to do, but the truth is better than uncertainty.

Make sure that you make a great effort to work with the current staff members. Remember that they may have a great deal of respect for the previous owner/administrator and be sure that you respect that. Get to know one another and work to get everyone on the same page. Explain your beliefs and hopes for the site. Try to ask them for their thoughts if you feel they would be valuable. And when you do, be sure to listen and respond appropriately. I was once a staff member at a site that was bought by a person who annoyed me. Why did he annoy me? Because he asked us for feedback and then appeared to not give it a second thought. Or that was the perception that I got. He didn't make me feel like he considered what I said at all. It's not that he needed to do what I said, but conveying to your staff members that you appreciate their perspective is an important part of leading a team.

Some people feel that when you are making changes to a community you have purchased or acquired, you should make them slowly. Although there can be benefits to that, I'm rather indifferent on speed. If you go slowly for the sake of going slowly, you are delaying progress. Just make the changes at the pace that is appropriate. The sooner you make a change, the sooner you can move forward.

There will be people who will not fit in with your strategy and goals for the site, and they may have to move on. Not everyone will like you, not everyone will like what you do, not everyone will stay. This is natural. But, by listening, by conveying to people that you are listening, by being understanding, by explaining yourself and being open to questions, you will put yourself in the best position possible and give yourself the highest chance of winning people over and being successful.

What Skills and Characteristics Do You Need to Have?

What is the most important piece of the initial cultivation and development of your community? You. You, as the community administrator, determine a lot. You will be a major factor in the success or (hopefully not) failure of your community. You don't have to know everything and you don't have to be God's gift to community administration. You do need to be open to new ideas, open to learning, and committed to doing the best work that you can. Nothing is handed to you—you will have to work.

You need to have good people skills and good communication skills. You need to be able to communicate clearly to users and staff. To that end, you must also be able to understand people and not discriminate based upon the way people type or communicate online. It helps if you have a healthy knowledge of Internet lingo and lingo related to the community's subject matter so that you can understand as much of what people say as possible. However, if you don't know what someone is saying, you can usually look it up, pick it up as you go, and/or ask for further clarification.

You need a great deal of patience. You'll be dealing with idiots and, if your site is large enough, plenty of them—people who will, quite frankly, love to and even want to cause trouble, upset you, or rattle your cage. Nasty messages? Venomous hatred? Get ready—they are now a part of your everyday life. You need to accept this, laugh it off, and stay on point.

You need to be accessible to people (via private message, e-mail, and/or otherwise) and be comfortable with it. You are the boss, and any communication method you list on your community profile is fair game. You can't be angry when people use them. For example, an administrator should never, ever have "no private messages!" in his or her signature. If you don't want to be contacted, don't be the administrator. If you put your instant messenger name on your profile, expect people to contact you. You can't get angry at people for using contact information that you made available to the public. You're on twenty-four hours a day. Your mistakes are magnified. Don't forget it.

The best administrators that I know are active participants in their communities. It's a good thing for people to see the administrator posting along with them, welcoming them to the community, etc. It helps to lower the disconnect—it helps them to think of you less as some higher figure of authority and more as a person. It also gives you the opportunity to set a posting example that others can follow. Even on KarateForums.com, I still participate actively where I feel comfortable, despite my lack of martial arts knowledge.

You need to be able to avoid taking things personally, otherwise people will easily offend you. Respond without thinking and you will damage your community. You are held to a higher standard than your users, and you should hold yourself to one, as well.

Although you shouldn't take things personally, you still need to care. You need to care about what happens in your community; you need to care what people think, how they feel, and how they are. Caring about what you do is important, and you have to know when to care and when not to care—when things are really important and when they are not.

You have to be able to make hard choices. Sometimes, this means deciding between what is right and what is easy. Don't do the popular thing unless the popular thing and the right thing are the same thing. You will have to make choices that will make you lonely. You will have to make choices that may cost you users and may cost you staff members (that, hopefully, can be minimized through explanation and through involving your staff members in the process). But part of being a good manager is the ability to make these tough decisions—to step up to the plate when it's not fun or pretty.

Technical knowledge is one thing you don't need. You do not need to know how to program (I don't), although if you did it would serve you well. However, there is no reason you can't pick up small details here and there in the course of your work. It's not a good idea to be so reliant on someone else for all of the technical aspects of your community that you are completely helpless because you don't know how to do simple things like upload a file, repair a corrupted MySQL database table, and so on and so forth. It's not a good place to be when it's 11 p.m., your site has been hacked, and you have absolutely no idea how to get it back online. You should continue to learn every day.

Everywhere you go and everything you do will reflect on you and your community. Do not ever forget that—always carry yourself with this in mind.

Conclusion

This chapter discussed some of the things that you have to think about and decisions that you should make before you jump into managing an online community. Having this understanding will help you to manage your community and give you a better chance at success.

CHAPTER 2

Developing Your Community

In this chapter, you'll learn how to lay the physical and technical foundation of your community, ensuring that you get off to the right start and don't make life any harder than it already is. And if your community has already launched, use this section to identify areas where you can adjust and improve.

Choosing a Name and a Domain Name

Choosing a name for your community may be one of the first things that you do. Generally, if a website is worth creating, it's worth giving it its own domain name. The cost of a domain name is so low that there is really no reason not to have one. Owning your own domain name gives you control—control over your brand and control over your URL.

Here is one example: One of the downsides to a lot of free, remotely hosted community services is that they do not allow you to have your own domain name. Your URL ends up being something like http://yourname.their name.com. So, if you spend your time promoting this URL and then you want to move to another service or to your own domain name, who controls the original URL? You don't. You have to promote your new URL all over again and you may not even be able to forward the old one properly. Just skip all of that and register a domain name that you control.

Choosing a domain name might not seem like the most important decision, but don't take it lightly. A poor choice will make your job harder because it will make your site harder to find, harder to promote, and harder to remember. There is no reason to give yourself a handicap to start with or to make this any harder than it already is.

Communities for New or Existing Content Sites

If you are adding a community as a new section of an established site or launching a new one where the forums are a section of a larger site (but not the primary focus of the site), choosing a name and/or a domain name is usually pretty easy. In almost all cases, you can just add "Forums" or "Community" to your website's name (example: SiteName.com Forums) and create a /forums subdirectory on your existing domain name (example: http://www.sitename.com/forums). Some people give their communities their own domain names, such as sitenameforums.com.

Generally, I recommend going with the subdirectory option because people will be familiar with your domain name and it makes it that much easier for people to identify your overall brand. If your site is fairly established, you may want to register sitenameforums.com (or whateveryoucallyourcommunity.com) and redirect it, just to protect the brand. If, for some reason, you end up giving your community a domain of its own, be sure to utilize my domain name selection advice later in this chapter.

Naming a Stand-Alone Community

Now, if you are creating a stand-alone community, you have to be a bit more creative. I have launched several of these. One popular method that I and others have had success with is to name them in a "ContentForums.com" format. That is, describe the content and add the word *forums* to the URL. KarateForums.com, SportsForums.net, and PhotoshopForums.com are examples. Usually, I prefer the *forums* moniker over others, but *community, talk, chat,* etc. can work just as well. If the word or term is very common, like *sports,* there is a good chance that all or most of these combinations (with a ".com" extension) will be taken. But, it's always worth checking and considering.

You certainly don't have to have *forums, talk, chat,* or any of those things in the domain. The important thing, generally speaking, is that the name relates to the subject matter of your community. For example, Community Admins.com is a good name for a community for people who run forums. BadBoyFans.com is a good name for a Bad Boy Entertainment fan community.

Of course, this isn't a be all and end all. You can certainly choose a name that isn't related to the subject matter of your community. After all, *Google* and *Yahoo!* didn't mean a heck of a lot to people until they became recognized Internet brands. However, having a domain name that is related to what your community is about will make it easier for you to promote the site, and using a domain with related keywords in it has search engine benefits as well.

Don't forget to check out expired domain name auction services like SnapNames (http://www.snapnames.com), Pool.com (http://www.pool.com), and NameJet (http://www.namejet.com) as well as aftermarket services like The Domain Name Aftermarket (http://www.tdnam.com). Some people shy away from these things, but if you pay just a little attention to them, you can come away with some great deals and land a great name for your site.

Several factors go into choosing a good domain name. Here are a few guidelines to get you going in the right direction.

Extensions A ".com" extension is absolutely the way to go. In nearly every case, it is worth using a halfway decent ".com" URL over a great anything else. Most users automatically type in ".com." So, if your URL is site name.net, people might remember "SiteName" but not the ".net," type in ".com" and get an entirely different website. In a way, if your site has any other domain name extension but ".com," your work will probably help, in some small way at least, the person who does own the ".com."

If you have a domain name other than ".com," you really have to make the extension a part of your branding. In the previous example, if you have sitename.net and you go around calling the site "SiteName" without including the extension, it'll make it harder for people to remember. And, when they don't remember, chances are that they will assume it's sitename.com or, if you're lucky, they will search for your site and hopefully (again, if you're lucky) find it. Eliminate the guesswork and make your extension a part of your branding if you don't have a ".com" URL. But, again, you probably shouldn't go in that direction to begin with.

If you have a really, really good ".net" or ".org" domain name, it might be worth going for. For instance, I wanted to start a sports discussion site and I really felt that sportsforums.com was the perfect domain name. To my disappointment, it was taken, but sportsforums.net was available. I decided that it was a good name and worth the effort. In hindsight, I probably would have been just as well off—or better—finding a ".com" alternative that was available at the time. Even though I certainly wish I had the ".com," it has worked out pretty well. Nonprofit organizations may also prefer the use of a ".org." However, you generally shouldn't venture much further than ".com," ".net," or ".org" into the mass of domain name extensions that are available today.

There are rare cases where this guideline may not apply. For instance, if you are starting a Japanese discussion community about Japanese events in Japanese, getting a ".jp" (the Japan extension) domain name might be wise. Be warned: There are restrictions on who may or may not own many of these country-specific domain names. So be sure to check it out thoroughly before you buy.

Dashes and Numbers   I strongly recommend that you not have any dashes (-) in your domain name. When you start a site, you should think long term. In the long term you are better off without a dash. People need to be able to recall your website's name and your domain name easily. People may remember the name of your site, but will they remember that your URL had a dash? It's the same as not owning the ".com" of your domain name. They will remember "SiteName," but will they remember "Site-Name"? Similarly, the dash can hurt word of mouth or vocal marketing, as well. Although it's generally not that big a deal, if you own site-name.com, it might also be worth registering sitedashname.com.

The same goes for numbers. Avoid them.

Spell It Correctly!   Don't fool around with spelling. Some people try to play around in this area, but domains like "gurl-gamerz.net" just don't cut it. Don't try to spell something phonetically (the way it sounds when spoken). Don't sub 0 for o, such as y0urname.com—it'll only hurt your community. Spelling the word(s) in your domain name correctly will ensure that people will have an easier time finding your site and remembering the name. Spell it correctly and move on.

Length   Try to keep your domain name to a reasonable length, but don't skimp for the sake of having a short name. For instance, KForums.com isn't as good as KarateForums.com, if you are starting a martial arts discussion community. I would say a safe maximum would be around eighteen characters (not including the extension), with a good average of ten to fourteen.

Prefixes   Although the name of my network has a prefix, I usually try to avoid prefixes (generally, *e* and *i* are really the only ones worth considering) with my community names. An example of a domain name with a prefix would be esitename.com. If you are unable to find a good domain name and a solid ".com" option with a prefix is available, it may be worth considering. It's better than a dash or a number, and it's probably better than going to a non-".com" extension.

Don't Curse!   Avoid profanity. Putting any sort of expletive in your name will shock people—and not in a good way. It doesn't convey the best image, and even if your site has the greatest content in the world, many people simply will not visit. (Unless, of course, your site is crude and vulgar by nature . . . then, hey, a crude domain name might fit, right?)

You can overcome a bad domain name. Your efforts will be the deciding factor on whether your community becomes a success. However, there is no reason to make it any harder than it already is. Selecting a good domain name is part of selecting a good name. It's important that you take the time to do this. Choosing a poor domain name can set you back from the start. You don't need anything extra weighing against you—trust me.

Domain Name Registrars

Finding a domain name registrar is pretty easy. Ask your friends for a recommendation. Different registrars provide different options. If you are just buying a domain name that you are going to use for a live site, most registrars will be perfect for you. However, if you plan to buy other domain names that you would like to redirect, it's not hard to find a registrar that provides free (and ad-free) redirection services. Find one that has the features you need at a competitive price.

Web Hosting

As with choosing a domain name registrar, ask your friends for a recommendation. There are plenty of bad hosts out there, but there are also plenty of good hosts out there—a personal recommendation from a friend or trusted associate can help ease the confusion of picking a host out of the masses. If you have an established site or have been working in web development for very long, there isn't much that I can tell you that you haven't already heard.

Communities can sometimes be resource intensive. The larger the community, the more intensive it is. Large communities sometimes need to tweak their server settings and/or script settings to minimize this and even give a community its own server or even an army of servers. (This is just for your information, however, as if your community is new—you are no where near needing to think about this unless you expect to be profiled by *USA TODAY* or the *Wall Street Journal* tomorrow or something like that.)

If you're just starting out and you plan to be just a basic discussion community, you can probably begin with a basic plan that won't put much of a hole in your wallet. PHP (the coding language that many community software options are written in) and MySQL (a database management system that many of those same options use to store your community's posts, member information, and other data) are popular solutions (although there are others). If you go that route, make sure that your host offers at least PHP and MySQL so that you are able to host your community site. You should check the community software's resource sites for recommendations on how much space and bandwidth it would be wise to start out with. Be sure to contact any potential host and ask if you can upgrade your plan to a larger one at the drop of a hat. It is important that you have this flexibility in case your community grows suddenly.

The larger your community gets, the more bandwidth, space, and resources it will require. You need to be able to host all community files (including users' uploaded avatars, images, attachments, and more) as well as the database and backups of the database. To make the most of your money and server space, you should probably go through the server from time to time and remove anything that isn't needed. As an example, many servers have stat programs installed by default. The longer your site runs and the more visitors it gets, the larger these files will be. If you find them useful and want to keep them, you may want to download them to your computer and then delete them from your server to free up that space every once in a while.

All hosts go down from time to time, but you want a host that minimizes its downtime and has excellent support. Downtime itself is not a reason to leave a host. How a host responds to downtime and how often it occurs are, however. It is beyond the scope of this book to go into any great detail about hosting or the technical aspects of managing the server that will be home to your community.

Choosing Your Community Software

When it comes to community software, there are a lot of options out there. They come in an array of programming languages and database types, and some are free. Several have quite a following. It is quite likely that you will be using a PHP and MySQL-based program, because that is what most people seem to use, including myself. In line with that, in this section, I am going to mention a paid option and a free option. There are other good software choices, but these are the two that I recommend based on my experience.

vBulletin

This is the paid option. It's called vBulletin (http://www.vbulletin.com), and it is a well-established and fully customizable community package. It has a great feature set, is widely used, and has a large support community as well as a paid support staff, as you would expect. It's affordably priced: At the time of this printing, vBulletin costs $85 for a leased license (which allows you to run the script and have access to the members area for one year, where you can download updates to the software) and $160 for an owned license (which allows you to run the script for an unlimited period of time, but you only get one year of member-area access—you can renew your access at a rate of $30 per year).

The software has a large and active hack and template community, with vBulletin.org (http://www.vbulletin.org) being the largest resource. Hacks are code/software modifications that improve the program in the eyes of the administrator (or satisfy a need or a user request, etc.).

phpBB

This is the free option and the one that I use on my own sites. Although vBulletin offers the benefits that you would expect from a commercial package and may be a more complete program overall (phpBB does not offer the comprehensive out-of-the-box feature set that vBulletin does), I believe that if you put the time in, phpBB (http://www.phpbb.com) can fill your needs just as well.

I have used phpBB in a live environment since March of 2001, going all the way back to version 1.2.1, if I recall correctly. It's an open source program released under the GPL (General Public License; for more information, visit http://www.gnu.org/copyleft/gpl.html). This basically means that phpBB's code is available to everybody for modification and use. Once a program is released under the GPL, all persons who create and modify the script are bound to the terms of the license, including the original author. So, modifications of the code must then be released under the GPL, as well.

Like vBulletin, phpBB has a great hacking community. There are many hacks, templates/styles, graphics, and utilities that are available for the script. A site that I own and run, phpBBHacks.com (http://www.phpbbhacks.com), was the first site dedicated to phpBB hacks and is the largest source of phpBB-related downloads, granted with author permission, on the Internet. It also features a friendly support community and other phpBB-related resources.

Due to its functionality, active development, flexible license, and large support and customization community, phpBB is extremely successful and widely used.

Your site can be successful with either program. Really, as long as you have a good one running in your community, your efforts (yes—you, the person running the community) will primarily decide the community's fate.

Basic Options

There are many basic options that you will have to decide on before your community launches. Or, if you've already launched, you might consider making some adjustments. In this section I'll explain some of the more common choices.

Software Options

These are options that deal primarily with the configuration of your community software.

Requiring Registration to Participate   You should require users to register to post and participate in your community. Besides opening up a world of options to your members, being a part of a community means just that—being a part of it and having an account that everyone can identify with. This allows all posts and activity from a given account to be associated with said account. It eliminates impersonation and allows you to effectively deal with troublemakers (through bans, etc.). If a user doesn't have an account, it gets noticeably harder to associate any negative (or even positive) activities with him specifically, to document his activities properly, and to take action.

Allowing guest posting can lead to people posting more junk in your community. Because less commitment is required to actually post (i.e., no commitment at all), it will make your site more susceptible to hit-and-run posts including inappropriate content, advertising, and other unwanted activities.

In some cases, it may be a good idea to allow guests limited posting access to your community. These cases are exceedingly rare, however. In almost every imaginable case, requiring registration is the way to go. If you are selling a product and you have a presale questions forum, allowing guest posting might make some sense there. But even then it's questionable because it simply invites spam and other junk. So, if you allow guest posters, it will increase the time it takes to moderate your community and make the forum easier to abuse.

Smilies   Smilies, also known as emoticons, are usually little cartoon faces depicting particular emotions. For instance, inserting a happy-face emoticon into a message will mean that you are happy, a sad face will mean you are sad, and a mad face will mean you are mad. Or something like that.

Add as many of these as you desire. As with any content in your community, you should monitor smilie usage so you can ensure that users are utilizing them within your user guidelines. There are users who will use them a lot and there are users who will not use them at all. You can always add new ones as they are required and/or if you feel they are worthwhile.

Flood Controls   Flood controls prevent users from repeating a certain action (posting, sending a private message, using your search function, etc.) within a specific period of time. For instance, if you have your posting flood control set to twenty seconds, it will prevent a user from making two posts within twenty seconds of each other. It certainly won't stop spammers, but it will slow them down. You cannot set your flood control too high, however, as it will annoy your users. For this reason, you should generally place it between ten and twenty seconds.

Word Censors   Word censors are a great way to help prevent people from posting vulgarities and other inappropriate messages in your community. A censor will bleep out (so to speak) the profane word or term until one of your moderators can get to it. A great way to set it up is to replace censored words with a single asterisk (*) so that members will be less bothered by what the actual word is (for instance, * is better than f***—if people can't read the actual word, it has less impact) and your moderators can catch it, remove it, and contact the violators.

There are other things that you can do with word censors, of course, but this is usually the most effective out-of-the-box use. You want your users to learn that certain language is not acceptable. Do not use your word censors just to delete a word totally, because there will be no lesson learned and people will just get confused and angry.

Be mindful of the fact that word censors can also censor words that you may be OK with. Most often, this occurs when you institute wildcard censors that flag words starting with, ending with, or containing certain letters. If this becomes an issue, you may want to force the censor to act in a more specific way, so that only the word itself is censored, instead of words that contain a certain sequence of letters.

As an example, the first three letters in the word *assault* form a word that I do not allow on my communities. So, I have the censor set to censor the word itself (those three letters when posted alone) and vulgar variations of or including the word, but not any word that begins, ends, or contains that three-letter sequence. Sure, people use that word in other vulgar terms and we will have to remove their posts, but there are too many words that start with those letters to justify censoring it with a wildcard.

Don't forget, you can never censor every vulgar term. Don't even try. It's not possible. You should add words to your censor list as they present themselves, certainly, but it will never be 100 percent complete. People will use words or come up with new ones that you didn't or can't censor and you will have to remove their posts. For this reason, do not institute an "if it's not censored, it's OK" type of guideline.

You can also use your word censor to change one word into another. There is rarely, if ever, a good reason to do this, however. If you have a problem with something that someone is saying, you should remove the post and contact the user privately—don't play games.

There is an incredible use of the word censor feature detailed in the "Innovative Tools" section of chapter 6.

Post Counts   A post count is a tally of the number of posts a user has made on your community. Usually this information will display next to the user's posts and on his or her profile page as well as in other potential locations.

How much someone cares about his post count varies from person to person. Some people don't care at all about anyone's post count, let alone their own. Some care. And some care a little too much and try to boost it artificially. This is where it can become a problem.

To combat this, some communities have tried to reduce the importance of post count or limit the impact of posts perceived to be of little value. Some communities have done away with post counts altogether. I'm not a fan of this. For people who don't care about post count, it doesn't mean anything to them that you display it. So, there is no harm there. If people care about it, it's not going to bother them either, because they want you to display it. What will bother some people (as well as yourself, potentially) is when people bump up year-old threads with replies that only say "cool" or "yeah." People usually make those posts to increase their post counts.

Another method that some communities have tried is to make posts in specific (usually off-topic) forums not count. The idea is that posts related to the subject of the community are of a higher value than posts that are not.

I like to let all posts count. Sure, some posts are of higher value than others, but a post is a post. Making it so that posts in off-topic forums don't count will only limit abuse, it won't prevent it. If you see someone who is blatantly boosting her post count and contributing nothing of value to your forums, you should deal with it. And, unless it becomes a big, big issue, I'm inclined just to let all posts count the same, no matter where they are posted.

Post count is what it is. It's an indicator of how much someone has posted on your forums. It does have importance and those who have a high post count are most often worthy of some sort of praise, but it's not the most important thing in the world. You should always try to stress this—stress quality over quantity while also not saying that post counts are worthless, because that isn't true, either.

Old Posts   This isn't really an issue if you are just starting out, but it is something that you may think about as time goes by. What will you do with old content and posts?

Whatever you do, don't delete or prune them. As an online community, old posts are your history and your heritage. Keep them and treasure them. They will be something that you and your users will hopefully look back on fondly (for the most part). They are memories.

Old posts and content indexed by search engines can help new people find your site. Some people look at post count and decide to join a community based upon that. Also, if you ever happen to sell your community, the post count can directly affect your selling price. So there is little or no reason to delete old posts.

However, you may not want users to bump old threads. People who want to boost their post count artificially often look to old threads, choosing to bump them up. They welcome people who are no longer around or ask questions of people who haven't visited in a year or more, and it can be annoying. If it does become an issue, you could make it so that threads that have not been active for a specified period of time are automatically closed. You could always reopen them later, if need be.

To bring members' attention to the issue, you could display a notice above the reply boxes on threads that haven't been active for a set period of time. This notice might say something like, "This thread is twenty-one months old. With threads of this age, rather than replying to them, we generally recommend that you start a new thread."

But, whatever you do, don't permanently delete them.

Purging Accounts Some administrators choose to purge inactive accounts. But what constitutes inactivity can vary among communities. For some, it's never logging in. For others, it might be never posting or a combination of both and/or other factors. After a specific period of time, some administrators will delete these accounts.

The only accounts that I delete are the accounts that people never activate via e-mail. In other words, whenever someone registers, she receives an e-mail with a link she must visit in order for her account to be activated. If she fails to do this after a while, I will delete her account. When I delete the actual account, the user receives another e-mail letting her know of the deletion and encouraging her to come back to the community and register again if she is still interested in participating. But once she activates her account, I view it as a real account and will not delete it. Ever—even if she has zero posts. If someone thinks enough to register on my site and to confirm her account via e-mail, then she registered it, she wanted it, and that's cool by me. You never know what someone will do. Maybe one day she'll want to post. And if you delete her account, maybe she won't.

Just as with posts, some people look at the number of members that you have and join the community based upon that. I'm not saying it's a lot of people, but plenty join a community based upon the activity that it has—and member count is certainly a component of that. And, again, if you ever want to sell the community, some buyers value member count. Your count can and will affect their offer. They are legitimate accounts and they have value.

Remember that the accounts aren't hurting anything. If it gets to a point where you need to delete members or delete posts because your server somehow can't handle it, it's time to find a new server.

User Options

On most online communities, each user has a multitude of configurable options available. These can include options to alter the way that your community looks and acts and can allow your members to create their own public user profiles and more. Obviously, in adding, removing, or adjusting these options, do what you think is best. However, let's talk about a few notable options.

Signatures and Avatars Signatures are generally lines of text and/or code that produce font styling, display images, etc. and are attached to the bottom of every post and private message (and sometimes in other places, as well). An avatar is an image that is associated with an account. It is most commonly displayed near their username on posts and, potentially, in other locations.

Although there are exceptions, there is usually little or no reason to disallow signatures and avatars. If your members want to take advantage of them, they will. Those who don't, won't. You can even offer users the option to turn them on and off on a sitewide basis. Signatures and avatars allow your members to express their individuality—a lot of people like to be able to display their icons next to their usernames and to have their signatures at the end of their posts to give their fellow members insight into themselves.

You will probably want to make members upload their avatars to your server rather than allow them to link to other servers. The more servers that have to be called up on a given page, the more likely there is to be an issue with slowness. For example, let's say you have five users on a thread who have avatars linked to five different servers. If just one of those servers is down or slow, your users may experience a slowdown on that thread. For every avatar that is inaccessible or slow to load, it will be worse. Hosting all of your member's avatars will also help cut down on unauthorized hotlinking. This also goes for images in signatures, if you allow them.

As with any content in your community, you should have guidelines that apply to signatures and avatars. I talk specifically about crafting guidelines in chapter 3.

Username Changing If you allow members to change their usernames whenever they want, with no regulation, all by themselves, it will lead to confusion. Your members will be confused and you and your staff will be confused. It doesn't make it any easier to keep track of a user's actions on your site if he or she has a different username every week. This is why you shouldn't allow members to change their own usernames.

However, in general, there is nothing wrong with allowing users to change their usernames, just as long as you are the one changing it for them so that it can be properly documented. This will placate anyone who wants to change a username, and as long as the person doesn't want to change it to something inappropriate or already taken, it shouldn't be an issue. And by being the one to change it, you will be able to inform your staff when a particular trouble-maker changes his username, and you will be able to keep track of him or her.

User Titles and Ranks   One very popular use of rank titles (usually titles that display below a member's username in various locations within your community) is to create a set that change based on the user's post count. You could make these ranks relate to the subject matter of your site. For instance, at a martial arts discussion community, you might set the ranks to different belt colors, such as White Belt, Yellow Belt, Orange Belt, Black Belt, and so on. You could have different belt images depicting an actual belt in that color. On a sports site, you could have Rookie, Veteran, Hall of Famer, etc. On a movie site, you could have Usher, Extra, Supporting Actor, Star, etc. You get the idea.

You could also allow members to set their own rank titles. It adds one more thing to keep an eye on, certainly, but it's generally not that big of a deal. You could even make it so that only members with a certain number of posts may do it, making it an incentive of sorts.

On a related note, you can add custom profile fields (or use user titles) that let users specify personal information related to your community. On a martial arts site, this could mean a field for users to list the martial arts classes that they take. On a community for fraternities and/or sororities, you could allow them to display their Greek letters and shield. On a sports site, you might let them display their favorite team logos.

So, as you can see, there are a lot of different ways that you can go.

Ignore List   An ignore list allows members to ignore posts and not receive private messages from certain members. In practice, I don't like how it functions, due to what it encourages.

Think about the way that discussion threads work and evolve. You have a number of different people making posts. Some of these posts can stand on their own (except that they are in response to the first post) and some relate, either directly through quotes or indirectly, to more than one post on the thread. If you ignore posts by a certain member, then you will very likely not get the full meaning of any number of posts. This leads to odd replies where one member may have answered a question, but then another member had that person ignored, so he posted the same answer, which lead to replies mentioning X's post or thanking X and the person ignoring the poster and so on and so forth. It really creates a mess. It's better to require that your members respect one another and, if they don't, good-bye.

Even if you use ignore, staff members shouldn't. They must be able to see all of the posts inside of their areas of responsibility in order to do their jobs well.

Private Messaging   Private messaging is a way for members of your community to talk privately to one another on your site. In some communities, the use of private messaging is optional—it can be turned on and off in the members' profile settings area. If you do give people the option to turn it off (staff members should never do that, as they have to be ready to be contacted by members of the community), make sure that it doesn't affect their ability to send and receive private messages to staff members. Staff communications should go through your private messaging system because you can track it. With some software, you can see if someone sent a private message, who it was sent to and from, and if it was viewed. This is a crucial form of backup for you and your staff.

As an example, if a user trashes one of your staff members, you are in a tough position because although you trust your staff member and know that he or she must be telling the truth, you hate to have to take the staff member's word on something like that. This is why you want to require that all communication among users and staff members go through private message. That way you can always see the communication and point to absolute fact, which will give you a greater sense of ease with your decisions.

Allowing Users to Be "Invisible"   In some communities, members are allowed to mark themselves as "invisible." This will usually mean that they will not appear in your "who's online" area or appear "online" on your community anywhere (administrators and sometimes moderators can still see them, however).

In general, I think the value of this feature is questionable. Why would people want to be invisible? They don't want to be bothered. They don't want to be seen on your site. Those are the two main reasons I've found. If you are a part of a community, you are a part of a community. Do you want someone who wants to hide or doesn't really want to be seen on your site? Maybe you do, maybe you don't. If you do allow invisibility, make sure that your staff members don't take advantage of it—staff members are to be public, visible examples to your community. Don't hide them.

Setup Options

Let's talk about a few key items in the visual setup and early organization of your site.

What Guests See   Allowing nonmembers to view the posts that are already on your site will allow them to get a feel for it and could entice them to register, especially when they see something that they would like to comment on. But make sure that in order to comment, they have to register. Just as important, if not more, is making it so that search engines can find your content. If you require your members to log in to view all of your content, search engines can't find that content. That in turn will make your community immeasurably harder for potential members to find because, for most communities, search engines generate the bulk of their new members.

As an aside, showing your content has other benefits. You don't want members of your community to infringe upon the rights of others. The indexing of your content makes it easier for copyright holders to find violations of their rights, something that they will appreciate. Coincidentally, you'll notice that many music communities, for example, keep some (or even most or all) of their forums private. Simply put, it makes them look guilty.

How Many Forums Should I Have?   When you are starting a community, it's best to have as few forums as possible. However, you do not want to skimp for the sake of skimping—you should ensure that you have a solid, basic organizational structure that makes sense. The forums should be fairly vague and inclusive of the site's subject matter. For instance, if you are starting a web development community, don't have a forum for Adobe Photoshop, a forum for Adobe Fireworks, and a forum for Paint Shop Pro. Just have one forum for graphic design or something of that nature.

There are some cases where having a lot of forums can be a good thing. For example, if you are expecting a rush of posts about a certain topic, it may make sense to create a forum for that topic. However, cases like that are fairly rare.

You can order your forums by importance, arrange them alphabetically, or do a combination of both (such as A-Z with an "other" forum going at the bottom). Dividing your forums into appropriate categories is a good idea. For instance, if you run a sports discussion community, you might have a "Sports Discussion" category with all of your sports-related forums in it; an "Other Discussion" category for your general chat, off-topic, and introduction forums; and a "SiteName.com" category for your site-related forums, such as an announcements forum and a feedback forum. Obviously, this is just an example; your actual forums will vary. Try to divide them up in the way that makes the most sense.

As your community becomes more active, you will get a good idea as to when it is time to add a new, more specific forum and/or to adjust your structure to make it more specific as a whole. Don't just add a forum if one or two users request it. Make sure that adding the forum is a good idea and that there are either several users who want this forum and/or there are many current posts on your site that would fit into this new forum. When you do create a new one, be sure to comb through your existing forums and move any posts that are now appropriately suited for the new forum.

Later, if you do find that you have a forum that covers a subject that doesn't need its own forum, you can always merge it with another forum.

➤ **Advertising Forums**   Depending on the subject of your site, it may make sense to have an advertising (or perceived advertising) forum of some kind. Or, at least, a forum where people show off or ask for feedback on something that they are in some way affiliated with.

As an example, on the phpBBHacks.com Support Forums, we have a phpBB Review forum (http://www.phpbbhacks.com/forums/phpbb-review-vf5.html). This is a forum where users can come and create threads about their phpBBs. The purpose of the forum is for users to get feedback on their phpBB with the hope of improving them. However, one of the reasons that many of them post is to get traffic, which is understandable but shouldn't be the main idea behind posting the thread. The guidelines for this forum are as follows:

This forum is for phpBB forum reviews. Below you will find a few guidelines applying to both people asking for reviews and giving them.

Posting Your phpBB

This forum is not for advertising your community or for bringing traffic to your community. While those may be side effects, the purpose of your thread must be to get feedback on your community with the hope of improving it.

Be sure to present your URL in a prominent place. If possible, link directly to your phpBB. If you have specific things you want people to look at, mention them.

It is recommended that you actually spend time customizing your phpBB before posting it. Change the look of your site, install hacks that your userbase will appreciate—integrate them in an aesthetically pleasing way and customize it to your liking. Don't just install a phpBB and post it with its basic subSilver look and a different logo.

You will be criticized. Your site isn't perfect (no site is) and that is why you are posting here. Sometimes the opinions of users may be blunt. You can choose to ignore them or accept them, but you should not get angry at them. Reviews are made to help you improve aspects of your site, so most reviews aren't going to make you feel better—just hopefully allow you to improve your site. If you feel that anyone steps over the line and becomes disrespectful, please report them by sending a private message to me or a member of the staff. Please do not respond to them yourself, thereby aggravating the situation further.

This can probably go without saying, but your community must be running phpBB in order to post here. Posts asking for reviews of communities that run any other community software are not allowed.

Each phpBB is allowed 1 thread. In certain situations, a 2nd may be permitted, such as if a long period of time has elapsed since your previous thread was active and/or you have launched an entirely new design.

You are allowed one non informative bump to your thread, but it must come once the thread has been inactive for at least 48 hours. Beyond that, bumping can only occur for noteworthy changes. Your phpBB cannot require people to login just to view it.

Like any thread, your thread is subject to our User Guidelines. So, for example, phpBBs that are featured in the phpBB Review forum must not cover anything inappropriate for this community.

Your phpBB must feature some sort of ''Powered by phpBB'' statement. At the very least, a mention of phpBB on all phpBB-powered pages with a link to http://www.phpbb.com.

If these guidelines are not followed, the review thread will be removed.

Reviewing phpBBs

Read the first post in the thread, the one by the person requesting a review. If he or she is looking for feedback on specific aspects of the site, try to fulfill these requests.

Most users would prefer to hear comments about specific areas or parts of the site or design, rather than general observations.

Honesty is great, but be sure to be respectful when you are criticizing. Please do not make it a personal issue by doing things like attacking their taste in general. Stick to the content and design of the website.

You may want to include information about your operating system, browser, screen resolution, etc.

Please do not be critical of the phpBB's subject matter or the size of the phpBB (posts or members or how few one may have).

Like any posts, your posts in this forum still fall under our User Guidelines and are handled as such.

Thank you for visiting phpBBHacks.com.

In the actual online document, the mentions of user guidelines link directly to the guidelines in question. This saves people the time of locating the guidelines that you are talking about.

Another example would be PhotoshopForums.com, where we have a Market Place forum (http://www.photoshopforums.com/market-place-vf12.html) where people can buy, sell, and/or barter web and graphic design work. Shown next are the PhotoshopForums.com Market Place User Guidelines.

Welcome to the PhotoshopForums.com Marketplace. This is the place to buy, sell, and barter web and graphic design work. Before you post in this forum, please ensure that you read this thread in its entirety so that you know what is appropriate and what isn't.

Thread Starters

You may not post more than one thread for the same job or piece of work within 60 days. Please be as descriptive as possible in the initial post. If you are holding a contest here or selling something here, you must accept participation here. You can post listings at other sites, but please include all pertinent details in your post and don't tell members to go to another site where you are accepting entries or bids. They should be able to post entries here or send them to you privately.

It can also be helpful to include your preferred method of contact, if you do not want people to post in the thread. You can ask them to private message (PM) you (please keep in mind that even if you have under 25 posts, you can still receive and reply to PMs), to e-mail you (provide an e-mail address or ask them to e-mail you through our site—make sure that you elect to display your e-mail as public in your profile), or to contact you through an instant messenger and so on. Due to the fact that you cannot initiate a PM conversation or send an e-mail through our forums until you have 25 posts, it is recommended that you at least offer an actual e-mail address in your post, if you want people to contact you privately, so as to allow members with less than 25 posts a definitive means of contacting you.

In the initial post, if you are looking to pay for some work or buy something, you must include the specific compensation being offered, even if you are not offering any at all. In such a case, please simply say that you are not offering any. Freebies are allowed, at this time, but please keep in mind that this is actual work that is worthy of compensation. It is nice and appropriate to offer something—anything: advertising, a link on your site, some cash, whatever—in return. The level of compensation that you offer can also affect the quality of the entries and the amount of attention that your listing receives.

Similarly, if you are selling something, please include either the sale price or a minimum bid (even if that minimum is $0). If you give your listing a minimum of $0, please do not be offended when you receive a low bid.

If you are offering some form of compensation, selling an item, or requiring a minimum bid, please be specific. For example, please do not say, "I have a small budget," say, "I have $25 to spend on this job." Please do not say, "I am looking for between $25 and $50," say, "I am looking for $50." If you are offering part-time employment or something of that nature, a payment range is acceptable. But please be as specific as possible. If you are offering full-time employment or similar, you are not required to provide specific compensation, but we recommend providing some sort of guidance, at least.

Designers and Buyers

Please read the thread starter's posts completely and make sure that you understand what they are looking for or what they are selling. Please follow their instructions for contacting them. If they say that they want to be contacted in a certain way, please contact them in that way or do not contact them at all.

Contact them in regard to what they are asking for help with or selling—do not send them vague, general advertisements for your services as if you didn't read their post at all—this will be regarded as advertising.

Please do not make uninvited remarks about the compensation or sale price that has been offered. If you are not comfortable with the amount, do not contact them or participate in their thread. Do not harass anyone in regards to this.

Acceptable Uses

Below, you will find a list of most of the popular uses (or attempted uses) of this forum. As time goes by, we may add to this list. Please note, however, that this is not an all-inclusive list. There are items that may or may not be allowed that are not listed. If you are ever in any doubt, please feel free to contact us first for a definitive answer.

Allowed

- Design contests
- Once-off template sales (no resold templates)

- Once-off logo and graphic sales

- Specific web and graphic design jobs and positions

Not Allowed

- Check out my design/domain/hosting/other services (service providers are not allowed to advertise their company or work)

- eBay (or similar) links

- Vague web and graphic design jobs (i.e., "We have projects we are looking for people to undertake.")

- Join our community, etc. type posts

- Website sales

- Domain name sales

- Write tutorials/articles for my site

Please note that PhotoshopForums.com is in no way responsible for any transactions that take place in this forum. You assume all responsibility for your transactions, whether it is on the buying end or the selling end.

Thank you for visiting PhotoshopForums.com.

Finally, the SitePoint Marketplace (http://www.sitepoint.com/market place) is a sort of online classifieds area where people can post their web development (and generally related) ads, from selling websites and domain names to advertising services and employment ads. It's well integrated into the SitePoint Forums (http://www.sitepoint.com/forums) with unified log-ins, profiles, and more. To encourage positive participation within the Marketplace, there is a set of auction guidelines (as of August 2007):

The following guidelines apply to any members participating in a SitePoint auction, including sellers, commenters, and bidders:

Guidelines for Sellers

1. Linking to or providing the URL of pages containing explicit, obscene or vulgar language or images is not allowed. This means that adult websites may not be sold at SitePoint.

2. Auctions may not be used to sell: access to services, memberships, subscriptions, "leased" services or discounts thereof. Such services should be advertised in the "Advertise Your Services" Marketplace category. Auctions must be used to advertise items for outright sale, rather than temporary, non-exclusive or leased licenses. When selling domain names, the buyer must be given full control and ownership of the domain name, including the ability to transfer the domain name to another registrar.

3. The seller must provide full details of the item for sale (including a URL if they are selling a website) in the auction. Sellers may not intentionally hide information from public view. This includes the use of statements such as "PM me for more information." If a moderator sees evidence that the seller is not publicly disclosing information, the auction may be suspended pending changes.

4. Sellers may list an item for sale on other sites simultaneously, provided that they do not link to the other sites and they allow people to bid on the auction at SitePoint. It is against our guidelines for sellers to require or encourage SitePoint members to go to a third-party site to make a bid.

5. Linking to external sites is restricted by SitePoint's self-promotion policy, which states that linking to your own web pages or pages from sites which you are affiliated with (including affiliate links) will be deemed as self-promotion and could result in the loss of your membership. However, sellers may link to the site for sale if they are selling a site or to web pages which solely contain information about the item they are selling. In particular, sellers are not allowed to link to other items for sale which are not a part of the auction.

6. Sellers must ensure that they place their auction in the correct category, according to what they are selling. See also: Definition of turnkey sites below.

7. Sellers may not create an auction if they have no intention of selling (for example, if they only want a valuation). If an auction indicates or implies that the seller does not intend to sell, it may be suspended or removed by a moderator. A seller is allowed to change his or her mind and decide not to sell after the auction has started. When this happens, the seller must cancel the auction to ensure that no more bids can be made.

8. The seller may sell more than one item in a single auction, but the items must be sold together as a package. The seller is allowed to change his or her mind

later and sell the items individually. When this happens, the seller must cancel the auction in which all the items are listed together.

9. SitePoint does not oversee the process of money changing hands and is unable to offer assistance in cases where the sale does not go as planned. All sellers should take due care when selling any item.

Guidelines for Buyers and Participants

1. Comments should be made only by those who are seriously interested in buying the item for sale. Frivolous comments, even if they are well intentioned, are discouraged and may be removed by a moderator.

2. Negative comments about or criticism of the seller or item for sale is strictly not allowed. This includes accusations of fraud or theft, even if they are well-intentioned (for example, to warn others). If any member has a dispute with a seller, it must be solved privately and not be referred to publicly in auctions. A member who posts negative comments or accusations about a seller may have their posts removed or may be banned permanently.

3. SitePoint does not oversee the process of money changing hands and is unable to offer assistance in cases where the sale does not go as planned or the item is not delivered as described. All buyers should take due care when purchasing any item.

Definition of Turnkey Sites

The section describes what is considered a turnkey site. Turnkey sites should not be listed for sale in the Established Sites For Sale category, and non-turnkey sites must not be listed for sale in the Turnkey Sites For Sale category.

Turnkey sites are sites which do not yet earn any revenue. Content sites without complete content and e-commerce sites without any products yet also qualify as turnkey sites.

If your site meets the following criteria, it is not considered a turnkey site and must be listed in the Established Sites For Sale category.

1. The site generates a reasonable amount of revenue (i.e., enough to cover the cost of hosting).

2. If it is a content site, the site already has enough content to be reasonably useful to a visitor.

3. If it is an e-commerce site, the site already has one or more products for sale.

However, if your site meets any of the following criteria, then it should be considered a turnkey site and should be listed in the Turnkey Sites For Sale category.

1. The site generates no significant revenue—not even enough to cover hosting cost.

2. The site is in an unfinished state such that it is of no use to visitors yet.

3. The site is based on a commonly available script or piece of software and does not contain any unique content.

Reporting Offenders

A team of SitePoint Advisors and Mentors regularly view the auctions. However, they may not notice every guideline violation immediately.

If you notice anybody breaking these guidelines, it should be reported to a Site-Point Advisor privately. Please do not complain about a member breaking the guidelines publicly in a comment. Your comment may be removed and you may receive a warning.

In settings like those in the preceding shaded boxes, advertising forums make some sense. But there are a bunch of instances where a site really should not have an advertising forum, because it doesn't usually make sense to encourage advertising that lacks purpose or relation to your community. For example, a rock band fan site doesn't need an advertising forum. It's not common for a site to "need" such a thing. It really depends on what your site is about and what you want to get out of it. For some communities, like a design community that has a forum for design reviews, it's a no-brainer, because you couldn't picture the site without it. If you do have an advertising forum, make sure that you outline a set of guidelines for it.

One potentially bad thing about having an advertising forum is that you may find users who will just register to post in that forum and only that forum, not really adding anything else to your community. Depending on the goals of your site, this may not fit in. If it becomes a problem, there are some things that you can do, save removing it entirely. You can require users to have a certain number of posts before they are able to post new threads or listings in your advertising section, or you could require users to have accounts for a certain number of days or months before they are able to do so. This way, access to the advertising forum becomes a benefit of being an established member of your community.

Reward-based participation aside, you could make it so that the forum is invisible to guests and visible to registered or logged-in users only. That way, when users discover the advertising forum (unless someone else told them about it), they will have probably already registered because they wanted to join your community. This cuts down the number of registrations for users who just want to post an ad and leave.

Remember, though, that when it comes to straight-up advertising forums and sections, no one "deserves" to advertise on your site. If you decide to allow it, that is your choice—it's a benefit and a privilege but not something that is deserved. These sections create additional moderation responsibilities, and advertising on your site has value, even if you decide to give it away.

➤ **Private Forums** Besides staff forums and the like, some communities have forums that are only available to certain members. The purpose of these forums will vary. Some are temporary (planning a new feature, getting feedback on design ideas, etc.) and others are more permanent, such as a forum for members who have X number of posts or a forum for members who are considered to be experts.

In practice, I'm not a fan of exclusionary forums like these. I like to see everyone in the community participating together in a respectful manner. However, if your needs require such a forum, you should do what you can to make sure the forum is not flaunted. You shouldn't deny its existence or anything, but it might be in poor taste to parade it around in excess. Don't list it on your index-page list of forums for regular members, for example. This helps to limit feelings of being left out.

For those who have access, you should also draw attention to the fact that those forums are private and explain who has access. For example, add something like this to the forum description: "This is a private forum. Its contents are only viewable to users of the X user group and staff members." This will help users distinguish between public and private forums.

➤ **Other Forums** Once you have come up with the forums that are relevant to your subject matter, it's a good idea to add at least one general chat forum where users can discuss anything else. I mean anything else: music, movies, sports, cooking, favorite colors—whatever! It helps keep the general off-topic chatter out of your other forums, and it often allows your users to bond and to get to know one another. And that will help you to build a good atmosphere.

As your community grows, you may notice that some subjects are discussed in the general chat forum more than others. You can grow that structure and add new forums over time as opportunities present themselves. For example, if you see that movie discussions are loading down your general chat forum, you could add a forum for movies. If your general chat forum is looking clogged up by game threads like "What song are you listening to right now?" or "Word Association Game," you could add a forum specifically for game threads.

Another forum you may want to add from the start is an introductions forum where new (and sometimes old) members can introduce themselves to the community. This helps to get people acquainted and makes them feel more comfortable within the site. Members should be allowed to mention their websites and/or things that they are affiliated with in one way or another. Their threads shouldn't be all about their ventures and shouldn't beg people to visit their sites, but mentioning what one does and who one is associated with is often a part of introducing oneself and should be allowed.

Finally, think about site-related forums: namely an announcements forum and a feedback forum or a single forum that functions as both. The benefit in separating them is that, hopefully, your announcements will have less of a chance of getting lost in the list of topics. In an announcements forum, only the administrator (or sometimes other members of staff) has the ability to create a thread and, usually, anyone can reply to that thread. In a forum that caters to both, anyone can start a thread.

➤ **Why You Don't Want a Feedback-and-Suggestions Forum** If you look at a lot of communities online, there seems to be an unwritten rule that communities have a feedback-and-suggestions forum of some kind. In fact, before pulling mine, I am not sure that I had ever seen a community without one—although I'm sure that they must have existed. It's an established convention of sorts. So when I made the change myself, I considered it to be a sort of changing of the rules and felt that I had good reason for doing so.

You see, there were two main reasons people used my feedback forum: either someone had an idea or someone had a problem (perhaps a complaint).

In the first case, final approval on any new ideas will come down to the administrator. You can't simply let users decide if a specific idea will be put into place with no management oversight. You must feel that it's worth doing. So, when someone suggested a good idea or a potential change, I left the thread as it was and either said that I would make it happen or that I would like more feedback, inviting more users to respond. If it was a bad idea or a change that really had no chance of happening, I replied to the thread and then probably closed it.

I thanked the user for the suggestion and expressed that I would keep it in mind but that it would not happen at this time or in the foreseeable future. I never said never, but I provided a more detailed explanation as to why, if applicable. I closed the thread because I didn't want users to think the suggested change was a distinct possibility. I didn't want to mislead anyone. Obviously, some people didn't like to have their threads closed, but I didn't want to breed false hope for something that just wasn't happening—only for me to strike it down later. I didn't want to play with people's emotions and waste people's time, in other words. Either it would happen or it wouldn't—I want users to know because it was the right thing to do.

In the second case, most of the time the post would be directed at me. I would be the only one who could fix the problem, answer the member, or be the first person to respond. For instance, on database problems I am the only person who has access to the database, so I am the only one who can fix it. Sometimes, other users could help with other problems (like "How do I upload an avatar?" and that sort of thing) and would respond before I could. But compared to other posts in the forum, that definitely was less frequent.

The forum would also serve as a storage point for guidelines ("sticky threads") and a place where users would praise site features.

So as you can see, most of the topics either needed my attention or approval in some way, could be fixed only by me, or had me as the first person to respond. This brought about the idea to eliminate the feedback forum altogether. Now I ask people to contact me directly (with a link featured in a visible area on every page of the site). The link is to a contact page with a form on it that people can fill out and send—it also includes a direct and clickable link of my e-mail address for people to use in case they would rather not use the form. Our header and footer features this link on every page, as well as in my signature, at the top of the forum listing on the index page, in various site-related documents (like our user guidelines), and elsewhere.

Let's go over how this affects the benefits I mentioned. First, the easy ones. We can use any forum to store guidelines (I use my announcements forum) or we can create separate pages for those things. Praise, although appreciated, doesn't need its own forum. These comments can also be directed via e-mail. However, if someone is praising the people in the community, my staff members, etc., then I'll probably just allow that in the general chat forum. If someone is praising the site itself or me, then I'll probably remove those and thank the person privately.

Now, the harder ones. Obviously, I still want to get user feedback on ideas that could actually happen. So, we use the announcements forum for that. For instance, let's say somebody suggests an articles section where users can submit articles. This idea has potential, but I want to see what others think and I want to see if people would actually submit articles. So, I make an announcement ("New Idea: Articles Section—Would You Use It?") and I ask people to post their feedback on that thread. This allows us to get feedback on the ideas that have a chance of happening and limits feedback on ideas that won't be.

There is no way to create a forum just for problems that other users and staff members can help with. This is a downside. I don't think it's a big one, but it's one nonetheless. People will not differentiate database errors from problems like "How do I upload my avatar?" and even then, they would use the forum for other things. You could definitely make it work, but a "special-problems" forum would most likely add to your community's required moderation time in an unnecessary way.

Another negative is that of perception. The lack of a feedback forum may give some people the idea that I don't care what they think and don't want their feedback. This is untrue, of course, as I will ask for it with a very plain and visible link on the forums, but perception is still perception and people are slanted. Does this make the whole thing not worth it? Far from it—the upsides outweigh the downsides. Another positive is that, especially if your community is of a decent size, it can help you see comments that you may have missed if they were posted in the forums. Even if something is posted in your feedback forum, maybe your cookie expires; maybe you didn't see there was a new topic posted and you miss it and then the user thinks he's being ignored. But, with a good e-mail system, that is generally less likely to happen because you are going to see everything that comes in and you can make it so that the subject line in the e-mails that your contact form generates is something that you will notice right away.

You might think that this would add to your workload as the administrator. But that is not what I have found. Keep in mind that you are dealing with inquiries that you would most likely be dealing with anyway. The only difference then is that now they are more efficiently handled, which actually allows you to save time.

So if you don't have a feedback-and-suggestions forum, what happens when someone posts feedback in the forums, anyway? With the exceptions I listed (people praising members of the community, my staff, etc.), I remove the thread. In our guidelines, we include a bit of text basically saying that all site-related questions, feedback, error reports, etc. should go through our contact form or through a member of staff. When we remove a post, we contact the member and we use a contact template (see the contact templates in chapter 5). These contact templates also include language that allows staff members to answer user questions, if they can (questions like, "How do I upload my avatar?" for example). If the staff is unable to respond to posts (as may be the case with messages from banned users or when members ask about advertising), then they simply say that I will contact the member as soon as I can. The staff member notifies me in our staff-only member-documentation section and I contact the member directly with the answer, referencing the member's original post.

This system has worked well for me and I believe it can work well for you. Still, if you want a feedback forum, have one. When you get down to it, it's not that big of a deal—most communities have it—I just feel that my system is a more efficient method of handing feedback, suggestions, problem reports, and the like.

If you do have a feedback-and-suggestions forum, it may be a good idea to set guidelines regarding the scope of the feedback you will accept. For example, do you want people questioning administrative decisions (thread removals, closures, bans, etc.)? Do you want people criticizing your staff members? Things like that. If you are going to have a feedback forum, make sure you respond to the threads that are posted. It's not a pretty sight to see feedback forum threads with no replies from someone with authority. It makes it look like you have ignored your members.

Starting with Staff

Should you have a staff for your community when it launches? It is not necessarily needed right from the beginning, but if you know some good people who are interested in the subject matter of your community and would like to become staff members, why not just go ahead and bring them on? They can bring activity to your community, which will be very useful. Make sure that they understand that their primary function in the beginning will be to help start topics and stimulate the flow of discussion. As the community becomes more active, they should become moderators and help you manage the community as appropriate.

If you do decide to have a staff, read chapter 5, "Managing Your Staff," for information on how to get started.

Design, Layout, and Customization

"Talent is cheaper than table salt. What separates the talented individual from the successful one is a lot of hard work."

—STEPHEN KING

If you are going to do this the right way, you need to have a unique, custom look. Your users will identify you by your name, but they will also become familiar with your color scheme and the look of your site. It will be a part of your brand and overall community experience. Your colors will remind users of your site.

Think of design as a means of promoting your community. That may sound a little strange, but consider this: you visit two different sites about the same subject—one that has a custom, usable, well-put-together design and one that has the default template that you've seen a million times. What is your immediate impression? It's probably that the first may be something unique, and the second may be just another community. As superficial as it may seem, appearances and first impressions do count. You need to have something that, at the very least, won't hurt you. Something that is unique, usable, easy to look at. Having a bad design or the default design will hurt you.

Some folks like to treat design like an ugly stepsister. That is to say that some people will sit there and talk about how they care about their community's environment and say that design isn't important. Some will even treat the issue of design as something that only people who don't care about their community's environment will care greatly about. That's baloney. That's not excellence and that's not the pursuit of excellence, which is what you should be concentrating on. These people make comments like, "Well, I hate it when a site has a great design that takes forever to load. Great to look at, but it's not a good idea for a community." Nonsense. The problem with that viewpoint is that the situation the critic is describing is an extreme. There are opposite extremes, and neither is the way it has to be or should be. Terrible, quick-loading design. Great, slow-loading design. These are extremes.

Good designs need not be "heavy" or graphic-intensive. Good designs are unique, usable, and do not take forever to load. I don't want you to worry just about having a good community environment. Don't get me wrong; environment is the most important thing, but I want you to be greedy, want it all, and get as much as you can with the abilities and resources at your disposal. Be selfish in this area—aim to be great in every aspect.

Don't Just Install a Ready-Made Template

There are many great templates available for phpBB, vBulletin, and other software options. However, you should use these templates as a base for your custom template and not simply slap them up and leave. You should give your site its own flavor—perhaps customize the colors, change some graphics, create a custom logo—in other words, customize the template so that it's uniquely yours. Don't just install a premade template (or worse—use the default template) and quit! You want your site to be a complete offering, and for that to happen, you need to have your own distinct layout. Even if it bears a strong resemblance to what you started with, making adjustments to make it yours will put you in a better position to be successful.

Designing for a Community

When designing a layout for a community (or having someone design one for you), keep in mind that this is a layout that users (including you) will have to load and look at over and over and over again as you log in, view topics, read posts, and more. The layout should make key areas of the site easily accessible, should not have anything that hurts the eyes, and should be mindful of load time. Keep it as light as possible and people will appreciate it.

Stick to One Look

You may be tempted to install more than one template for your community. For most people, it's just not a good idea. As I said earlier, users will come to see your community's look and color scheme as part of its overall persona, and this connection can be important. Plus, consistency is an important part of usability—be consistent in the design and structure of your community.

That doesn't mean that everything has to be the same, however. Feel free to add subtle accents to your layout during holidays, special days, and what have you. An example of this would be putting snow on your logo and/or graphics during the winter holidays or displaying pumpkins around the site during Halloween.

If, for some reason, you have more than one template installed, you should have your official "normal" layout set as the default, making it the one that guests and logged-out users always see.

However, there is one sizable disadvantage to having multiple templates when it comes to some community software: When you install a hack or make some sort of adjustment that requires changes or additions to your template files, you will have to adjust those files for every template that you have installed. This means that when you have to make changes, those changes will be more time-consuming than they would have been if you only had one template.

Customizing Your Community

What happens when your chosen community software is missing something that you need or want to have? You customize it by installing a hack. Hacks are modifications to the code of your community software. They add, alter, or remove features or functions. This is not the illegal or malicious kind of hack. These hacks are installed with the community owner's permission and are not discouraged by the creator of the software.

To find out what hacks are available (or, potentially, to request that a hack be written), you should check the big resource sites dedicated to your community software. If you are using phpBB, check out phpBBHacks.com (http://www.phpbbhacks.com). If you are using vBulletin, check out vBulletin .org (http://www.vbulletin.org).

Although the right hacks can definitely add some great stuff to your community, don't install a ton of hacks just to install a ton of hacks. The idea isn't to have more hacks than anyone else. Having hacks that you don't need and/or adding hacks in a sloppy fashion will take away from your site instead of adding to it. Speaking generally, install hacks that you feel are going to improve the usability of your community, add a feature that your community needs to be successful, add a feature that your users have heavily requested, or make your job easier. The next four sections illustrate an example of each case.

Improve the Usability   On all of my communities, I have installed two specific phpBB hacks that really help people use the site.

By default, phpBB allows users to change the way the date display on my forums is formatted when they are logged in. They change that format by changing the PHP date function code in their profile section. However, most users have no idea what that is (including me without having a good look at the manual). Does "D M d, Y g:i a" mean anything to you? Maybe it does, maybe it doesn't. But, the point is, it's too complicated. Date formats may not seem like a big deal to you, but date formats differ around the world. Some people will feel more comfortable in your community when they see a date format that they are used to. A hack that I have installed lets members quickly and easily choose from a preset selection of date formats in a drop-down menu.

I installed the second hack after discovering that I'd lose my cookie once in a while when I browsed my community. Posts that had been marked as "new" would now be marked as "read"—even if I hadn't had a chance to read them yet. When it happened (which, again, was not all the time), it was annoying. So I installed a hack that allows users to view a list of threads that have been active in the past hour, two hours, six hours, twelve hours, one day, and so on. Now, even when a cookie is lost, I can still pull up a list of threads with new posts within a given period of time.

Add an Important Feature   When I was setting up PhotoshopForums .com, I sat down and figured out what hacks I absolutely had to install. I decided that the community would definitely need to have a file-attachment hack installed because it was a graphic design community and people would expect to be able to attach their graphics to their posts.

The hack for this specific task was a complex one, but the feature was definitely needed, so I did install it. The community would simply not be as good or relevant without it. That is why it is so important.

Add a Requested Feature   You should always consider member suggestions and requests, including feature ideas. That doesn't mean that you'll add them, though—you should think about it carefully. Even if a bunch of users request a feature, don't feel obligated to add it. Use your best judgment to decide if the feature is not just a fad and will have real value to your community in the long term. The more hacks that you install, the tougher it may be to upgrade your community when the developer of your software releases a new version. A lot of the time you will have to reinstall the feature, and sometimes that will be quite difficult because it will require solid programming knowledge. If you don't have that or don't have access to that, you may want to limit your hacks to those that don't add data to or alter the database you want to keep or the default database tables. In other words, know your limitations and respect them.

Make Your Job Easier   There are also hacks that will go unnoticed or unseen by users, but you may not be able to live without them. I am speaking of administrative-function hacks. Generally, these modify existing administrative functions or create new ones that will help you manage your community. Like any hacks, however, you should only install the ones that you need and/ or feel you will benefit from.

One example of a hack that makes my job easier is the one I have installed on my sites that allows me to delete all of the inactive users (users who have not confirmed their accounts via e-mail) with a couple of clicks. It also allows me to confirm those accounts (or to only confirm certain accounts), to send the members a reminder e-mail, and more. Obviously, users do not have access to this hack, but it's very useful as it allows me to delete junk accounts, spam accounts, unconfirmed accounts, etc. easily.

Another example is a hack that allows me to remove all posts made by a specific user in one shot. So, if I have a spammer who joins and makes ten spam posts, I don't have to delete them one by one. I just log in to my admin area, enter the spammer's username, and all of those posts are removed to the trash forum. This is a time saver.

Whatever hacks you install, make sure that you document them. Save all of the original hack installation files, database changes, and so on and so forth. This documentation will make it easier for you to remember what you have installed and what changes you have made, making your life easier when it comes time to upgrade your software and make other changes. Don't forget, every hack that you install adds a bit more to the maintenance time required for your community. So, consider all hacks carefully before you install them. Think before you hack.

Be Smart, Be Safe

Part of managing your community is making sure that it is as secure and as safe as you can make it. It is beyond the scope of this book to cover all of the ways that you can secure your software and your server, but here are a few common, recommended practices.

Follow the Instructions and Recommendations

I am sure that, to some of you, this seems to be common sense—yet, not everyone does it, so it is worth noting. If the instruction manual for your particular forum software tells you to run "install.php" and then delete it, run "install.php" and then delete it! Follow any and all instructions and security recommendations that the manual makes. The manufacturer wrote the software and, chances are, it made the recommendations and rules for good reason.

Check Your File and Folder Permissions

Keep an eye on your file and folder permissions. You don't want to be any more liberal with them than you absolutely have to be. Only in rare cases (a folder where members can upload their avatars, for example) will anything need to be writeable by everyone. Besides that, only allow what you have to—generally this means 644 (-rw-r-r-) for files and 755 (drwxr-xr-x) for folders.

Protect Your Admin Areas with .htaccess

If you are on an Apache server, there is a very simple way to protect the admin areas of your community. They may already be secure, but an extra level of security can never hurt. With .htaccess you can make certain directories require that a user enter a correct username and password combination before accessing that directory. So, for instance, in phpBB you have the admin directory where all of the administrative actions take place. This is a directory that you want to protect. If someone tries to access it, not only would the user have to have administrative access granted to his or her phpBB username for your community, but the user must also have the correct username and password for your .htaccess protection. So, if for some reason someone hijacks your phpBB account, this system may stop the hijacker from making any changes in the admin section. It's a nice, simple, extra level of security.

If you have cPanel (http://www.cpanel.net) installed on your server, you can easily protect a directory with the Web Protect/Password Protect Directories feature. If you have a different control panel, you may be able to make the appropriate adjustments in it. Failing that, it's not hard to set it up manually. There is a very useful .htaccess creation wizard located on Web Design Forums.net (http://webdesignforums.turtletips.com/tools/htaccess). If you wish to learn more about the code that powers your .htaccess protection, you could read the "Comprehensive Guide to .htaccess Password Protection" article at JavaScript Kit (http://www.javascriptkit.com/howto/htaccess3.shtml).

When setting your .htaccess password, be sure to make it different from any of your other ones, such as the one that you use on the administration account of your community. It's a good practice to avoid using the same password for more than one function and/or at more than one website. Which brings us to . . .

Have Separate Passwords for Everything

Have one password for your community software-administrator account, one password for your .htaccess protection, one password for your database, one password for your FTP log-in, and so on and so forth. Do not use the same password over and over again. Use unique passwords for everything that requires one.

This makes it harder for someone to access everything if he gets his hands on one of your passwords.

Create a Separate Database Account for Each Database

To that end, you should also create a separate database account for every database. Don't use the same username and password combination for multiple databases and, especially, do not use your main cPanel/web hosting control panel log-in as the database username and password. Create one specifically for each and every database. If a hacker somehow accesses one of your database username and password combinations, this will help stop him from accessing more than one database or from accessing your web hosting control panel so he can do more damage.

Backup Your Database—Constantly!

You should be constantly backing up the database that houses your community's posts, member information, and other data. If you are on a Linux or Unix server, you could set a crontab, which is a means of automating tasks on your server, to run every evening to backup your database. In line with that, it's a good idea to have enough server space so you can have a backup or two of your database on your server and not have to worry about running out of space. For a backup system to be anywhere near reliable, you can't have all of your eggs in one basket—or in this case, on one server. So, you want to make sure that you have a recent backup of your database on at least one server or computer that doesn't host your site.

If you can manage it, download your database onto your own computer or hard drive whenever possible or, better yet, at regularly scheduled intervals. A backup system that doesn't happen automatically is a backup system that is doomed to fail because if you have to remember to do it yourself, you'll forget, put it off, or not backup as frequently as you should. Plus, there are better uses of your time.

My current backup system looks something like this. First, we have the main, live copy of the database, of course. Second, either my host offers me nonguaranteed backups (it backs up my files at least daily, but it doesn't guarantee it—i.e., it's not a feature I pay for) or I have a second hard drive on the server that my database automatically backs up to at least daily. Third, I have a crontab that, everyday, automatically exports a copy of my database to the folder above the public_html folder. Fourth, I use CuteFTP's (http://www.cuteftp.com) scheduling feature to download that copy to my computer every two days automatically. Fifth, the copy on my computer is automatically backed up every day (on days where it hasn't been updated, it isn't, though) to an external hard drive. So, at any given time there are at least five copies of my database that are no more than three days old or so. These copies reside on at least three different machines in at least two different locations. The presumable worst-case scenario (other than all five copies tanking and me crying myself to sleep for the rest of my life) is that I have a database copy that is three days old. Most likely, it'll never get to that point. But it's good to know that if it does, I'll be prepared. Are there better backup systems? Certainly! Loads better. But this is a good, affordable solution that provides me with a great amount of security and safety.

My backup system may sound expensive, but it wasn't. It consists of a 250 gigabyte hard drive with an external enclosure, software that automatically backs up my data (SyncBackSE, http://www.2brightsparks.com/syncback/sbse.html), and my FTP program (CuteFTP Home). This sort of system can be had for a few hundred dollars or less. You need to have a high-speed connection to download the database files at a decent pace, but besides that, it's totally worth the investment for your community and for your peace of mind. Be sure you have some sort of backup system. The more comprehensive it is, the better off you'll be. This goes for all of your site's files—not just your database files (I mention those first because they change more often, usually).

The cPanel software has a built-in feature that you can use to set up crontabs, but you will still need to know what to type in. For this information, you can always contact your host. You could also check out the "Diary of a Webmaster Part 4—Backing up with MySQLDump" article at SitePoint (http://www.sitepoint.com/article/backing-up-mysqldump).

I cannot overstate the importance of routinely backing up your database. So many things can happen where you can lose all of your data. Do you want to lose every post, every member account, and all of the members' details? If you want to be successful, you don't.

Keep Your Community Software Updated

When your community software developer releases a security fix or a new version that patches up a security issue or issues, upgrade or, at the very least, patch the security vulnerabilities. Don't wait for someone to attack your community before you upgrade.

Conclusion

In this chapter, I covered a majority of the issues that you'll face relating to the technical and physical aspects of your setup. Having a complete community is about being good in all phases—everything from your domain name and your look to your technology and security. Give them the attention that they deserve and ensure that they are running in the fashion that gives you the greatest chance of succeeding.

CHAPTER 3

Developing Guidelines

Ο ne essential to building a truly successful community is to have a set of well-thought-out guidelines that users must adhere to and respect in order to participate in the community. There are also bound to be at least a few legal issues to consider, as well. Please bear in mind that the contents of this book cannot be construed as legal advice and you should always consult with qualified legal counsel if you need such information.

You'll notice that I said *guidelines* and not *rules*. Guidelines allow for some flexibility, some discretion. Rules are more likely to be enforced in a hard and fast manner, which can leave little room for interpretation and will probably lead to you having to deal with more nutcases who insist on reading them fifty times backward and forward in hopes of finding an angle where they think you are being inconsistent.

Your user guidelines are a key communication tool for you. They are a type of vision statement for your community. By putting your expectations of users in writing, you are letting everyone know what your vision is for your community. By communicating this, people will know what they are in for and will either get behind you (and participate) or get away from you. Either way, they will at least know what your community is all about, and having this level of communication is vital to your success.

Your user guidelines are very much a living document that will change and grow with your needs. In this chapter, I'll help you to get a good idea of what they should cover and how they can be formulated and delivered.

Guideline Ideas

In this section, I am going to give you some ideas that may be useful to you as you craft your own guidelines. Please keep in mind that these are general guideline ideas. They will not all apply and you may have more specific needs that will, depending on the nature and content of your community, require you to craft explicit guidelines for their handling. For example, as mentioned in chapter 2, if you have an advertising forum, you should come up with a list of guidelines just for that forum so users know how it is meant to be used.

Another good example would be the user guidelines at the DrGregHouse .com Forums. This is a fan community for the *House* TV show. I run it. Although we want to maintain a community that is generally clean and family friendly, sometimes things are said or discussed on the show that we would otherwise not allow on the site. Yet, it would be kind of odd for us to prohibit discussions about things that have actually happened on the show. So, in light of this, we came up with an addition to our user guidelines:

However, there are exceptions that are made when you are directly quoting dialog from the show or discussing events that have happened on the show. During these times, you may be allowed to post content that would otherwise be considered vulgar and/or inappropriate. If it has been said on the show or has happened on the show, chances are that we will allow you to discuss it, as long as it is not overly gratuitous or discussed or speculated on in an overly gratuitous manner.

It must be necessary and relevant and the discussion must focus on exactly what happened, what was said, or what the original topic of the thread is. It cannot turn into an unrelated discussion that would otherwise be a violation of our User Guidelines. For instance, if there was a religious issue on the show, what happened on the show can be discussed—but it cannot be treated as a means to introduce more general topics of religion, which are not allowed on this community.

For these exceptions only, if you are quoting a word or term that would normally be considered vulgar or inappropriate on this community, you may censor or abbreviate the word or term and post it (an example of self-censoring would be h*****). Absolutely no vulgar (self-censored, abbreviated, or otherwise) or inappropriate content can be posted on anything outside of posts, including signatures, profiles, avatars, etc. Some *House* episodes contain language that is not appropriate here. If you use it, you will not be able to participate.

What Do They Apply To?

What do your user guidelines apply to? Posts, profiles, private messages, what else? Make it clear that your user guidelines apply to all of the content posted in your community.

It's wise to apply your guidelines to private messages (if you allow them) in your community. If you don't have the ability to view private messages easily when you need to, install a hack that allows you to do so. Make it clear that you can read private messages but that you only do so when someone reports an issue or you have a legitimate reason. This can be a sticky subject for some, so I've tackled it in depth in the "Violations in Private Messages" section of chapter 6.

Cross-Posting, Duplicate Threads, Etc.

Cross-posting is when a user posts the same thread in two or more locations. It is best to have one thread so that you can find all of the responses and information in one place, rather than having it spread across two or more threads. It adds unnecessary clutter and can be a waste of your members' time. Ask your users to post their topics in the most appropriate forum, given your organizational structure. If the duplicate thread(s) has already generated helpful replies, close it and add a reply, linking to the one thread that you intend to leave open. Remove any duplicate threads without helpful replies.

Posting the same thread in the same forum more than once is also something that should be discouraged for the same reasons and handled in exactly the same manner. If the two (or more) threads were posted within a very short period of time, you can deduce that one was an accident and simply remove it. However, if one is posted more than five minutes or so after the other, chances are it was not an accident.

If your software has a merge feature, where you can place posts from one thread into another, you may want to move any helpful replies off of cross-posted or duplicate topics and onto the one thread that you intend to leave. Then you can simply remove those extra threads instead of closing them.

Post-Count Boosting and Bumping

As I discussed in the "Software Options" section of chapter 2, sometimes people take their post counts a little too seriously and try to boost it artificially through the mass creation of short and/or meaningless posts. You can use your guidelines to discourage this behavior. If you allow game threads like "Word Association Game," "What song are you listening to right now?" and the like, you may want to include guidelines about those, as well, such as to not post consecutively within a short period of time.

Bumping is when you add a new post onto a topic for no apparent reason other than to get people to look at it again and/or bring it back up to the top of the active-topics lists (hence "bumping" it up). For a lot of communities this isn't much of a problem. But for others (especially support or help communities), it can become one. It did on the phpBBHacks.com Support Forums. So we allowed one noninformative bump (i.e., a post that doesn't add anything to the thread or reply to anyone) per topic that must come no sooner than forty-eight hours after the last activity on the thread.

We took it a step further and installed a hack that actually prevented the thread starter from making two posts in a row on the same thread if the two posts were within forty-eight hours of each other. This requires them to either wait forty-eight hours, edit a post they've already made on the thread, or wait for someone to reply to them. This has substantially reduced the time that my staff and I previously had to spend on removing bumps.

Styles of Communication (No CAPS!)

It's not something that will always be needed, but you may find it useful to specify guidelines relating to styles of communication. This includes things like not typing 100 percent in CAPS, forming complete sentences, resisting the temptation of shorthand (like *r* for *are* or *u* for *you*, for example) and the like.

When someone is especially bad in one of my communities, I send them a note asking them to adjust the way they post, but that has been so rare for me that it hasn't been worth adding to my user guidelines. That could always change.

On the other side of the coin, prohibiting your users from making uninvited remarks about spelling, typos, posting styles, etc. can help to keep threads from degenerating into nonsense. They aren't necessary and only serve as a sidetrack. If someone has an issue with how a fellow member is posting, she should report it to a staff member.

Advertising

I prefer to use the word *advertising* instead of *spamming*, as it seems a bit less inflammatory and accusatory. Assuming you don't want solicitations to override your community, you should come up with guidelines that cover advertising in your community. If you allow widespread, unregulated advertising, people will get sick of seeing it and they will leave. If someone wants to advertise, he can pay for it. You can even sell ad threads, as we'll talk about in chapter 9, if it's all that popular. Spammers tend not to be the buyers of ads (not that you'd want to sell to a spammer, anyway). Most of them just want to spam and leave.

How strict you want to be is up to you. I'm really strict on advertising. Generally, if a user starts a thread to bring attention to something that he is (or appears to be) in some way affiliated with, it is removed. I do not say things like, "Well, such and such ad may be useful to my users, so I am going to allow it." If you are relatively strict on advertising (you don't have a dedicated forum or forums for it and you don't really care for it popping up in your forums), you would be getting into some potentially difficult waters if you allowed threads that you felt advertised something that would be useful to your user base. Not only is it not always easy to guess just what might be useful, but when it comes time to reject one, you'll have to be ready to explain why that one thread wasn't "useful" and why it was different from other threads that you have allowed. And then, of course, people probably won't agree with you. Not that it matters, but why make it harder than it has to be, right?

Sometimes, when you pull someone's post for advertising, the member will complain that his or her site is a personal website, has no ads, and/or it is nonprofit and that he or she was just trying to help. For this reason, I've included language in my guidelines saying that it doesn't matter if a site is commercial, personal, or for a nonprofit—advertising is advertising. This helps to get everyone on the same page. Of course, if you want to apply different policies to different types of websites, that would be helpful to declare as well.

For the most part, the only time that I will allow people to link to their own sites is if it is necessary (e.g., in a website review forum, it is necessary for members to link to their own sites) and when it specifically answers a question that someone is asking. And even then it must be a link to the specific page or area with the answer, rather than a general link to a homepage. The link must be needed—if the answer can simply be posted without the link, that is the way to go. This can vary by community, however. For instance, in a martial arts community, you would allow people to post links to pictures or videos of themselves performing or practicing—as long as said pictures and videos don't include website URLs, advertisements for sites or companies they are affiliated with, etc. So, you will need to find the balance that is right for you.

You may also want to keep an eye out for people who are posting excessive numbers of links to their own sites (even if they do answer questions specifically) or utilizing any "sneaky" advertising methods.

An example of excessive linking would be a user who appears to be simply looking for opportunities to mention his or her site. A mention here or there that answers a question (as described earlier) is fine, but watch out for people who seem to be asking questions where their site can be an answer (or, worse, creating pages on their sites because of questions they see on your site).

Sneaky advertising methods include things like representing a link as something other than what is; acting like a third party that is unaffiliated with the item or entity being discussed; trying to hide links in posts by linking smilies, periods, and so on. For more on this, please see the "That Doesn't Look Like Spam . . ." section of chapter 6.

Make sure that people keep their signature links in their actual signatures in their profiles. Generally, people try to sneak signatures into their posts to get attention or (especially when people try to mimic the default appearance of signatures in your community) to get the post spidered by search engines even if you already allow your member signatures to be spidered. Doing this makes it harder for you—and them—to remove their signatures from their posts, edit their signatures, etc.

Affiliate Links

These are links that lead directly to the user earning cash, banner impressions, credits, points, etc. Although I don't mind these in signatures and profiles (although you might), they are definitely a problem if they are included in a post. They are not always easy to spot, but if you look at the link carefully, a lot of the time you can pick them out. If a product is really worth recommending, your members can post the link without their affiliate codes tacked on.

Copyright

Your community must respect the laws protecting copyright and intellectual property. I am going to speak as someone who lives in the United States, but your country most likely has copyright laws.

You must not allow your users to post complete written works (stories, poems, news articles, editorials, interviews, and so on) if they do not have the permission to reproduce those works. Under fair-use provisions, you may allow your users to quote small portions of an article and link to or cite a source. Do not allow them simply to quote small portions without a source. Do not allow them to post the whole thing with a source. Require that they both quote a small portion and link to or provide a source. Even then, if the author or rights holder asks you to take this content off of your site, you should comply. As long as you require your users to quote only a small portion and provide the source, most people won't have a problem (chances are, they'll even like it). But the original work still belongs to the author, and if the author wants it removed, you should remove it.

You should never assume that someone has the rights to a work. Quite often, it can be fairly easy to spot a questionable situation. If you have a member who hardly ever posts more than ten words and doesn't know where the period key is located on the keyboard and then, all of a sudden, discovers an expansive vocabulary and posts a 2,000 word exquisitely written article . . . well, something might be up!

If you see an article quoted from ESPN.com, the *Wall Street Journal*, or *USA TODAY*, you can assume that the poster probably doesn't have the right to reproduce it. Sometimes, it can be harder to determine whether the poster has rights to reproduce written works from smaller or less prominent sites.

Doing a bit of research can often clear things up. For example, use Google to search for a phrase taken from the post. Do any pages come up? Check them out. This will allow you to see if the article was taken from another site and, if so, which one(s). After giving it a quick look, if you are reasonably suspicious, pull the post. If someone does, in fact, have the rights to reproduce the work, he or she can always offer some proof and then you can reinstate the post, if appropriate.

You should be ready to handle claims and reports of copyright infringement. You want people to contact you before they go further up the chain (your host, your datacenter, etc.) because when they get to those people, they will be getting into the Digital Millennium Copyright Act (DMCA). With the DMCA, they might not be too choosy in what they pull down. In fact, they might pull your entire site down in a heartbeat. You don't want that, so make it so that people can contact you without a lot of fuss. Don't make people register or log in to contact you. Don't make it harder for them to find infringers and report them.

Read these reports as soon as you can. Investigate and handle them as appropriate. If the complaint goes directly to your host or higher, you'll be notified (possibly after they have pulled your site) and, as long as the infringement isn't particularly heinous, they'll usually give you the opportunity to remove the content from your site or send a counter notification that the DMCA complaint is not valid. Don't take this as an opportunity to play games, though—if you think you could be in the wrong, you probably should comply. I'm not saying all DMCA notices are valid—they're not. But it's often not that hard to make an educated guess that you might be violating the rights of another.

Depending on your situation, you may want to look into designating a DMCA agent for your community through the U.S. Copyright Office (http://www.copyright.gov/onlinesp). If you qualify, doing so can afford you protection under the act's Safe Harbor provisions, limiting your liability.

That said, you should be proactive—not reactive. I've dealt with administrators who think that they can let people distribute anything on their sites until the rights holders contact them. That is such a backward, disrespectful position to take.

It isn't just limited to written works, either. Pictures, audio, video, and other creations are also protected. Due to the mass of online piracy, the biggest issues are with audio and video. For whatever reason, some people think they have the right to distribute and/or illegally download copyrighted media. Don't let these people use your community for these activities in any way, whether it is the actual distribution of files or the promotion of this behavior. If you want people to respect your rights, you need to respect theirs.

In addition to that, such activities limit your potential as a community. What respectable companies and individuals would choose to associate themselves with a community that promotes theft? Hosts, advertising networks, and companies that are highly relevant to what you do will not. Think about that. Let's say you are a fan site for *The Simpsons* TV show. You'd like to have some sort of contact with Fox, right? If you allow people to illegally trade/share/distribute (*steal* is a simple-enough word there) episodes of *The Simpsons* and Fox finds out, it'll want nothing to do with you nor should it. So be careful. You don't want to do things you'll have to hide or that you'll be ashamed of if they come to light.

It is beyond the scope of this book to address further the legalities of running a community. For definitive and complete advice, be sure to seek the services of qualified legal counsel.

Illegal Activities

In addition to avoiding copyright infringement, you should not allow your community to host any discussions of illegal activities or illegal content. No warez (illegal trading of copyrighted works), cracks (circumvention of software copy protection and activation systems), or law breaking of any kind. This includes posting information that a user has obtained illegally.

Hotlinking and Bandwidth Theft

Hotlinking happens when you link to a visual element (graphics, etc.) so that it embeds into your site but is called from a server that you do not have permission to link to in this fashion. Your site gets the benefit of the file, but the person who pays for the server foots the bill. The result is bandwidth theft.

Hotlinking means that you are using bandwidth that you have no business using. Here's another example: If a user links her avatar to a server that hosts the image but she does not have permission to link to that server, she is hotlinking. It's costing the owner of that server money and resources. It's not fair and it could get you in trouble.

Hotlinking can sometimes be hard to detect. But if you keep your eyes open, you can minimize occurrences in your community. Discourage it, disallow it, and combat it when it's brought to your attention. Just as with copyright infringement, make it easy for people to report it to you and then make sure you handle those reports appropriately.

Providing links to files on other servers is also hotlinking. (For example, consider this link: http://www.somesite.com/images/notmine.jpg. Based on the jpg extension, you can tell that this is a link to an image file rather than a website. It's hotlinking, and it's not OK.) This includes links to images, video, audio, documents, archives, and more. People should link to the *page* with the file on it—not to the file itself. Linking directly to a file allows people to view it or download it directly without viewing the website that hosts it. Website owners have these files on their sites to give people a reason to visit those sites—accessing them directly just sucks up their bandwidth without giving them an actual visitor.

If the website owner gives permission to hotlink (a lot of the time, this will be posted on the site), then fine. But, if the owner doesn't or you are unsure, then it's a no-no.

Encourage your members to use your attachments feature (if you have one) or to use one of the many, many free image, video, and file hosting services out there, such as ImageShack (http://imageshack.us) and YouTube (http://www.youtube.com). However, this doesn't change anything that I said as far as copyright infringement. Don't encourage people to upload the latest *Harry Potter* movie or Diddy album, for example. Nothing they can do would make that OK.

Legal Advice, Medical Advice, Suicide Threats, Etc.

Depending on the subject matter of your community, you may want to create a policy for discussing these sensitive matters. For example, in my martial arts community, health and fitness are very much a part of the subject. So we have a policy about discussing those topics.

Your policies should make it clear that any advice given on your site is for informational and educational purposes only, that it is not verified by you or anyone else for accuracy and as such, it can be inaccurate. Make it clear that what appears on the site is not to be construed as actual, professional advice. People are responsible for their own health care, their own legal responsibilities, and so on—not you. Outline this and encourage your users to seek the counsel of qualified professionals.

As far as suicide threats are concerned, it's simply best not to allow your community to get involved. You should remove the post or message and you or your staff should send a private message to the person encouraging him or her to call 911 and/or go to the hospital.

Personal, Real-Life Information and Privacy

Keep personal, real-life information such as home addresses and home phone numbers out of your community. You don't want to be responsible for a member being harassed by a nut job. If members wish to share this information, they can share it privately.

Depending on context, you may also want to prevent the posting of private communications like e-mail conversations. It can be a nasty business because not only are they private, but you don't know who is making up what or putting what into whose mouth.

English Only, Please

If your community is an English-speaking community, requiring posted content to be in English will ensure that the site's intended audience can understand what is being said and, more important, helps you properly monitor and administer the community. If you can't understand what people are saying, how can you tell if it's bad?

If your site is for speakers of a language other than English, the same idea still applies for that language.

Respect

Members of your community must treat you, your staff, and one another with respect. They don't have to like one another or agree with one another, but inflammatory and disrespectful comments cannot be allowed.

This includes disallowing the posting of potentially false or slanderous information in your community. Although you may be protected by The

Communications Decency Act of 1996, which prevents content hosts from being sued over defamatory content that their users have posted (unless you are the one making the defamatory remarks, of course), you may very well get dragged into any mess that one of your members creates, and that is a waste of your time. Even if you are OK with that, you don't want to be a community that is known for allowing defamatory statements.

Use some common sense here. When a member says, "Patrick O'Keefe, the author of that book you read, stole a plasma TV from Wal-Mart," is that really something you want on your site? If the statement is untrue, it would defame me and tarnish my reputation because it is an accusation of criminal activity. You don't want that on your site. If someone committed a crime, people should report it to the proper authorities—not to you.

The difference between fact and opinion is important here. There is a difference between saying, "Patrick is a jerk," and, "Patrick defrauded me." If I'm a jerk, that's your opinion—but, if I defrauded you, that's either a fact or it's not. It's best that your community simply stays out of these things.

Do not allow your site to become a soapbox for someone you believe has some sort of agenda. Even if the person is referring to someone who is not a member of your community or is speaking of an entirely different website altogether, you need to be mindful. If someone got banned from XYZ Forums, he doesn't need a thread about it at your site. It's not relevant.

Obstructing the Flow of Discussion

Or that's what I call it, anyway. Basically, in an opinion-based discussion, you will find users who will make statements like, "There is no argument." Or they'll say things like, "Are you serious?" or "Are you kidding me?" when the user was clearly already serious. You'll even have people who appoint themselves as some sort of opinion judge, where they sit there and decide whether an opinion is valid and evaluate each and every opinion on the thread. These types of remarks obstruct the flow of discussion. You want to keep it flowing, so hold those kinds of remarks to a minimum.

Vulgar Language and Offensive Material

To ensure that your community is inviting and approachable, you can disallow strong vulgarities on your site. I want users of all ages and backgrounds to feel welcome. Allowing profanity does not make for a welcoming environment. You should also not allow users to post any offensive or inappropriate material in their posts, profiles, signatures, avatars, or anywhere else in your community. This includes pornography, racial slurs, sexually motivated content, and depictions or descriptions of extreme violence. Make it clear that abbreviations of vulgarities as well as attempts to self-censor (one example of this is when a user intentionally puts asterisks in a word, such as *s****) or circumvent your existing word censor also violate this guideline. You should decide what words you are comfortable with and set a standard through active and consistent moderation.

Obviously, there are exceptions. If your community is about sex education, well, there is going to be sexually motivated content. If you are a fan site for a TV show that discusses topics that would otherwise be inappropriate (see the example at the beginning of the "Guideline Ideas" section), you'll have to make some adjustments.

Freedom of Speech

I touch on this in a more meaningful way in the "Real People, Real Cases" section of chapter 6. It's sufficient here to say that "freedom of speech" has no place in any professional or responsibly run community. It is your site and it is your responsibility to set the guidelines that all users must adhere to. Contrary to what you may hear from "experts" (also known as angry people crying foul on you for removing their posts) in the field, you have no legal obligation to allow them to say whatever they want, whenever they want, however they want—or, in their eyes, to "uphold free speech."

Multiple Accounts

Allowing one member to hold more than one account? Sounds like fun! Why wouldn't you want your members to play dress-up in your community? Because it complicates things unnecessarily. When you search for all posts by a specific user, you want to get all posts by a specific user. You don't want to have to search multiple user accounts to find all of this data. If the person doesn't make his identity widely known, he's being dishonest with your entire user base. Finally, and perhaps most important, it is easier to track the member's violations or issues when he or she only has one supposed username and you know what it is.

If you feel that someone may have created more than one account, you should contact the member and ask for an explanation of the similarities between the accounts. If the member says the other account is for his or her brother, mother, girlfriend, hamster, etc., you really have no choice but to give the member the benefit of the doubt. If you find out that the user is actually using two accounts or if you get an answer that is less than favorable, you may want to take action, such as locking one or both accounts.

When is there no doubt? Well, let's say you get two new members and their first posts on your site look like this:

Poster 1: Have you ever stopped by SiteName.com? It's awesome!

Poster 2: Wow, never seen that one before. Thanks!

Poster 1: No problem, glad to help.

Poster 2: Yeah, I'm still on there right now. Loving it!

Poster 1: hehe.

If they both used the same Internet Protocol (IP), there is no doubt and you'll want to ban both accounts. But I have also had members create new accounts because they couldn't get into their old accounts or they weren't sure that their accounts still existed. In these cases, I try to identify the members and either help them to get back into their old accounts or close their old accounts and let them use the new ones. In either case, I make it clear that creating multiple accounts is not acceptable and that they shouldn't do it in the future.

Automated Account Creation, Participation, and Scraping

You don't want people to create accounts or posts automatically or to steal your content by scraping it. Scraping is when someone or something takes (scrapes) content from your community, placing it on another site or in another format. Will a guideline stop them? Maybe, maybe not. But, at least you'll have something to point to if and when you need to take a little action.

Signatures

Signatures are lines of text and/or images that display at the end of your member's posts. These can get out of control (I've seen signatures that took up two screens), so you want to have guidelines in place to keep them in line.

One thing to consider is whether you want to allow images in signatures. I'm not a fan of them, but if you must, limit their size (both screen size and file size). It's not a happy moment when you're sitting at your computer waiting for somebody's huge signature to load or you have to scroll a page and a half every time that person posts. For text signatures, be sure to set a line and/or character-per-line limit. You may also wish to require that members not use certain BBCode tags or that they not use BBCode to make the text larger than a certain size. BBCode is formatting code that is used on your community, usually in posts and signatures. Also require them to keep their signatures readable by not using colors that are harsh on the eyes and so on.

Avatars

Usually your community software will allow you to set a maximum avatar size that it will enforce. You may wish to describe these limits in your general guidelines. You can limit avatar size and even prohibit animated avatars, but unless you are dealing with a particularly sensitive demographic, that is not usually necessary. For the reasons discussed in the "User Options" section of chapter 2, make users upload avatars to your server rather than having them link to other servers.

Privilege Restrictions

Do any of your community privileges have prerequisites? For instance, do users have to have a certain number of posts before they can initiate conversations via private message? Must they have a certain number of posts before they can have avatars or signatures? If so, you should include this information in your user guidelines to prevent confusion.

Deleting Accounts and/or Posts in the Future (Leaving Your Community)

What happens when someone tells you she wants her account deleted and her posts removed? This is something that comes up when people are leaving your community (maybe because they disagreed with your policies) or when they are banned. You need to have a policy that covers it. You should not comply with vague requests such as, "I'm leaving, remove all of my posts." If a long-time user wants all of his posts removed, doing so could remove a lot of useful posts from your community, make other posts (made by other people) less useful or relevant, and deflate your numbers in a truly unnecessary way.

However, I think it's fair for you to compromise when you have someone who no longer wishes to be associated with your community. I do this by allowing members to request that their accounts be closed. What this means is that their accounts will be banned if they aren't already (so they cannot access them, post from them, or change them), the usernames will be changed to something nondescriptive (such as username85673), and the profiles (e-mail addresses, signatures, and the rest) will be cleared. We still document that information internally, just in case they try to sign up again. I make it clear that this is not something to take lightly and it's irreversible. No posts are removed.

Why treat it so seriously? You don't want people playing games with you or your community. You don't want someone coming in, making a bunch of posts, and then getting all of those posts removed. Everything posted in your community becomes a part of the community, even if a particular member no longer is.

Now, if someone wants a post removed for a legitimate reason, that's fine. If I ban someone who wants pictures of herself removed, that's an understandable request and I'm happy to comply with it. What I'm not going to do is a mass purging of posts for no other reason than somebody wants me to. That would be opening my community up to harm.

Who's the Boss?

It's important that your members respect the decisions that you and your staff make. To ensure that this happens, make it clear that administrators, moderators, and/or staff members have the final say and are responsible for interpreting and enforcing the guidelines of your community. At the same time, be sure your guidelines say that if there is a complaint about a decision relating to the guidelines (if someone believes you wrongfully removed his thread, for instance), the complainant should contact the administrator or staff member (your choice) via private message and not publicly. This includes things like "They deleted my post," "Why did you guys delete my post?" and "My post got deleted because I did this and that."

To encourage a member to revise a post that violated the guidelines, you can allow the member to request a copy of a post that you removed. You can then decide whether to provide a copy of their post (if it was a pretty good post other than small violations here and there) or not (if it was full of violations, it may just be better to tell the person to start over).

If You Break the Guidelines, There Are Consequences

In order for people to respect your guidelines, there must be consequences for those who choose not to do so. Those who disregard you, your staff, and your guidelines run the risk of losing their ability to participate in your community, and you should be upfront and honest about this fact.

The Guidelines Are Not All-Inclusive

Your guidelines will never cover everything 100 percent. So, it's important to convey that they are not all-inclusive and to allow yourself room to work within them. You want to give people an outline of what you expect. You cannot hope to address every situation specifically, nor should you try or represent that you have. Discretion is a big part of managing a community. Explain that your user guidelines are subject to change at any time without notice and that you reserve the right to deactivate any account and to remove any content without warning.

We Can't Watch It All!

Chances are that your forums (or at least, most of them) allow people to post and have that content displayed immediately. This means that you do not sit there and approve each post one by one before it is actually visible in your community. To ensure that everyone is aware of this, you can make it clear that the live nature of your community makes it impossible to monitor and/or verify the accuracy and/or validity of content posted.

This also extends to violations of your user guidelines. You simply cannot find them all. You do the best you can and you get a lot of them, but you should encourage your users to help you. If a user responds to a guideline violation with a guideline violation, handle it appropriately. Just because a person acts a certain way does not give others license to act that way as well. Responding to violations publicly does nothing but magnify those violations and encourage further ones. You want your users to contact you or a staff member privately when they believe they have witnessed a violation, and then you want them to forget about the violation all together—in other words, you don't want them to respond to it publicly. You and your staff can make the appropriate determination from there.

Even better, if you have a "report posts" feature (as described in the "Post Reporting System" section of chapter 6), be sure to use your guidelines to encourage members to use it.

Have Fun! And, If You Need Help, Let Us Know!

A majority of communities are there for some sort of enjoyment, however small. Even if they are there to help or to learn, they are still there to create a positive experience while doing so. Encourage your members to keep it light, to have fun, and make it enjoyable. And if they have any questions or need any help, encourage them to contact you.

■ ■ ■

In this section, we dealt with some of the more popular issues that you can outline and discuss in your guidelines. There are more ideas that I am sure you will come up with as your community evolves. No matter what you do, be sure to give your users the benefit of the doubt in initial, nonsevere violations and enforce them with patience and understanding.

Real-Life Examples

Here are a couple of real-life, in-use examples of what happens when (some of) the guideline ideas in this chapter come together. Both examples have their differences and they should hopefully give you plenty to think about as you craft your own guidelines. I recommend that you use a simple, direct approach, as it makes for a shorter, more easily comprehensible document. Tell people what you expect of them.

These are the user guidelines from KarateForums.com, which is a martial arts discussion community that I run. I didn't come up with all of it—my guidelines are the culmination of my work and ideas as well as work, ideas, and suggestions made by others. You should always keep your eyes and mind open. Let others inspire you, and if another community has a guideline that inspires you, drop the administrator a line, tell him or her how great it is, and ask if you can use it on your site. A lot of the time you don't legally have to ask (assuming you just want to use the idea, not copy the language, which you can't do without permission, of course), but asking demonstrates common courtesy and respect. Treat people as you'd like to be treated.

Participation in the KarateForums.com website constitutes agreement to the following guidelines, which apply to posts, profile information, avatars, signatures, any other content on this site and participation in general. This includes private messages, which we have the ability to read, but only do so when a violation is reported to us or we have a legitimate reason. Although rare, it does happen. You cannot initiate any conversations via private message or send any e-mails via the site until you have reached 25 posts.

Because of the live nature of the discussions on this community, it is not possible for us to review and/or confirm the accuracy or validity of a message before it is posted. If you believe that someone has violated our User Guidelines or you have spotted content that may otherwise require attention, please click the report post icon (exclamation point (!) button) in the upper right part of the post where the violation is located. If the thread has numerous violations in it, you need not report each post; simply report one post and note that you spotted other violations in the thread, as well, in your report before you submit. Include a brief description of what you believe is wrong. After you send your report, forget that the post(s) exists. Do not post "I have reported your post"—do not further reference the post in the thread in any way. If you feel that the report post feature is not appropriate for reporting a certain type of violation, please feel free to send a private message to a staff member or contact me.

Notification is strongly encouraged—we need your help to keep up the quality that KarateForums.com is known for. It is also voluntary and anonymous, but in no case should a user respond to a situation personally, thereby aggravating the situation further. Responding to a violation in an inflammatory manner is a violation in itself and will result in appropriate action.

This is a for-profit website that will attempt to generate revenue through avenues that we deem appropriate. Any content that violates our User Guidelines will be removed. Interpretation of our guidelines is at the discretion of the staff.

1. Cross-posting is not allowed and will result in the removal of one or more posts. Cross-posting is defined as posting the same information in two or more locations. When posting your topic, please try to post it in the most appropriate place within the organizational structure of our community. Identical topics posted in the same or different forums will be removed.

2. While member post count has meaning, it should not be taken too seriously. Attempts to artificially increase your post count are prohibited. This includes the mass creation of short or meaningless posts. When participating in game threads such as ''Word Association Game'' or ''What song are you listening to right now?'' please do not post consecutive replies within a short period of time.

3. Advertisements are not allowed. Generally speaking, posts made specifically for the promotion of a website, product, or service are considered advertising or, at least, posts made that unnecessarily send people to a website that you are in some way affiliated with. It does not matter if it is a commercial website, a personal website, a nonprofit website, etc. We do authorize and/or sell advertisements on a case-by-case basis. If you are interested in utilizing this option, please contact us.

All signature links must be kept in your signature in your profile. Anyone found to be posting excessive links to their websites or suspected of using ''sneaky'' advertising methods is in violation of this guideline. You may only post a link to your site/a site that you are in some way affiliated with if the link specifically answers the question that is being asked and the answer cannot be simply posted without the link. Even then, link directly to the page where the information can be found. General and unnecessary links will be tagged as advertising. If you are found to be excessively posting links to your site (or you appear to be seeking out threads where your link may be relevant, so that you can post it), you may lose the ability to post links to your site.

4. You are not allowed to post an affiliate URL that leads to you earning cash, banner impressions, credits, points, etc. Such links are only allowed in signatures and profiles, but may not be referred to in posts.

5. Do not post personal, real-life information such as home addresses and home phone numbers. Do not demand of or continually press other users for personal information, including their background in the martial arts. Ask once, if you must. If the person you are asking does not want to answer, do not press them further.

6. As this is an English-speaking community, we require that posted content be in the English language, so that it can be well received and properly monitored. This excludes martial art and technique names (which must still be posted in English characters) as well as pictures of organizational badges which may be posted or used as avatars.

7. Vulgar language and inappropriate material is not allowed and will be removed. Abbreviations, self-censoring, and attempts to circumvent the word censoring feature of the community software also violate this guideline. If your post contains a word that is censored by the software, you must remove that word or the post will be removed. If you feel that the censor is acting in error, please contact us.

   We try to maintain a family friendly atmosphere whenever it is possible within the main subject matter of this community. Please keep this in mind when participating.

8. When linking to outside websites, you must ensure that the content of the link is appropriate for our community, in line with the guidelines laid out here. This includes mentioning or referencing a site, even if the mention is not hyperlinked. If you post a link and that link is automatically censored, it is considered to be an inappropriate link and you should remove it from your post immediately. If left, all posts that feature inappropriate links will be removed.

9. Posts that discuss illegal activities, transactions, or websites such as warez, cracks, etc. will be removed. This includes the posting of information that you have obtained illegally.

10. Non martial arts related political and religious discussions are prohibited. If it is believed that the end result of a discussion will be political or religious (with no relevance to the martial arts discussion taking place), the post may be removed. Likewise, strong political and religious sentiments should be kept out of profiles, signatures, and other content.

11. Do not post copyrighted materials (articles, videos, audio, etc.) that you do not have permission to reproduce or distribute. For text articles, most of the time you may quote a small portion of the article (usually no more than 1/5 or 1/6) and you must link to the source (if online) or provide the source (if offline).

Posting the entire article, even with the source, constitutes copyright infringement. This is not the place to illegally trade or distribute copyrighted (or those with questionable copyright status) video or audio clips.

12. When posting and linking to images, videos, files, etc., please refrain from hotlinking. This is the direct linking to images (.jpg, .jpeg, .gif, .png, etc.), video (.avi, .mov, .mpg, .mpeg, .wmv, etc.), audio (.mp3, .wav, etc.), archives (.zip, .rar, etc.), or otherwise downloadable or streamable files on servers that you do not have permission to link to, instead of linking to the page where the item can be found. This includes providing a direct link to the file, even if that file is not embedded into your post. This practice costs the server owner money and resources.

13. Respect is the name of the game. You must respect your fellow members. Please refrain from inflammatory and defamatory comments as well as flaming, taunting and general disrespect. Do not simply put down the opinion or advice given by others. If you don't agree with it, say why—respectfully. Don't just tell them they're wrong. Do not make uninvited remarks about typos, duplicate posts, posting styles, etc. This is not the place to aggressively pursue attacks and accusations on one's chosen style or background. We all have different opinions and different backgrounds.

When an opinion-based discussion is being had, do not state things like "there is no argument" as if your opinion is the only one or the only one that matters. When someone has clearly stated their opinion, do not say things like "Are you serious?" and "Are you kidding me?" Remember, this is not a debate club. This is a friendly discussion community. Allow people to have their opinion. No one is to act as some sort of opinion judge, responding to each one to say whether they agree or not or whether or not it is a valid, well-thought-out opinion.

We do not allow threads to be started to discuss who or what is the most overrated, who or what is your least favorite, etc.

14. Any and all health and medical advice and information given on this community is intended for general discussion and educational purposes only. It is in no way intended to serve as actual, individual medical advice. In no way does participating in these forums constitute a formal or informal doctor/patient relationship. These forums are not limited to physicians, doctors, or other health professionals. In fact, all members are invited to participate. Because of this, we assume no responsibility for any posts. It is possible that some information may be inaccurate, incomplete, or otherwise flawed. No information is endorsed or verified by KarateForums.com or any health professionals. Your health is important and

you are responsible for your own health care and well-being. If you have any medical concerns at all, you should consult a physician or other health care professionals as you deem necessary.

15. We do not allow discussions debating what the best martial art is nor do we allow discussions debating what martial art has the best something. This includes discussions such as ''What is the best martial art?'' or ''What is the best martial art for street fighting?'' or ''Does BJJ have the best kicks?'' or ''What martial art has the best footwork?'' and the like. The exception to this is for individuals who need help choosing a martial art. In these cases, the person who needs assistance must make it clear that they need help selecting a martial art and must list the martial arts that are available to them in their area. They cannot simply ask what the best martial art is for them—there must be a list of arts. They must offer some details (even if they are few and vague) about their needs and their situation (body type, environment, etc.).

16. Signatures are limited to 5 lines of text. This includes blank lines. No images. The text in the signature may be customized by the BBCode in use on the forums. It is recommended that you stick with readable fonts and colors and that the size is not too large. You may mention websites and ventures that you are in some way related to, as long as they are otherwise appropriate for this community. Focus on things that you like, not things that you don't.

17. Each user is allowed to create one account. If you would like to change your username, please contact us and, most likely, we can do it for you while you can keep all of your profile data, posts, and other content.

18. Automated account creation, participation, and content scraping is not permitted.

19. We know that people will have to leave our community (of their own free will or otherwise) from time to time and to that end we do not delete accounts, posts, or other content posted on our community. All content is granted to us with perpetual electronic publishing rights because any content posted on this community becomes a part of the community, even if you no longer are. You may request an item to be removed at any time, but we will decide when and if to remove content from our community. If you wish to no longer be identified with our community, we will be glad to close your account and alter your profile information to remove all identifying characteristics. After account closure, you will no longer be able to participate in this community and this action is not reversible.

20. Moderators and the administrator have the final say on anything. If you have a problem, you may make a complaint to them directly and not publicly on the

website. Creating threads or posts that question or reference administrative decisions or potential administrative decisions, such as post removals and thread closures, is not permitted. We are not perfect and if you feel that we have made a mistake, please privately contact a staff member and we will review the situation. If you would like a copy of your removed post so that you can adjust it and repost, please contact us. As long as we wouldn't prefer you to simply start over, we'll be glad to send you a copy.

21. If you ever need clarification on any part of our User Guidelines or have a question, suggestion, a bit of feedback, or a problem with the site, please feel free to contact me directly to ensure that it receives the proper attention. Please do not post it in the forums as it will be removed.

22. Whenever you are participating in this community, please keep in mind that we strive to create a fun, friendly, and inviting atmosphere. So, please have fun and enjoy the forums!

Freedom-of-speech rights do not extend to privately owned websites, such as this one. These guidelines detail the types of behavior and activities that are allowed here.

If a user violates our guidelines and shows a disregard for them, our staff, and our community, they run the risk of losing their account. We reserve the right to deactivate any account and to edit or remove any content without warning. These guidelines are subject to change at any time without notice.

Do you have a question about our User Guidelines or anything else? Do you have a suggestion? Do you want to offer some feedback? Or are you experiencing some trouble with the site? Well, no matter what it is, please do not hesitate to contact me and I will be glad to help in any way that I can.

Thank you for visiting KarateForums.com.

Next, in order to give you a different perspective and additional angles to consider, we'll take a look at the SitePoint Forums (http://www.sitepoint.com/forums) Community Guidelines from August 2007.

This is a community of webmasters, hobbyists, newbies, experienced, and inexperienced people.

Respect Is the Key

The SitePoint Forums (SPF) is a place where it's okay to be yourself—be that harried, jovial, silly or sad—as long as you always act with respect for your fellow SitePointers.

Pretend you run these forums; in essence, you do. Before you hit the submit button think if you would allow that post on your own site or forums. Only you can prevent spam and cross-posting.

If you've been caught or accused of a wrongdoing, please don't be irrational. When we revoke privileges, we do so to preserve the professionalism of the forums, not as a personal vendetta.

Republishing Your Words

We know that your words are filled with knowledge of how things work in the real world. Because of this we have dedicated ourselves to bringing the best of our community to a larger audience. We do this by including links to your posts throughout the network and using discussion topics for the basis of new articles and features. We reserve the right to quote your discussion forum posts in newsletters, throughout the SitePoint network, and in SitePoint promotions. When republishing your quotes for wide distribution, we will identify you only by your SPF member name.

How to Report a Problem or Get Help

If you come across any violations to these guidelines or have any problems navigating the site, do not hesitate to let us know by using the "Report Post" links at the bottom of each post or through the SitePoint Contact Form.

We'll be happy to address your concerns.

Here at SitePoint we encourage everyone to participate in and enjoy the community through the following Guidelines:

Welcome Newcomers

One reason the SitePoint Forums is so special is that we welcome all newcomers, regardless of their level of knowledge or experience. Help new members learn about how to find information and resources and how to get involved in the community.

Don't Attack One Another

Don't attack others. Personal attacks, including accusations of wrongdoing, are not allowed in the public areas of the forums, even if they are well intentioned (i.e., to "warn others"). SitePoint is not a place to air your grievances. If you have a dispute with somebody, please keep it in private or risk having your posts removed or being banned. Thank you.

Only One Account Per Person, Please

We only allow one account per person. We enforce this very strictly as it helps us deal with problems. If you lose access to your account, do not create another one as it may be banned. You should contact an Advisor for help.

Keep Personal Information Personal

Before you post, consider that what you post will not only appear on our forum, but may also come up in searches and on external search engines. If you do not wish to make a piece of information public knowledge, do not post it.

Keep Your Posts Clean

There may be places where explicit, obscene, or vulgar language, graphics, or behavior is appropriate. However, SitePoint is not one of them. Discussion forum posts that contain explicit, obscene, or vulgar language will be removed. Similarly, discussion forum posts that solicit or offer explicit or X-rated GIFs, JPEGs, or similar content files will be deleted without notice!

Be Courteous: Avoid Duplicate Posts

Do not post the same discussion more than once on a discussion forum or on many forums. Duplicate discussions can be frustrating for other members, especially for those whose time and energy is limited. Duplicate discussions will be deleted. Reposting the same message repeatedly can be interpreted as spam and could result in the loss of your membership.

Advertising

The SitePoint Forums has a strict, no-self-promotion policy. Linking to your own web pages or pages from sites which you are affiliated with (including affiliate links) will be deemed as self-promotion and could result in the loss of your membership. Under certain conditions, links to your site can be placed into your forum signature (see Signatures) or in designated areas of the forums (such as the Marketplace) only.

Avatars

Avatars are small images that can be included in your user profile. These images must be 75 by 75 pixels or less and a file size limitation applies.

The SitePoint logo, in any variation, can not be used by anyone who is not a member of the SitePoint staff.

Signatures

Each SitePoint Forums membership comes with the ability to display a signature. This signature can be used to promote your site, business, or other ventures as long as they relate to you personally. You may not allow others to use your signature nor can you rent out the space for use. Your signature is not a commercial entity and cannot be sold; anyone found to be breaking these guidelines will be warned. Repeat warnings will result in a permanent ban.

Your promotional signature must follow these guidelines:

1. Signature size is limited to 4 lines of 65 characters.
2. You can put in links that lead to your site(s) or a product page.
3. You can't run sales ads in your signature.
4. You can have a slogan (i.e., ''UK's Best Hosting starting at £19.99.'').
5. No affiliate or referral IDs. (Links to Outwar or any other similar type of scheme have been deemed acceptable under the grounds that it is just a game. However, all links to the Outwar site must not be seen as misleading by our members and it should be obvious from the outset where the links lead to.)
6. No scams or unenforceable offers (i.e., ''Earn $10,000 a month selling suntan lotion to dolphins.'').
7. Pre-approved BBCode is acceptable but must adhere to the following restrictions:
   - Center and Right align tags are not to be used.
   - Code, Quote, PHP, HTML, Edit, Off-topic and Spoiler tags are not to be used.
   - The HR tag is not to be used.
   - The maximum font size permitted is size 3.
8. Signature cannot contain images.
9. Signatures cannot be sold, nor contain offers to buy or sell other signatures. This includes but is not limited to linking to websites that solicit the selling of signatures.

Posting Content from Other People or Websites

Copying any content from another person's work, or another website, is not allowed without express permission from the creator/owner of the original work. Even if you attribute the article correctly, it is still copyright infringement. Do not reproduce substantial parts of articles or news items from other sites in the forums. If you don't have permission to copy something, then always err on the side of caution and simply post a link to the material at its original location or quote a short excerpt only, indicating where the quote came from. SitePoint shall not be held responsible for member-posted information that violates copyright.

Using the Private Message System

The private message (PM) system of the forums allows you to send messages to other members in private. Where applicable, the same guidelines apply to the private message system as apply to messages posted on the forums.

Sending any unrequested commercial and/or bulk message through the private message system may result in an immediate suspension of posting privileges. Furthermore, any reports of harassment via the PM system will be fully investigated. To report an abusive or unwanted PM, please use the SitePoint Contact Form.

Marketplace

The SitePoint Marketplace is a section of the forums in which members can advertise their sites, domains or templates for sale or hold contests. In order to ensure the Marketplace runs smoothly, replies to threads in the Marketplace must be relevant to the original poster's topic and must contribute something. Replies that are critical of the item for sale or thread starter will not be tolerated. If you have a dispute with a seller or contest holder in the Marketplace, please contact them privately.

Finally, We Reserve the Right

SitePoint Pty. Ltd. and its assigned agents reserves the right to remove a post which does not relate to the topic being discussed in the forum. In addition, SitePoint reserves the right to organize discussion forums in order to best serve the majority of our members. For example, narrow interest or minimal activity topics may, at SitePoint's discretion, be relocated to a more appropriate discussion forum or deleted entirely.

SitePoint Pty. Ltd. or its assigned agents also reserves the right to prohibit or delete discussions that are thought to violate applicable law or that may be harmful to other members, the sites that comprise SitePoint or the rights of SitePoint Pty. Ltd. or others. That said, SitePoint does not have the practical ability to restrict conduct or communications that might violate these guidelines or the Terms of Service prior to transmission on AOL or the web, nor can we ensure prompt removal of offending discussion forum posts.

We also reserve the right to remove your membership from you should you violate these guidelines.

Again, at least one of the mentions of specific pages, such as "contact" or "SitePoint Contact Form" are linked to an actual page with a contact form, making it so that users do not have to search around to find it.

Hopefully, with these two examples and the ideas highlighted earlier in mind, you will be able to construct your own set of user guidelines that fulfills your needs. Although you should craft your own guidelines, a set of general, ready-to-use user guidelines (with blanks for you to fill in) is featured in appendix B and is available in a downloadable archive from the book website (http://www.managingonlineforums.com). You can use these as a starting point for your own user guidelines.

The Children's Online Privacy Protection Act of 1998 (C.O.P.P.A.)

The C.O.P.P.A. (http://www.ftc.gov/bcp/conline/pubs/buspubs/coppa.htm) basically says that you cannot collect information from a person under the age of thirteen without the permission of a parent or legal guardian. This act is enforceable internationally. Many community software programs have C.O.P.P.A. support built in. This is usually in the form of a dialog that appears before a user can register. It asks the user for his date of birth or if he was born after or before a given date. If he indicates that he is below the age of thirteen, he is either denied registration or his account is deactivated and he receives an e-mail. The contents of this e-mail will usually be a document that can be printed and signed by the parent or guardian. The user must then fax, mail via regular mail, or e-mail (by scanning the completed and signed form into his computer) this document to you. Upon receipt, you can activate his account. Be sure to keep these documents, should you ever need to refer back to them for any reason.

You may think that a person who is under thirteen may just lie and indicate that he is older, and you would be right. That does happen. However, if he does, it is not your concern unless it comes to your attention. You simply can't know when a user does this. Again, unless the user contacts you later (or posts in your community) and says something like, "I'm twelve and . . ." you have no way of knowing. However, if you do spot an underage user, it is your responsibility to deactivate his account and require him to comply with the C.O.P.P.A.

Privacy Policy

It's generally a good idea to have a privacy policy for your community. Some people feel more comfortable if they see one. Some advertising networks require that you have a privacy policy in order to be considered for admittance. The Direct Marketing Association has an excellent privacy policy generator (http://www.the-dma.org/privacy/creating.shtml) that you can use.

As I said before, this book should not be considered legal advice, and if you have any doubts or questions, you should always seek the counsel of a qualified professional.

Get Them Out There!

Now that you have crafted your user guidelines, get them out there. Whether you put them on a separate page or in a closed sticky thread, be sure to add a link to them on all pages of your community and wherever else it makes sense. You can add a link to them next to the input text boxes for posts and private messages (with a linked message, such as "Participation constitutes agreement to our user guidelines"). You could force users to view them before they register, if you'd like, but because they change from time to time, linking to them from various visible areas within your website is a requirement.

If you put guideline-related content in closed threads on your forums, you may want to post them from a separate username that posts nothing but those types of posts. For instance, create a user named "Guidelines." Then, if users want to locate all of your various guidelines, they can just search for all posts made by "Guidelines."

Conclusion

It's hard to overstate the importance of guidelines. They tell people what the goals of the community are and they give you a constant point of reference in your pursuit of those goals. They are essential when it comes to managing how your members are supposed to act and contribute while on the site. Any well-run community must have guidelines of some sort.

CHAPTER 4

Promoting Your Community

"I do not know anyone who has got to the top without hard work. That is the recipe. It will not always get you to the top, but should get you pretty near."

—Margaret Thatcher

With your community developed and set up for success, you need to help people find it. Even if you have the greatest community setup and infrastructure in the world, it won't count for a lot if no one knows that you exist. The easier it is for people to find you, the better off you will be.

The focal point of this book is community management. Going over the intricacies of search engines and marketing and all that good stuff is beyond the scope of this book. However, in this chapter, I'll discuss some popular community-promotion ideas that you can use. They should give you a solid base of knowledge that you can then work with and expand upon.

You

Promotion starts with you. You should be proud of what you have created. If you know someone who is interested in the subject matter of your community (an acquaintance, not just someone that you know of), you should tell that person about your website. If you meet someone who is interested, you should tell him or her about your website. But, don't go seeking random people just to tell them about your community. They will ignore you and, eventually, label you as a spammer—a reputation that can follow you.

You should be a walking billboard. Not in the sense that all you talk about is your site, but in the sense that you should have your website linked in all of your e-mail and community signatures, in your instant messenger and social networking profiles, and so on. If you have more than one website, link them together. If you are a member of a community that has an advertising forum, use it. But, only advertise in areas where you are 100 percent sure that it is acceptable. If you are not sure, always ask a staff member in that community. As I said, if you turn into a spammer, it will only work to your disadvantage. If you want members of other communities to respect you, you must respect them.

If it's possible, establish yourself in the subject area of your community. This is certainly not required or needed, but it can be helpful. You can do this in a number of ways; the easiest is to participate in an existing community (perhaps one much larger than yours) for a similar subject or write articles for a major site in the genre, if one exists. It is important that the site have signatures and bylines or bios where you can mention your website(s), or you will not get the intended effect. For instance, if you were starting a web development community, you could post on the SitePoint Forums and submit articles to SitePoint with mentions of your site(s) in your signatures and bio. Of course, you should want to participate in these communities, rather than just doing it all for the sake of advertising. That's no fun.

What Is Not Considered Promotional Can Be Promotional

There are things that are not considered promotional but can and will affect the attractiveness of your community and, as such, the activity of your community.

For example, consider your design. If you have a nice, unique design, it makes people say to themselves, "Hey, maybe there is something different here—maybe this is worth my time to check out." As superficial as it may be, design often makes the first impression, and first impressions can be very important. Some people will dismiss your community if you are running the default template from your chosen community software. You may have the greatest atmosphere in the world, but you often need to attract people for them to figure that out. Running the default template with little changed is not going to inspire people to sign up or to give you a closer look.

Activity and your domain name are also promotional. Activity breeds activity. Whether they're in an articles section or are actual forum posts, the more posts there are, the more content there is and the more attractive your community will be. Likewise, a great domain name makes it easier for you to promote your site and makes it easier for people to remember your site. It's not unheard of for someone to dismiss a community because it didn't have its own domain name or, at least, to prefer one that does have one over one that does not. So, again, everything that can help your activity or attract new users is not always labeled "promotion." Keep that in mind.

Preparing Your Community for Search Engines

Before I start talking about search engines, let me just say that this is basic stuff for the most part. I'm not a search engine optimization (SEO) expert. I'm just giving some basic tips here. So, search engine optimizers and search engine marketers—don't jump all over me!

Getting on the major search engines is a big step in the right direction. With rare exceptions, a majority of your new traffic (and, perhaps, all of your traffic) is going to come from search engines. I've never really spent a great deal of time optimizing my sites for search engine rankings, preferring to spend the time that I do have on developing and improving my communities and websites. My idea is that if the site is truly of high quality, people will link to it and visit it.

Links help you and they help your rankings. There are some things that you can and should do, however, that can help people to find you with search engines. As I said, I'm not someone who spends a ton of time on this sort of thing, but I have made the adjustments that I'm going to discuss here.

Some people get really into SEO and, as long as you have the time, that's fine. But SEO is no substitute for good content, and some people get carried away. For example, I've seen people who make it so that they have no outgoing links (links that go to a different domain than the one that the site is on).

They do this because although incoming links (links from other sites to yours) can help your rankings, outgoing links can hurt them. They sometimes achieve this by sending links through an internal link-redirection script so that the URL looks something like this: http://www.theirsite.com/redirect.php? http://www.othersite.com. The search engines count it as an internal link (where the site is linking to itself), but when a visitor clicks on it, he or she is actually taken to http://www.othersite.com. If a site is worth linking to, it's worth linking out to and giving it the credit that comes along with that. You might ask, what search engines are the popular ones? SearchEngineWatch .com has a helpful links directory (http://www.searchenginewatch.com/links) covering major search engines, specialty search engines, and more. Do not submit your website for indexing until it is actually open.

Make Your Community Spiderable

If search engines are going to spider (or crawl—a term that means that a search engine indexes a given page or site) your topics and forums, they have to be able to actually access them. Why wouldn't they be able to access them?

First of all, spiders don't log in. You need to make it so that log-in is not required to view forums or posts. Also, session IDs, which pass a user's session information from one page to the next, can cause a problem. This has to do with the structure of your URLs. If session IDs are kept in the URLs (usually it is a mix of letters and numbers, such as "s1dsJKA1HJa12"), it can prevent the search engine spiders from doing their work. Question marks (?) and id variables (id=) can also cause trouble (such as http://www.sitename .com/viewtopic.php?id=11211984). Luckily, hacks can often make your community more search engine friendly (including the integration of search engine–friendly URLs) if your community doesn't come with the right functions out of the box. You should search the leading resource sites for your particular community software for one of these. The one that I am using inserts the forum or topic name into the URL, which can help rankings as well. This is what it creates:

> *Before: http://www.sitename.com/viewforum.php?id=3889*
> *After: http://www.sitename.com/forum-name-vf3889.html*
>
> *Before: http://www.sitename.com/viewtopic.php?id=71498*
> *After: http://www.sitename.com/topic-name-vt71498.html*

You don't want to change URLs anymore than you have to, so you should try to start with search engine–friendly URLs. If you don't, make sure that the old URLs will at least still take you somewhere, even if it's your index page. Better yet, keep them working or use them to redirect visitors to the new URLs.

Descriptive Page Titles

Descriptive and dynamic page titles can affect where your site ranks. So in general, your index page should describe the content of your site. If you are viewing a forum, the name of that forum should be in the title of your page. If you are viewing a topic, the name of that topic should be in the title of your page. Get rid of any extra, generic text. Here are some examples:

Not Good: KarateForums.com—Index
Good: KarateForums.com—Karate and Martial Arts Discussion Forums

Not Good: KarateForums.com—View Forum
Good: KarateForums.com—Martial Arts Entertainment

Not Good: KarateForums.com—View Topic
Good: KarateForums.com—How Do I Tie My Belt?

The "good" titles will make it more likely that people will find your site when they search for a topic that has been covered in your community. For instance, in the earlier example, if someone searched for "How do I tie my belt?" that particular topic would now be more likely to pop up in search engine results.

Another benefit of descriptive page titles is that they make your link more attractive in search engine results, leading to more visits. For example, if you did a search to find out how to tie your martial arts belt, what would you be more likely to click on: "KarateForums.com—View Topic" or "KarateForums.com—How Do I Tie My Belt?"

You may also want to try putting the topic title or the forum title first in the actual page title, ahead of your website name. Some people have found that doing so leads to more visits from search engine users because the first thing they see is the content of the link, not the name of the site.

Welcome Messages

This is not specifically tied to search engines but can be very helpful when trying to entice random guests to join. A welcome message is a dialog at the top of your site displayed only to visitors who are not logged in. It encourages them to create an account (including a link to the registration form) and it can also explain a little bit about your community and/or the benefits of registration. Users who are logged in do not see the message. Some people have set their sites up so that the search engine term the visitor used to reach the site is repeated in the welcome message as well.

Here are a couple of examples. See figure 4-1 for the Top Hosting Deals Forums (http://www.tophostingdeals.com/forums) welcome message, which details the site's content and some of the benefits of joining the community.

In figure 4-2, you can see that at CommunityAdmins.com (http://www.communityadmins.com), we simply implore users to sign up for an account to start posting.

Figure 4-1. Top Hosting Deals Forums' welcome message.

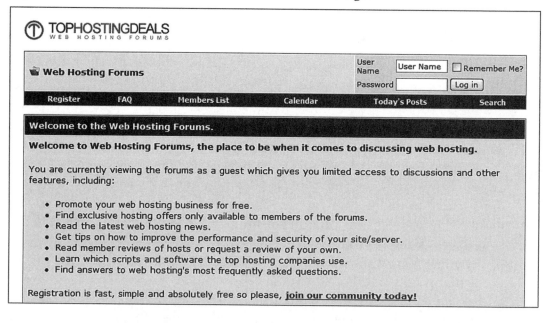

Figure 4-2. CommunityAdmins.com welcome message.

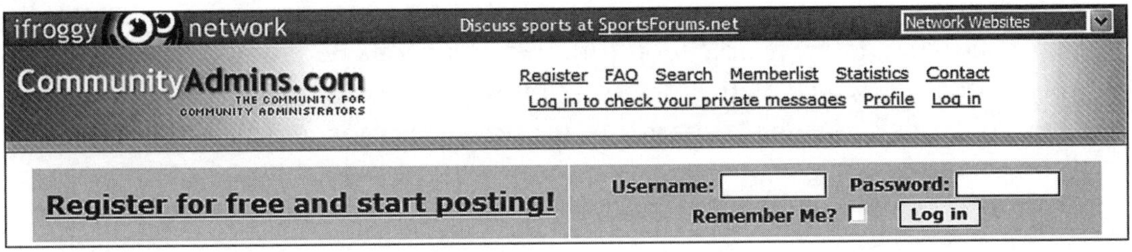

Before You Launch

"What IS your fascination with my forbidden closet of mysteries?"

—Chief Clancy Wiggum

If you can help it, don't just launch right out of the blue. At least a couple of weeks before the launch, you could at a minimum put up a simple page with the logo or the name of the site and the specific date and time (don't forget time zone!) that you will be launching. Be sure to launch at that exact time (a few moments before, actually). Don't set a date you can't keep, and don't be late. Depending on the traffic, you may also want to set up a simple mailing list on which users can sign up in order to be e-mailed when the site launches. If someone takes the time to sign up, he or she is probably seriously interested in checking out your community when it goes online. You are building your user base before you even launch.

Make sure that people have something to come to, however. Before your site goes live, be sure to post some threads and get some topics going with the people (as many good people as you can find) who are helping you out at the start. You should have active threads before the site launches. To do this, give some people prelaunch access. People will be more likely to sign up if the community is, at least, relatively active.

Don't stop posting, either. Visit every day (more if you can) and post new threads and reply to existing ones, welcome users, and so on and so forth. Keep it hot.

At the beginning and during less active stages of your community, you may want to prevent your forum software from showing dates on the index page. If the last active topic in one of your forums has no recent response, some users will dismiss it even if the content is still current and valuable. By not showing dates, people won't immediately consider your content inactive or outdated, which will, hopefully, allow additional people to discover it. But obviously this is no substitute for active threads and new posts in your community.

Directories

There are a ton of website directories online. Some of them are very general and cover a majority of interests, and some of them are very specific. Most of them won't generate much traffic and some will question if it's worth the effort. But at the end of the day, if you have the time and it's a free listing, a link is a link. It can't hurt. You can use your favorite search engine to find noteworthy directories and directories related to the subject matter of your site.

The most important directory online is the Open Directory Project/Directory Mozilla (DMOZ; http://www.dmoz.org). Not only is it heavily trafficked and linked to, but many websites use its data to create directories of their own. So, if you get a link in the DMOZ directory, you may very well see your link pop up in a number of other places as well. One very notable example would be the Google Directory (http://directory.google.com).

However, it can be difficult to get your link into DMOZ. Many people have trouble doing so and wait times can be quite extreme. On top of that, there are bad editors (I've had my own experience with one—a banned user who became an editor of a category in which we were listed proceeded to remove our link from the category and add a link to his own site). But, you can't let that overshadow everyone—there are good editors, as well. Still, because of its established presence on the web, you should definitely submit your site and hope that your link gets approved.

Partnerships

Promotional partnerships bring you to someone else's audience while bringing them to yours. The idea behind it is simple: By sharing your audiences, you both aim to be better off in the long term. For a community, an example might be a partnership with a content site.

Having a content arm or partner gives your community more to discuss. Placement on that content site will also bring you more traffic. But both sides must benefit or it will not work. So before you approach any potential partners, be sure that your community—your offering—is in tip-top shape: Well-thought-out design; capable and competent staff; good atmosphere. Basically, it should be a professional setup that your potential partner would be proud to be affiliated with.

What Can You Offer a Partner?

Here are few things your affiliates might get out of a partnership you.

- **Your Effort.** You run your community. They don't have to. This is less of a burden for them, which means they can spend their time on their website and have faith in you and your team to handle the community in an efficient manner. For example, they won't have to handle the moderation, which some people consider to be tedious and time-consuming.

- **Traffic.** You must link to each other via prime real estate regions of your respective pages. Unless, of course, you have far less traffic than your partner does or vice versa. In that case, you may have to link to your partner more heavily or your partner may have to link to you more heavily to help balance the difference. In your community, this may mean linking to your partner's site in the header of every page, maybe the footer of every page, and/or in some other noticeable spots. Maybe you could display your partner's five or ten most recently published articles or resources.

- **Flexibility.** If you aren't flexible, people will just disregard you. Your community has advertising guidelines. But maybe they don't always have to apply to your partner. For instance, you can choose to allow your partner to start threads for articles that are featured on its website. Let your partner have forums that relate specifically to its site in your community. For instance, it could have a forum for its staff to discuss issues that are relevant to its site or it could have a forum for users to give suggestions or feedback for its site.

What Can a Partner Offer You?

- **More Fodder.** You will have one website that you can feel good about linking to. You can use it to bring issues up and to start discussions. Sure, you can do this with any website, but it's easier when the site is a partner and all of its users come right back to your site for discussions, rather than looking at some other site's community.

- **Traffic.** As I said earlier, you should be exchanging prime real estate. On the content website, this could mean that the partner links to you as its "Forums" or "Community" on every page of its site. Maybe it displays the five or ten most recently active threads from your forums. Your partner could also link to you in other noticeable areas, such as a "Discuss This Article" link that goes to your site.

When you contact a potential partner, be sure to stress all of these points (and any others that you come up with) and explain why your community is worth partnering with. I have done these deals before and they definitely can benefit both parties. Make sure that you choose a website that you want to be affiliated with, not just any site that looks popular. You have to like the site and like the people behind it because maintaining a good relationship with your partners is imperative to having successful partnerships.

Buying Advertising

As I write this, I've spent virtually nothing on advertising my network. Your decision to advertise rests on your budget and available resources. I have so far decided not to conduct any noteworthy campaigns. So don't think of it as any sort of requirement. But that doesn't mean it cannot be a great way to promote your site. It can be the quickest and most efficient way to grow your traffic. Many great sites grew very large on an ad budget of very little or nothing.

Regardless of what you spend, you don't want to waste your money. Don't rush into it and just start throwing money around. You want to look at advertising as an investment, so it's important to identify opportunities that allow you to get the best bang for your buck. To find out how to make the most of an advertising budget, I interviewed Ted Sindzinski, a marketing consultant who has helped major web communities and Inc. 500 companies increase their marketing and advertising effectiveness.

Here are some frequently asked questions about marketing and advertising your site.

Q. *How should I get started?*

Before you begin any sort of promotional campaign, you need to take the time to establish your goals. Are you looking to grow by fifty members a day? To double your traffic? Aside from wanting to be the largest community on the Internet, you should have a few realistic short- and long-term goals that you can work toward. Without defined goals, it is difficult if not impossible to gauge your progress as time passes.

All that separates free promotion methods like link exchanges and search engine optimization (SEO) is the investment required. Because advertising causes you to spend money, chances are you are looking to make your money back from the traffic and members you drive in—either in the short or long term. You need an advertising goal that can be measured in terms of return on investment (ROI). Although you probably don't know what an individual member will bring you in terms of revenue, you can make an educated guess. Take the number of unique visitors you have per month and divide it by your gross revenue. Do the same calculation based on the number of members you have and write down both numbers. You can compare your revenue per visitor and revenue per member with your cost per acquired visitor and cost per acquired member as part of your ROI calculation.

If you are looking to grow a lot, chances are you are going to experience a negative short-term ROI as a result of your desire to drive in a high number of members. It's even more likely if your site focuses on a very commercial topic like web hosting, movies, or medical advice. The more interest companies have in the niche, the more competition you will have for ad space both from big brands and others. Although this should not exclude you from using paid advertising, you will need to evaluate carefully what you are willing to spend to grow your site and what that expense will bring you. If, however, you are looking to supplement your existing traffic or promote an already successful and larger site, you may be able to generate an even or positive ROI. Figure out what you can spend on advertising, divide it by how much you are willing to spend per member, and you have your acquisition goal.

Q. *How should I prepare my site to receive visitors derived from paid ads?*

Advertising a site that's not optimized for advertising is a tremendous waste. Even a well-thought-out and well-executed campaign will dramatically depress its results if the ads just lead people back to your homepage. You need carefully designed pages developed for capturing visitors and funneling them toward your conversion process—a concept known as "landing pages."

Paid ads are everywhere. They are on nearly every established commercial site. Unlike SEO or most forms of free promotion, paid ads let you direct traffic wherever you want and control the environment the user ends up in. For example, in a commercial environment, if you search for "4x DVD-R," you find that the ads don't just display the names of companies selling DVDs or the term *DVD-R*. They display the entire search term. When clicked, most of these ads take you to pages with a specific product or group of products matching the search term. This allows you to see quickly if the site has what you want and to make a purchase decision in as few steps as possible.

When someone clicks an ad, you want him to see a page that explains your site and gives him something specific to do—like register. If you just send people to your homepage, you are asking them to leave. The last thing you want people to do is browse around to try and understand what your site is for. From your ad through to your landing page, everything needs to have the same message and push the person toward registration. By doing so, you'll be able to capture significantly more new members, and once someone registers the chances of her returning on her own (or as a result of your welcome letter, newsletter, or other e-mail) go way, way up.

Q. *What does a landing page consist of?*

At a minimum, it contains a description of your site as it relates to the term being searched for. If, for example, you ran a site about computer games and someone searched for "The Sims," your page would need to speak to that. What sort of value do you offer to someone interested in that game? Think of everything that a potential user could benefit from and write it down—those are your selling points. The selling points and your description form the bulk of any landing page, but they shouldn't be long. A key tagline followed by a sentence or two for a description and a few bullet points is all you need; few people will read more than that. Images that show your site features, relate to the term, or help convey your value can work wonders as well.

Finally, your landing page should include a conversion action that is as simple and easy to get to as possible. This means clearly defined registration links or, even better, a short version of your registration form right on the landing page. The easier to sign up, the better.

The goal of your landing page is to speak to what you are advertising and sell the user on your site. It's estimated that you have fewer than eight seconds after someone clicks an ad to sell him on your site and even less time to get him to determine if he wants to be there. Your homepage probably isn't designed for this and isn't designed to tell a new visitor how to register. That's why landing pages are important and why you need to have a landing page for each campaign type and category.

Q. *How can I track the performance of my campaigns?*

Measurement is probably the most important part of any campaign. If you don't track, you can't tell if you've met a goal, blown past it, or failed to get a single visitor. You may as well take your money and go to Vegas—at least you'll know what your odds of success are there. Tracking is one of those issues forum owners seem to overlook because it seems difficult. It's not. It can be done many different ways without additional cost and with minimal time.

Presumably you are looking to track registrations and visits, but you may also want to track things such as registrations to another system, visits to a contest, etc. This can be done by installing analytic tools such as Google Analytics (http://www.google.com/analytics) or WebTrends (http://www.webtrends

.com) or by using a third-party ad-tracking system such as Google AdWords (http://adwords.google.com) or AdWatcher (http://www.adwatcher.com).

With any of these, you'll need to place some code on your landing and registration pages. Once in place, it will report back on any tracked visitor with all sorts of useful things like where people are dropping off in the process, which ads are doing best, etc.

Q. *What's the most popular way to advertise a community online?*

Contextual advertising is probably the most common advertising method used by communities. With these ads, you generally bid on specific terms or sites and pay on a per-click model ("pay per click," or PPC). It doesn't guarantee results, but it does mean your ad will show up in front of the people who are interested in the subject, and you'll only get charged if they click on it.

The key to any PPC campaign is matching your site to the search term. For example, if someone searches for "The Sims cheat codes," you have a good idea that she already owns the game and is looking for information about a specific part. If your community has a section on cheat codes, this would be an ideal match and you want an ad that reflects it. Therefore, rather than displaying "XYZ Game Forums, a video game community," you could use "Free Sims Cheat Codes! Find the latest codes and get tips." By using a specific ad, your ad becomes more relevant and more likely to be clicked on.

As you advertise on broader terms, it is even more important to use the proper ad copy. A user searching for "The Sims" may not be looking for info on the game but for where to buy it. Therefore, it's important that your ad explains that you are a community/content site and not a site on which to buy the game. This lowers the number of clicks from broad search terms but drives in a more qualified visitor, and because registrations and repeat visits are the goal, the more qualified the user, the better.

This type of advertising gives you the ability to drive in qualified visitors and explain your site before you pay for a click. But there can be major downsides. Advertising on major sites like Google and Yahoo! for a competitive search term is often expensive. If you aren't careful, you can spend your entire budget on unqualified traffic. There are also concerns over click fraud, which can be a serious challenge if you have highly competitive forums. To avoid these issues, stick to the ideas I've mentioned. Pick specific, relevant terms; use ad copy that speaks to what you offer; and track your ads carefully so you can identify possible fraud. Following these rules, you should be able to drive in visitors for five to twenty-five cents each with conversion of 5 percent or higher.

Q. *What about advertising on smaller sites?*

Small targeted sites are a great place to find cheap ad buys without competing with larger companies on major websites. Here you will tend to find individuals rather than large companies meaning the terms and rates are more flexible. The more relevant the site, the better it will be for you, and you may even find that you are able to position yourself in an exclusive spot.

If the campaign works and runs for a long enough period of time, users will start to associate you as the forum for that site, leading to increased user loyalty and word of mouth. The main downside with advertising on smaller sites is their volatility and limited traffic. Smaller websites do tend to come and go, and even if the site is stable, you may not find much traffic to expand your buy or effectively run a small ad. Carefully monitor your results over time as you saturate the user base.

Q. *Should I advertise on related communities if they allow me to?*

Other communities, although very similar to targeted sites, are a different issue. Because there are so many forums and most have a tough time capitalizing on their traffic, it's often possible to find forums that practically give away ads. Don't let the cost fool you. If you're promoting a community on what could be considered a competing site, odds are that few people, if any, will register with your site and if they do, few will stick around. The fact is people in one community don't tend to run off to another unless there is a major problem. The only exception may be if you find a noncompeting but related site, but be careful. Any negative PR and you're likely to get no visitors, or worse, abusive members who just want to cause you grief. Unless the match is perfect and the deal is once in a lifetime, avoid trying to push your community on the members of another one.

Q. *How should I approach advertising campaigns of substantial cost?*

Large buys tend to be reserved for major branding and sites with financial backing or a revenue source. If you're lucky enough to have the funds available to advertise on a large network or site, you may get amazing results. A major difference between advertising on larger sites and smaller ones is the attention paid to ROI. You'll want to be diligent and limit the cost per registration. But, advertising on a top scale is normally done as a part of long-term awareness building.

To be effective, you can't make one $20,000 buy and expect to be known around the world. Branding is most effective when you pursue it continually. Even if you don't want to brand, you may get good returns by advertising on a larger scale with a closely related site. Look for secondary ad spots and alternative placements rather than ads that are front and center, which tend to demand high prices. As with a smaller buy, track the expenses and results carefully and set realistic goals ahead of time.

Q. *What about advertising offline?*

Offline ad opportunities can be a great way to promote a site, especially if your site crosses into an offline niche. For example, if you hold regular events or have a topic that's regional, look into buying ads in a local paper, sponsoring an event, or getting your name on a billboard. These venues tend to be more reasonably priced than you may think, and if you're really strapped for funds, consider distributing fliers at events.

For sites that are not tied to geographic areas, tradeshows can be a phenomenal way to drive in members and establish yourself with advertisers. Find an upcoming show, purchase a single booth, get a nice sign, bring a laptop or two, and start taking registrations. Shows tend to be expensive, but if you're known in your space, even to a limited extent, people are likely to come to you. If you have the money, distribute key chains, stickers, or other promotional items to extend your branding. Finally, consider advertising in a national magazine. This tends to be the hardest type of advertising to track, but the reach is different from that of an online ad, especially if the magazine is passed around. Before taking the plunge, review each publication to see how many other companies advertise websites in it. Some print publications don't drive web traffic.

Q. *Any final advice?*

There are a lot of opportunities out there and many sites and businesses that want your money. Before you pick one, evaluate all the possibilities rather than just jumping into the first available. You may also want to diversify your ad purchases so that you can test how contextual ads compare to a targeted site and so forth.

The idea is to maximize your advertising's effectiveness. To do this, you need to make the process iterative. Don't simply buy new ads every few months; spend time reviewing your results. Try changing your landing pages—even small tweaks to the copy and colors can help. Figure out which sites perform best, which keywords drive in higher conversion rates, and what sort of look or copy people respond to. Use that knowledge to cut what doesn't work and expand what does. As you continue your education, you'll find that you're able to hone in on good opportunities and exceed your goals without spending huge dollars.

■ ■ ■

Link Exchanges

One very popular and well-known promotional tactic is to exchange links with other websites. You are advertising for one another. When done with a discerning eye, it can definitely be beneficial. It helps in two main ways: It increases traffic and increases search engine rankings. You can exchange links on certain pages of your community, on every page, or just on a links page. If you want to link to a site that isn't particularly popular or well linked, you can exchange a link on your links page for a link on all of the other site's pages.

If the website is as popular as yours or more popular, you may consider exchanging links on every page, on your index page, or a like-for-like exchange (links page for links page, for example). If your site is less popular than the other site, then you may be the one who needs to exchange a link on every page for a link on the other site's links page. Remember, not all link exchanges are about getting loads of users to click. You can exchange small, out-of-the-way links that some users will find, that you will get some traffic from. Again, every little bit helps.

What I mean by "a discerning eye" is that you should choose your link partners with some caution. I reject pretty much all link exchange requests (a majority of which appear to be sent out by some sort of software). You want to exchange links with good sites. You want to associate with people whom you feel comfortable with, not people who could damage your reputation. You don't want to exchange links with trash sites or sites that appear to be doing something devious, unethical, or illegal.

In the same vein, keep an eye out for people who engage in tactics that search engines frown upon. One example would be where people hide or vastly limit the visibility of the text on their sites (by making it smaller or a color that is similar or identical to the background) to get search engines to pick up that text and thus improve the site's ranking. No one respectable does that stuff.

Besides just text links, you can exchange graphic advertisements, as well. The same basic principles apply. You want to make a fair exchange, and you want to design an attractive ad that people will look at and not simply away from.

Contests and Giveaways

Holding contests and giveaways can be a great way to attract people to your community. There are always two major parts to a contest—the prize and what people have to do to get it.

You can give away cash, gift certificates, merchandise (perhaps with your site's logo on it), advertising on your site, and more. A lot of companies are willing to donate products or gift certificates in exchange for some advertising and/or mentions in conjunction with the event. You can send out a general feeler to see what they might be willing to do or you can approach them with a specific offer in mind (i.e., a specific product in return for advertising worth X dollars). The amount should generally exceed the retail price of what you are after. All you have to do is ask, and if you offer them a good value, many companies will be more than willing. Sometimes you don't even have to do that. Once in a while, advertisers contact *me* to ask if I'd be willing to hold a contest and give away their products. Companies want the exposure and the goodwill it creates with members who identify their brands as those that "support" the community. This can lead to good things for them.

Now, what do people have to do to win? This can range from the simple to the complex. You could hold a random drawing of everyone who registers, or everyone who registers and makes five posts, or everyone who posts within a given month. You could ask people to help you with something to do with your site. For example, they could help you name a new forum, pick a slogan (the best one gets a prize), or help you design something on your site (good for a graphic or design community).

You could base the contest on the theme of your site. For instance, if you have a photography community, you could have an award for the best photo, as selected by you, your staff, or your members. You could have theme rules for the photos. In a sports community, you could have people predict the winners of games that week or that month.

You could reward people who refer the most new members, create the most new threads or posts, or contribute the most articles to your articles section. You could mix a lot of these principles by holding a contest that rewards them all. For example, you could give people credits or points for performing certain activities, and you could vary the numbers of credits for posts, articles, referred members, and so on and so forth. When it's all said and done, the person or people with the most credits win.

With contests, you have to take the good with the bad. You will get people (perhaps many people) who are just there for the contest. After it's over or after they have fulfilled their requirements, they're gone. In a referral contest, for example, people may just refer a lot of their buddies who may not be interested in your site in any way. That's just the way it is. But activity is activity, even if it is short-term activity. The hope is that some of the referrals become engaged in your community and decide to stay, but even if they don't, hopefully you'll have picked up some additional content—content that will go into the search engines and can help you attract even more people. Activity attracts activity.

You will want to come up with a detailed page of information for the contest. Tell people exactly what they can get and exactly how it will be awarded. Tell them what you expect of them. If the contest has to do with posting, maybe you don't want people making short, seemingly meaningless posts. Talk about how they can be disqualified. In doing so, discourage abuse and take a moment to explain what constitutes abuse. You don't want people creating multiple accounts or spamming other websites, for example. Disclose any and all restrictions (age minimums or location requirements, for example), how the winner will be notified, and how long he or she has to respond.

Post Exchanges and Paying People to Post

A post exchange is when someone posts in your community in exchange for you posting in his or her community. These users will usually have no other commitment to your community after a certain number of posts. Although it is possible that they may enjoy the community and decide to stick around after their commitments are fulfilled, it's not too likely and should not be counted on.

You have to take it for what it is: A short-term activity boost that can help you build up some content and lead to other people joining your community and taking part. So if you have the time to post in someone else's community, you might consider it. Even so, a better use of your time may simply be coming up with topic ideas for your own forums.

Paying users to post (or compensating them in some other way) also provides a short-term boost in activity. However, it's not without its downsides. Paying people to post isn't building community. It's superficial. Their posts certainly have value as pieces of content that will add to the size of your community and attract more users, but what happens when their paid time is over and one of your users wants to know why so-and-so disappeared or wants to know if you banned the person? What do you say then? "Well, I paid him to make a certain number of posts to help the community grow. His paid time was up and he left." That's not something to be ashamed of, but you should decide whether you will be comfortable with having to address it in the future. Likewise, how will you respond if someone says, "Well, my posts were better than hers and you didn't pay me." I don't see a lot of people (reasonable people) taking that position, but if they do, you could say that it was simply a short-term promotional endeavor. But again, you need to make sure that you will be comfortable with that before you decide to pay people to post.

If you do choose to pay people to post or to exchange posts, make sure that each account created is for a real person. Don't pay one guy to create five accounts and post from them. That's dishonest and misleading to your users, unless you actually disclose the situation (and it's a situation that sounds pretty lame, doesn't it?).

Paying people to post is much better than creating a bunch of different user accounts and talking to yourself. Just as you shouldn't pay one guy to pose as five, you shouldn't do it yourself. Again, it's misleading and you're basically living a lie. When you decide that it is time for your alter egos to die, what happens when a user wants to know why so-and-so is gone? What happens when someone e-mails so-and-so to say, "Hey, where have you been?" What are you going to say? "Well, actually, it was just me . . . the administrator. I was creating posts and talking to myself to try to get more people to join." You might as well say, "I tricked you." That's going to go over really well, so avoid the embarrassment altogether. Again, if you pay posters, make sure you're at least paying different people to post.

Offline Promotion

You don't want to get caught up in just the world of online promotion. Don't forget about the world outside of the Internet. There are so many ways to promote your community offline. I talked about it a little bit earlier in the "Buying Advertising" section, but I want to expand on it here.

The most obvious choices are publications such as newspapers and magazines. Although those can be great, a lot of people don't have the budget to advertise in them. Fear not, the world of offline advertising lends itself to the creative. If you keep your eyes open and use your mind, you can find effective, affordable means of getting your community in front of people.

Here's an example. For my martial arts community, I could print out some fliers, go down to the martial arts schools and academies in my area, and ask if I can put them up on their bulletin boards if they have one (and try to establish relationships with them). This is a simple, cheap endeavor. If one of the school's students logs on and really likes my community, he may just tell his buddies at the school about it. If they like my community, maybe they will tell *their* buddies, and maybe their buddies will tell *their* buddies and so on. I think I've had maybe half a dozen or more people from the same school posting at KarateForums.com at the same time.

When you create a quality website, people want to recommend it, but they have to find it first. You don't have to spend a lot of money to put it in front of someone. Take advantage of free bulletin boards and places designated for local businesses to leave their cards, pencils, promotional fliers, etc. If your site covers a subject a lot of people are interested in (travel, sports, finance), you can benefit from being seen in general, everyday places like grocery stores and coffee shops. Ask related local businesses if you can come by and post a flier, leave some business cards, pencils, or anything.

See what you can do to get your site in front of people who meet to talk about a subject. For example, there are plenty of investment clubs out there. If you run a finance community, that's a perfect match. Talk to the leader and see if there is any way that he might mention your site or allow you to leave some printouts at the meeting location. If you can afford to and there are enough people in the group, consider sponsoring one or more meetings. If you have the interest and time to participate in a group, all the better. You'll no doubt have the opportunity to mention your site when you introduce yourself to people, and you can even wear a shirt with your logo on it (but make sure it's OK with the group leader). To find groups like these, you can search online on sites like Meetup (http://www.meetup.com).

If you do have the opportunity to attend related conferences, events, and trade shows, you should always carry around business cards with your URL to hand out as you meet people. Again, you can wear clothing that has your site's logo on it, as well. You can ask conference speakers to post their notes on your site and mention your community in their talks if at all possible.

There are virtually limitless opportunities (varying in cost) to promote your community offline. Get out there, sponsor events, get a booth at and/or attend a conference, use print ads, talk with local businesses, and be creative. Use your imagination, keep your eyes open, and you will be able to come up with ideas.

Let Your Users Promote You!

There is nothing better than having happy users, especially ones who are loyal. They make it all worth it. Loyal users will tell their friends about your site. If they have personal websites, they may even link to you. Don't ever lose sight of the fact that every little bit helps.

Word of mouth is a great promotional tool and you can't buy it. People have to like you, like your site, and think your community offers something worth passing on. Word of mouth is not simply spoken. Word of mouth happens when people mention your link when they are instant messaging or e-mailing a friend, when they are posting in a chat room or in other forums, or when they are linking to your community from their own websites. Having a domain name that is easy to remember (as I discussed in chapter 2), can help this process along. Nothing helps it more, however, than having good content and treating people with respect. People don't pass junk sites on to their friends. They pass good sites on to their friends.

Why not make it easy and even fun (well, maybe) for users to promote your site? Have a "Link to Us" page and offer people an array of graphics in various shapes and sizes that they can use to link to your community. There are also the common "Tell a Friend" and "Send This Topic to a Friend" features that usually are not terribly effective, but nonetheless can't hurt. You can give people wallpapers that they can use on their computer and buddy icons or avatars they can use for instant messaging and on other communities. If you're creative, you can come up with other methods as well.

For instance, on KarateForums.com, I put together a feature that we called "Promote KarateForums.com at Your School." This feature was very simple: We provided a graphic both in color and grayscale (see figure 4-3) that users could print out on a single sheet of paper and stick on their school's bulletin board or elsewhere. I wouldn't call it a huge success—we didn't have that many users when the idea was launched—but it was one more way that

Figure 4-3. "Promote KarateForums.com at Your School" printout.

loyal users could promote the community. In that regard, it went over fairly well.

One example of a "cool" way to encourage users to promote your site is to give them access to some code that will allow them to display your community's ten most recently active topics right on their websites! All the topics are linked, so when people click on a topic they go right to your community. Not only will some people like to put this on their sites, but they are fairly attractive to potential clickers. You should check your community software's top resource sites for a hack or code that will allow you to do this.

As I said before: Be creative. When users link to you, be appreciative. Do not take anything for granted.

What Not to Do

I already advised you to avoid pretending to be other users. Along those same lines, don't lie. Don't be despicable. Do not engage in shady or unethical practices. Do not sign up in other communities and then send its members private messages, e-mails, instant messages, etc. asking them to join your site. Do not try to bend the guidelines of other communities and find ways to post links to your site. Keep yourself honest and maintain your dignity. This is very important.

If you operate in an unethical way, it will catch up to you and it will harm you. You may get some users to come to your site, but at what cost? If you make a habit of it, you will certainly get a reputation that will hurt you and make you regret doing what you did. And if you feel sorry later—too bad. The damage is done. Not many people are going to care (and that includes me), because you are getting what you deserve. Not only that, but chances are you'd get your site banned from ever being mentioned on some communities again.

As a community administrator, you need to have respect for those in the field. If you don't, they won't respect you.

Conclusion

In this chapter, I took a look at some popular methods of promotion for Internet communities. With these concepts in mind, you will be better able to handle other ideas that come your way. Obviously, it is beyond the scope of this book to go into technical or advanced concepts of marketing and promotion. However, I hope that what I have mentioned here will get you going in the right direction. Use your imagination and always keep your eyes open for professional and effective opportunities to promote your community.

CHAPTER 5

Managing Your Staff

Having an active and productive staff is vital. The larger the community, the more vital it is. It's important that you have confidence in your staff so that you don't have to be there at all times, can work on other things, or can even take a vacation with some peace of mind. Your staff members must be able to do their jobs in your absence and in your presence. Confidence starts with picking the right people, making sure that they understand their duties, and ensuring that the lines of communication between staff member and administrator are wide open. This chapter will help you to accomplish these objectives.

How Should You Lead?

"You don't lead by hitting people over the head. That's assault, not leadership."

—DWIGHT EISENHOWER

You should lead by example, plain and simple. There is no better way to lead. Set the example for everyone to follow. Go right into the trenches with your staff members. Participate in moderator duties (removing threads, contacting users, etc.). If you see an issue, take care of it yourself. Don't tell someone else to take care of it. Don't let it appear that certain duties are "beneath you"— such an attitude is disrespectful and damaging.

However, remember that you are still the boss. That doesn't mean that you should *remind* people that you are the boss. Many people send me suggestions and say things like, "But, it's your site, of course." Yeah, true. It's my site. So, what? My site is a ghost town without users. If I didn't want to consider suggestions, would I listen to them? Stress to your staff members (and to your users, for that matter) that suggestions are appreciated and considered, although you will not act on all (or even a majority) of them.

"Being a leader is like being a lady, if you have to go around telling people you are one, you aren't."

—Margaret Thatcher

You will inevitably have to make some tough decisions. Not all of your staff members will agree with these decisions. If you need to explain a decision, explain it with tact, compassion, and understanding. Explain that you considered the decision thoroughly, tried to take everyone's feelings and thoughts into consideration (which you should have done, obviously), and that, in the end, you made the decision that you felt was the best one.

It's inevitable that a staff member, even a good staff member, will occasionally veer off and do something questionable. So it's important to remember that there are varying degrees of severity. For instance, let's say that one of your moderators removes a thread and you feel it shouldn't have been removed. Unless it happens repeatedly, it really isn't that big a deal. Correct the situation by making the thread or posts public again and by offering a brief public explanation such as, "We removed this thread in error. I apologize for the confusion. Thanks." Be sure to say "we"—don't name an individual staff member or say this person did that or that person did this. That is unimportant—there is no reason to hang anyone out to dry. You are a team and your moderator probably thought he was doing what you wanted him to do. For the most part, you succeed as a team and you make mistakes as a team.

After you correct the situation, you can make a polite and thoughtful post in your private, staff member–only documentation area (or your problem users forum—see the "Moderation: The Process" section later in this chapter) explaining why this post was not a violation and that you have gone ahead and corrected the situation. Explain the situation in a friendly, nonaccusatory way. By posting, you are eliminating any doubts and suspicions and ensuring that everyone is on the same page—it's all a part of the learning process as far as nailing down what is to be removed and what isn't. Don't make it sound like a big deal; don't make it sound like you are making an example of anyone. Just explain what's up and thank them.

If there is an issue with an individual staff member that all or most of your staff are aware of, post in the staff forums for the reasons I just gave. But, if you must correct a staff member on an issue that no one else will be aware of, then contact the person privately. There is usually no reason to make it public, and the staff member will likely appreciate the direct contact.

Speaking of saying thanks: Do it often. Your staff members are extremely important to your community. In most cases, they are volunteers and see no real form of monetary compensation. In your posts to them, in your responses and your e-mails, be sure to include a thanks. "Thank you for your work." "Thank you for your efforts." "Thank you for your time." "Thanks." No matter how you say it, say it. It's important.

I once worked as one of the most active moderators in a community for somewhere around a year, making maybe 3,500 posts or so. I would have to say that the administrator thanked me for my efforts maybe a couple times in that entire year. I didn't feel particularly appreciated. And it affected me and the way I manage my communities and treat my staff today. I mean, I don't want to be thanked every day, but a thanks here and there does wonders. It does wonders because it's true—or should be. You should be thanking your staff members. I have had the pleasure of having many brilliantly selfless and caring individuals on my team, and I cannot thank them enough for what they do and did.

Don't hide from people—make sure that it's not hard for anyone to contact you. Your signature in your community should clearly identify at least who you are and what your position is. Although it is not absolutely necessary, it is also nice to include links to helpful site-related resources, exciting site features or news, or other relevant external sites. This helps you to create a professional appearance.

Leadership isn't the easiest subject to explain, and not everyone is comfortable with being a leader. But if you want to manage a community, that's who you'll need to be. Hopefully the information here will get you on your way to developing your own leadership style. Being approachable, professional, understanding, and hard working; being able to communicate and be friendly, yet firm . . . it's all in there. Lead by example. Be a real person. If you can do all that, you've done well.

Communicating with Your Staff

"A sense of humor is part of the art of leadership, of getting along with people, of getting things done."

—DWIGHT EISENHOWER

You should communicate openly with your staff members. Be light; find humor when there is humor to be found. Wherever possible, ask for their opinions on changes to your community. Get their feedback and allow them to be involved. Allow them to influence your decisions. In some cases, it can be extremely helpful to just put an idea out there and not infer a view of your own. It keeps staff members from being swayed into agreeing because they don't want to disagree with you. This can be a great thing to do when you receive a suggestion that sounds good, but that you aren't 100 percent sure about. Your staff members are in your community virtually every day. Often, they will know your community just as well as you do—maybe better in parts. You should consider them to be trusted consultants.

It's inevitable that you will have to correct a staff member from time to time. Do so with understanding and tact. Be upbeat. Be clear. Keep in mind that, although you know exactly how you want things to be done, you are the only one who has access to your brain. You shouldn't act as if a person should have already known this or that. Even if he should have, it's not productive. Instead of focusing on what he did wrong, focus on how he can better handle that situation in the future. Your job is to help each staff member understand how the job should be done, by doing it yourself, having established guidelines, and explaining things in a kind and encouraging manner.

From time to time, a staff member will take umbrage with something that you said. I've had staff members who liked to have their little rebellions because they didn't like that I reversed a decision or didn't like that I removed one of their posts or something like that. Maybe they'll change their signatures around a bit, maybe they'll disappear for a few days, maybe they'll remove your link from their sites. Some people don't always take this stuff well and that's a shame. As long as they don't become too personal or verbally abusive, it's not that big a deal as long as they are following your instructions and not undermining you or your decisions. Give them some space and some time to chill out.

Again, deal with these situations with tact and understanding. It is very easy for people to get their feelings hurt, and it can be hard to communicate over the Internet. Such conversations are never easy and are often stressful, but some relationships can be defined in these moments. Although some differences are irreconcilable, in most situations your objective should be to get things solved and move forward, assuming that the staff member is interested in doing so.

Staff Forums

It's important to have at least one forum where staff members can privately discuss issues relevant to the site, where you can ask for their opinions, where they can ask questions, and more.

In addition, feel free to add special forums as you find a reason to do so. For instance, larger communities sometimes have off-topic staff forums where staff members can discuss anything strictly with other staff members. This might include travel plans (a popular use of such a forum) or personal details that they feel comfortable sharing with the staff but not the entire community—it's just basically a lounge for the staff members and will help them to get to know one another better, which helps them learn to count on and respect one another. At the same time, these forums can sometimes hinder your staff's participation in your public off-topic forum. Part of a moderator's job is to be there for regular users and to be a presence in the public forums.

If you have a special event that the staff is bound to discuss in great length, you may see fit to add a temporary forum for the discussion of this event. You can then delete the forum (and move the posts to a more general staff forum) once it has served its purpose.

Talking Things to Death

"You can't build a reputation on what you are going to do."

—HENRY FORD

Although you definitely want to encourage your staff members to offer feedback, don't fall into the trap of talking things to death. Don't get into a habit of simply talking about things over and over and over and on and on and on without actually accomplishing anything. You need someone (you) who, at the end of the day, can make a decision and give everyone direction.

This isn't to say that you should just jump headfirst into something without proper consideration. Far from it. But keep staff discussions moving forward productively. Don't let them spin in circles, drone on forever, or stalemate without a resolution. Get it all out there, get everyone's feedback, consider it, make a decision, and move forward.

Staff Leaks

Staff leaks happen. I find that a lot of the time it is tied to some sort of administrative action toward a user, such as banning. Maybe the user is friends with one of your staff members (or befriended the staff member in order to use him or her—take your pick). Maybe that staff member shares with the user what you said about him or her. Not good.

You may want to keep some things just between you and the staff, but avoid saying things that would be totally embarrassing and humiliating if they went public. Only say what is true and right and it won't be a problem. But make no mistake; the privacy of your staff forums is very important and should be defended.

So, what do you do? Well, don't ignore clues. Keep your eyes open. But don't go on any witch hunts. That would only be good for the people who want you to suffer. Just go about your business as usual. The person to be pitied is the person who is violating the sanctity and trust of your team. There is nothing else that you can really do that is productive. Just treat your staff with the same respect as you always have and operate your business as usual. If something jumps out at you, investigate it. Often these things work themselves out on their own.

The Chain of Command

How many levels of staff do you need? In the beginning, you can probably get by with just you and a few moderators or fewer. But as time goes by, something may inspire you to expand (either in number or in tiers), such as increased activity or spotting a user whom you'd love to have on your staff.

If your forum is quite large and active, you may want to add staff members who have no moderator powers (these people are "guides"). The hierarchy might look like this:

Administrator (You) > Moderators > Guides (Powerless) > Users

Moderators have moderator power. Guides are essentially powerless; their main goal is to spot threads and posts that violate your guidelines and use your report posts system to point them out to moderators and you. All new staff members are always guides first. Such an organizational structure will allow you to get to know people a little better without having to give them full moderator powers in your community. You can then promote people to moderator based upon their performance. Not all guides will become moderators, though. Some will not have the free time or the drive to do so. Some will just enjoy the minimum requirement that a guide position demands, and as long as they fulfill their responsibilities, that should be OK. After all, you need guides and you need moderators. It's a team effort.

I have almost never had another user on my site who had administrative powers. I do all of the banning. This makes decisions more consistent and is the way to go, if at all possible—even on large communities. Sometimes you need to share the power, though. So, if you are thinking of doing that, ask yourself: Is it really needed? Perhaps all you need are more moderators or more power for your moderators. If you must give this sort of access (banning, the ability to edit user profiles, etc.) to anyone else, you should do so in a limited fashion under strict guidelines. Log all actions (date, time, who made the change, action taken, user taken against, etc.). All things considered, the fewer people who can ban people, the better.

Be careful about handing the keys to your community off to anyone else. If you do, make sure that you have checks in place so this person cannot shut you down and clear out all of your data, leaving you with little recourse. No one, besides you, should be all-powerful.

Regular Users Who Think They Are Staff

You will run into users who take it upon themselves to act like moderators in public threads. They may be telling users what to do, what not to do, saying that this topic should have been here or there, this topic should be locked, and what have you. This is not a good thing.

Encourage these users to report any violations (or posts that may require attention) to you or your staff privately, and tell them that after doing so, they should not reply to or reference the post in any way. After that, assure them that you will make an appropriate determination, whatever that may be (that doesn't necessarily mean you will agree with the person, however). You can send this notice via private message or e-mail. It is even better if your forum software includes a report posts feature (more information about such a system is in the "Post Reporting System" section of chapter 6) that allows users to report threads or posts with a few clicks and sends a message to a staff member or (preferably) automatically posts a message on a central page (that all staff members can access when they visit the site).

Moderators Policing Moderators

You don't want staff members policing their equals and confronting one another about problems. If a staff member has a problem with another staff member, ask them to contact you (or a supervisor) so that you can handle it as you see fit. It is in the best interest of the team atmosphere if directives come down from you and not from an equal, because resentment can develop and that is not good. Just avoid an unnecessary issue by having people report such things to you.

Only One True Admin, Please

Don't have a co-administrator. I don't mean don't give anyone else administrative powers, although you should certainly try to avoid that. No, when I say "no co-administrators," what I mean is that if you decide to grant other people administrative power in your community, do not place these other administrators at your level in the staff hierarchy. In other words, although you may all have similar "power" in your community software, make sure that you are the main administrator or head administrator or that the others are assistant administrators or something of that nature. Basically, make it so that you are the one who has to make any ultimate decisions.

I know you may be thinking, "Well, we'll be able to talk and come up with a consensus," and that's all fine and dandy, but you never know. Even if you know the person well, it's not a great idea. There are exceptions, but at the end of the day, you need someone (i.e., you) who can say, "This is how it is and this is the way it's going to be." Discussion is great, but it has its limits—decisions have to be made. You don't need to come to stalemates or talk things to death. You need to be able to make good decisions based upon everything on the table, if it should come to that. Just save yourself the stress and time.

Moderation: The Process

As far as this book is concerned, moderation is the viewing, monitoring, and, wherever necessary, removing of content in your community. The focus of this section is the recommended process for removing threads and posts from your site. This process is designed to prevent damaging content from festering, to make users aware of their violations, and to keep a record of user violations so that you can have an accurate idea of just how much trouble a user has caused.

Step #1: Recognizing Violations

You have written up clear guidelines. It is now important to make sure that they are enforced. Regular users or staff members without moderator power can help with this process by reporting violating posts. The interpretation of your guidelines is ultimately up to you, and through your application of them (and the supporting documents that you provide your staff, which I discuss in the "Staff Guidelines" section a bit later in this chapter) your staff members will come to understand what you expect. The wording of your guidelines should be clear enough so that they will have a good general idea right from the get-go. Nevertheless, make sure that staff members always feel comfortable asking you a question or getting clarification on an issue. If somebody makes a mistake, correct it and move on. Once a violation is spotted, remove it.

Step #2: Removing Violations

You can have a private forum that only staff members can see and access, and you can move all threads and posts that violate your guidelines to that forum. This effectively deletes them from your actual community.

There are some important benefits to placing all of these threads in a private forum instead of deleting them permanently or allowing edited versions to remain. These include better record keeping (you can simply link to removed posts rather than quoting what you removed), easier mistake correction (especially if your community software has a merge function), and comment minimization in response to the removals. Plus, if people know that you'll correct their mistakes, they'll be more likely to lean on you and less likely to actually care about what they post. Even if you edit out a violation, you should still contact your users directly to make them aware of it, rather than leaving a note in the member's post, which the member may never read again or may get hostile about. Without notification and consequence, no one is really going to learn anything. That said, it is very, very useful, for the sake of administrative action and documentation, to have the entire post as the user had posted it, free of any administrative edits, with the poster's IP attached and all that good stuff.

It's just a lot cleaner to split the posts off, as opposed to doing anything else. If you edit a post and leave it in the thread, what about the replies to the post? You'll either have to edit them all or create posts that make less (maybe very little) sense. Editing posts can get really, really messy and can lead to poor documentation, which will harm your ability to effectively manage your site.

Even if your software has a "soft delete function" where you can delete a post directly in the thread but not permanently delete it, it's still not as clean as it could be. And if those deleted posts aren't searchable, forget about it. As an administrator, I like to review posts that have been deleted. If they don't show up as new posts, it makes it harder for me to do that. There is nothing simpler or more helpful than having posts split off into their own threads in their entirety.

Now that a violation has been identified and removed, it is time to document the violation and the action that you will be taking.

Step #3: Documenting Violations and the Action Taken

"Put out an APB for a male suspect, driving a . . . car of some sort, heading in the direction of, uh, you know, that place that sells chili. Suspect is hatless. Repeat, hatless."

—Chief Clancy Wiggum

Next, you and your staff should document violations. One easy way to do this is by having a "problem users" forum where each user who violates your guidelines gets his or her own thread. Each thread is titled with that particular user's exact username. If the user changes his username, you should adjust the thread to include the new username and the old one. One way to do this is make the subject of the thread "New Username (Old Username)" and add a reply when the change has been made. If the usernames are too long to do this, just make sure that the current username is in the subject and all of the past usernames are mentioned at least once in the thread so that it comes up anytime you search for that username. Figure 5-1 shows what this forum might look like.

Figure 5-1. Sample problem users forum.

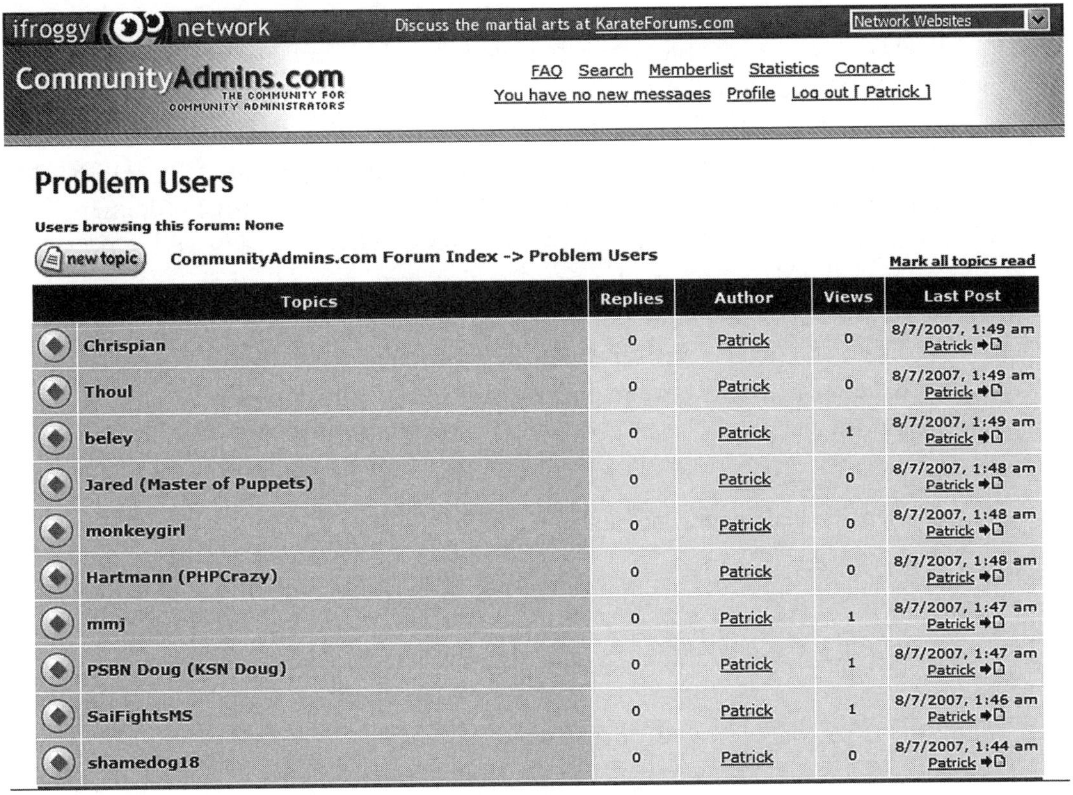

ifroggy network Discuss the martial arts at KarateForums.com Network Websites

CommunityAdmins.com THE COMMUNITY FOR COMMUNITY ADMINISTRATORS

FAQ Search Memberlist Statistics Contact
You have no new messages Profile Log out [Patrick]

Problem Users

Users browsing this forum: None

new topic CommunityAdmins.com Forum Index -> Problem Users Mark all topics read

Topics	Replies	Author	Views	Last Post
Chrispian	0	Patrick	0	8/7/2007, 1:49 am Patrick
Thoul	0	Patrick	0	8/7/2007, 1:49 am Patrick
beley	0	Patrick	1	8/7/2007, 1:49 am Patrick
Jared (Master of Puppets)	0	Patrick	0	8/7/2007, 1:48 am Patrick
monkeygirl	0	Patrick	0	8/7/2007, 1:48 am Patrick
Hartmann (PHPCrazy)	0	Patrick	0	8/7/2007, 1:48 am Patrick
mmj	0	Patrick	1	8/7/2007, 1:47 am Patrick
PSBN Doug (KSN Doug)	0	Patrick	1	8/7/2007, 1:47 am Patrick
SaiFightsMS	0	Patrick	1	8/7/2007, 1:46 am Patrick
shamedog18	0	Patrick	0	8/7/2007, 1:44 am Patrick

If it is the user's first violation, then the person who removed the thread from the community must start a new problem users thread for that user. If the user has already had a violation and, as such, already has a problem users thread, any subsequent violations by that user are noted in replies to the existing thread.

However, once in a while a staff member will create a new thread for a user who already has one. In these cases, simply close the new one, mentioning the old one when you do. In the old one, make a mention of the new one in a reply, so that that violation doesn't go without notice. If possible, have your community software prevent any new threads in that forum that feature similar titles. Then, have it list those similar threads (hyperlinked so that your staff members can locate the previously created threads). Sometimes there are no exact matches, so allow the staff to go ahead and post the new thread if they press the submit button again. That sort of function will pretty much put an end to duplicate threads in your problem users forum.

Each entry in a problem users thread should detail the violation and the action taken, and (if necessary) it should provide a link to the violation (which should now be located in your trash bin forum). I also find it helpful to quote the piece of the post that contained the violation—especially if it was a large post. It will show exactly what part of the post violated your guidelines. This makes it easier for your staff members to see why you removed a post, for you to see why they removed a post, and it makes it so much easier for you to review old removals, as well.

So, for instance, if a user made a post that contained vulgarities, you would move it to the trash bin forum and post something like this in a problem users thread:

http://www.yourdomain.com/viewtopic.php?id = 11211984
Vulgar language. PM sent.

*"I think you are acting like an * . . ."*

The link is to the removed post, "vulgar language" describes what the issue was, "PM sent" lets everyone know that you notified the user via private message, and the quoted portion is the part that violated your guidelines.

Ideally, you'd use the quote BBCode in your community software to quote it. If a user had a signature that was too long, you might say:

Signature too long (seven lines). PM sent.

Yes, it's that simple.

Documenting violations in this fashion will allow you to keep this information organized and accessible. This will help you keep tabs on each user and see just how many times he or she has violated your guidelines. Such information can be vital when determining whether to ban someone. It's also good to have it on hand for the sake of record keeping. As a side benefit, the problem users and trash bin forums are valuable training tools because they allow new staff members to see what types of posts are removed and how they are dealt with.

Finally, let's contact the user in question.

Step #4: Contacting Users

When a user violates one of your guidelines, she needs to be notified. If you removed a post, she will be wondering where it went. The tone of these messages should be polite, informative, and direct. It's important to document the process so that your staff members will know what to do and how to handle it.

One of the best uses of your private message system is for guideline-violation notification. This allows you to keep a record in your database of all conversations. You can then view all the details of a conversation if you need to do so. It's hard to verify the validity of an e-mail someone forwards you, but if you have a private message that clearly went from person A to person B, you have everything you need.

It's an excellent idea to have a series of contact templates that you and your staff members can use in your correspondence with members. Contact templates allow your staff to easily copy and paste messages that will, after filling in a few blanks, generally be ready to send off. They allow you to standardize the format and tone of the messages sent to your users, which will keep such contact as consistent as possible from staff member to staff member.

To give you an idea of what these should look like, here is an example of an actual contact templates thread—a post in your staff forums that includes your contact templates. The templates are presented in the format in which they are available to the staff. In other words, it includes the community BBCode that creates a link to the user guidelines, and that saves time for both the staff member (who no longer has to create the link by hand) and user (who no longer has to locate the guidelines manually).

LOG IN

This thread contains contact templates that you should use to contact users in regard to violations of our User Guidelines.

These templates should give you an idea of the type of verbiage to use when you must contact members in regard to violations. Whenever possible, please use the template in its entirety. However, if the template does not fit the violation perfectly or if you are contacting a user in regard to more than one violation, please feel free to combine templates and add additional, consistent wording that follows the usage and tone expressed in the templates posted here. Don't forget to change "post quoted below as it" to "posts quoted below as they" if you are quoting from more than one post.

If a template does not exist for a violation and you feel one would be valuable, please feel free to make one and post it as a reply to this thread. I will take a look at it and approve or deny it and edit it as I see fit.

Pay close attention to the text in capital letters in arrow brackets (< and >) as that is the text that you need to edit. Do not leave any of these elements in parentheses in the private message. When quoted posts are required, feel free to press the quote button next to the removed post and paste the output in the template, replacing the already existing quote tags, so that you do not have two sets of quote tags.

Thank you.

"Best" Discussion

Hello <USERNAME>,

Thank you for visiting KarateForums.com.

Unfortunately, I have had to remove your post quoted below as it violated our [url = http://www.karateforums.com/userguidelines.html]User Guidelines[/url] as creating a vague ''best'' martial art discussion.

<PASTE THE PORTION THAT VIOLATED OUR GUIDELINES>

We do not allow discussions debating what the best martial art is nor do we allow discussions debating what martial art has the best something. This includes discussions such as ''What is the best martial art?'' or ''What is the best martial art for street fighting?'' or ''Does BJJ have the best kicks?'' or ''What martial art has the best footwork?'' etc. The exception to this is for individuals who need help choosing a martial art. In these cases, the person who needs assistance must make it clear that they need help selecting a martial art and must list the martial arts that are available to them in their area. They cannot simply ask what the best martial art is for them—there must be a list of arts. They must offer some details (even if they are few and vague) about their needs and their situation (body type, environment, etc.).

Please keep this in mind to prevent further violations in the future.

Thank you for your time and cooperation.

Sincerely,

<YOUR NAME>
KarateForums.com Sensei

''Best'' Discussion: Additional Information Required for Help Choosing a Martial Art

Hello <USERNAME>,

Thank you for visiting KarateForums.com.

Unfortunately, I have had to remove your post quoted below as it violated our [url = http://www.karateforums.com/userguidelines.html]User Guidelines[/url] as a vague request for help choosing a martial art.

<PASTE THE PORTION THAT VIOLATED OUR GUIDELINES>

We do not allow discussions debating what the best martial art is nor do we allow discussions debating what martial art has the best something. This includes discussions such as ''What is the best martial art?'' or ''What is the best martial art for street fighting?" or "Does BJJ have the best kicks?" or "What martial art has the best footwork?" etc. The exception to this is for individuals who need help choosing a martial art. In these cases, you must make it clear that you need help selecting a martial art and must list the martial arts that are available to you in your area. You cannot simply ask what the best martial art is for you—there must be a list of arts. You must offer some details (even if they are few and vague) about your needs and your situation (body type, environment, etc.).

Please keep this in mind to prevent further violations in the future.

Thank you for your time and cooperation.

Sincerely,

<YOUR NAME>
KarateForums.com Sensei

Copyright Infringement: Text

Hello <USERNAME>,

Thank you for visiting KarateForums.com.

Unfortunately, I have had to remove your post quoted below as it violated our [url=http://www.karateforums.com/userguidelines.html]User Guidelines[/url] as copyright infringement.

<PASTE THE PORTION THAT VIOLATED OUR GUIDELINES>

When quoting an article or written work that you did not author or do not have permission to reproduce (which is our assumption in this case—if it is incorrect, please let us know and include some way for us to verify this fact), you may only quote a small portion of the article (usually no more than 1/5 or 1/6) and you must link to the source (if online) or provide the source (if offline).

Please keep this in mind to prevent further violations in the future.

Thank you for your time and cooperation.

Sincerely,

<YOUR NAME>
KarateForums.com Sensei

Cross-Posting

Hello <USERNAME>,

Thank you for visiting KarateForums.com.

Unfortunately, I have had to remove your post quoted below as it violated our [url = http://www.karateforums.com/userguidelines.html]User Guidelines[/url] as cross-posting.

<PASTE THE PORTION THAT VIOLATED OUR GUIDELINES>

Cross-posting is posting the same content in two or more locations.

Please keep this in mind to prevent further violations in the future.

Thank you for your time and cooperation.

Sincerely,

<YOUR NAME>
KarateForums.com Sensei

General

Hello <USERNAME>,

Thank you for visiting KarateForums.com.

Unfortunately, I have had to remove your post quoted below as it violated our [url = http://www.karateforums.com/userguidelines.html]User Guidelines[/url] as <DESCRIPTION OF VIOLATION>.

<PASTE THE PORTION THAT VIOLATED OUR GUIDELINES HERE>

Please keep this in mind to prevent further violations in the future.

Thank you for your time and cooperation.

Sincerely,

<YOUR NAME>
KarateForums.com Sensei

Hotlinking

Hello <USERNAME>,

Thank you for visiting KarateForums.com.

Unfortunately, I have had to remove your post quoted below as it violated our [url = http://www.karateforums.com/userguidelines.html]User Guidelines[/url] as hotlinking.

<PASTE THE PORTION THAT VIOLATED OUR GUIDELINES>

Hotlinking is when you link directly to a graphic, video, audio clip, archive (.zip, .rar, etc.), or otherwise downloadable or streamable file instead of linking to the page where that item can be found. Generally, people place this content on their websites as a means to bring people to those websites. When you link directly to the file, the person clicking the link does not visit the site, while using the site owner's bandwidth, which costs money and/or resources. Instead, you must link to the page where this content can be found, rather than directly to the content itself. This is unless you have permission to link directly to the content or the site owner has posted on their site that it's allowed. If this is the case, please provide us with information that allows us to verify it.

Please keep this in mind to prevent further violations in the future.

Thank you for your time and cooperation.

Sincerely,

<YOUR NAME>
KarateForums.com Sensei

Inappropriate

Hello <USERNAME>,

Thank you for visiting KarateForums.com.

Unfortunately, I have had to remove your post quoted below as it violated our [url = http://www.karateforums.com/userguidelines.html]User Guidelines[/url] as inappropriate <DESCRIBE WHY IT WAS INAPPROPRIATE>.

<PASTE THE PORTION THAT VIOLATED OUR GUIDELINES>

Please keep this in mind to prevent further violations in the future.

Thank you for your time and cooperation.

Sincerely,

<YOUR NAME>
KarateForums.com Sensei

Inflammatory

Hello <USERNAME>,

Thank you for visiting KarateForums.com.

Unfortunately, I have had to remove your post quoted below as it violated our [url=http://www.karateforums.com/userguidelines.html]User Guidelines[/url] as inflammatory.

<PASTE THE PORTION THAT VIOLATED OUR GUIDELINES>

Generally speaking, when a post is inflammatory, it isn't adding much to the thread outside of hostility.

Please keep this in mind to prevent further violations in the future.

Thank you for your time and cooperation.

Sincerely,

<YOUR NAME>
KarateForums.com Sensei

Report, Don't Respond: No Violation in Response

If the post they responded to was not actually a violation, please remove ''as it was in response to a post that had to be removed as it violated our User Guidelines.''

Hello <USERNAME>,

Thank you for visiting KarateForums.com.

Unfortunately, I have had to remove your post quoted below as it was in response to a post that had to be removed as it violated our [url = http://www.karateforums .com/userguidelines.html]User Guidelines[/url].

<PASTE THE POST THAT WAS REMOVED>

In the future, if you feel a post may be against our User Guidelines or may otherwise require some sort of attention, you should always report a potential violation by clicking on the exclamation point (!) button next to the appropriate post. After you have done so, forget that the post exists (do not reply to it further, even to say that you have reported it). We will then handle it appropriately.

We appreciate when members inform us of violations to our User Guidelines, rather then responding to them and making the situation worse.

Thank you for your time and cooperation.

Sincerely,

<YOUR NAME>
KarateForums.com Sensei

Report, Don't Respond: Violation in Response

If the post they responded to was not actually a violation, please remove "In this post, you were responding to a post that violated our User Guidelines."

Hello <USERNAME>,

Thank you for visiting KarateForums.com.

Unfortunately, I have had to remove your post quoted below as it violated our [url = http://www.karateforums.com/userguidelines.html]User Guidelines[/url] as <DESCRIPTION OF VIOLATION>.

<PASTE THE PORTION THAT VIOLATED OUR GUIDELINES>

Please keep this in mind to prevent further violations in the future.

In this post, you were responding to a post that violated our User Guidelines. In the future, if you feel a post may be against our User Guidelines or may otherwise require some sort of attention, you should always report a potential violation by clicking on the exclamation point (!) button next to the appropriate post. After you have done so, forget that the post exists (do not reply to it further, even to say that you have reported it). We will then handle it appropriately.

We appreciate when members inform us of violations to our User Guidelines, rather then responding to them and making the situation worse.

Thank you for your time and cooperation.

Sincerely,

<YOUR NAME>
KarateForums.com Sensei

Signature: General

Hello <USERNAME>,

Thank you for visiting KarateForums.com.

Unfortunately, your signature is currently in violation of our [url=http://www.karateforums.com/userguidelines.html]User Guidelines[/url] as <DESCRIPTION OF VIOLATION>.

<PASTE THE PORTION THAT VIOLATED OUR GUIDELINES>

Please adjust your signature as soon as you can and please keep this in mind to prevent further violations in the future.

Thank you for your time and cooperation.

Sincerely,

<YOUR NAME>
KarateForums.com Sensei

Signature: Too Long

Hello <USERNAME>,

Thank you for visiting KarateForums.com.

Your signature is currently <NUMBER> lines long, which is in violation of our [url = http://www.karateforums.com/userguidelines.html]User Guidelines[/url], which only allow for 5 lines.

Please adjust your signature as soon as you can and please keep this in mind to prevent further violations in the future.

Thank you for your time and cooperation.

Sincerely,

<YOUR NAME>
KarateForums.com Sensei

Site-Related Feedback, Problem/Error Reports, Etc. Posted in Forums

Hello <USERNAME>,

Thank you for visiting KarateForums.com.

Unfortunately, I have had to remove your post quoted below.

<PASTE THE POST THAT WAS REMOVED>

We ask that all site-related feedback, questions, problem/error reports and the like be sent via [url = http://www.karateforums.com/contact.php]e-mail[/url] or private message so that we do not miss them and can handle them in the most efficient manner possible. Please be sure to keep this in mind for the future.

<PROVIDE ANSWER TO THEIR QUESTION, IF POSSIBLE—IF YOU DO NOT KNOW THE ANSWER OR CANNOT ANSWER, LEAVE THE FOLLOWING> Patrick, our administrator, will be in touch with you as soon as possible regarding your post.

Thank you for your time and cooperation.

Sincerely,

<YOUR NAME>
KarateForums.com Sensei

Vulgar

Hello <USERNAME>,

Thank you for visiting KarateForums.com.

Unfortunately, I have had to remove your post quoted below as it violated our [url=http://www.karateforums.com/userguidelines.html]User Guidelines[/url] as vulgar.

<PASTE THE PORTION THAT VIOLATED OUR GUIDELINES>

Please note that if we do not allow a word or term, we do not allow a word or term—it doesn't matter if it is abbreviated or self-censored.

Please keep this in mind to prevent further violations in the future.

Thank you for your time and cooperation.

Sincerely,

<YOUR NAME>
KarateForums.com Sensei

In addition to this example, there is a set of general, blank contact templates that is available in a downloadable archive from the book website and is featured in appendix B. You can use these to craft your own templates that convey your own messages.

It's basically a given that some issues will not fit into a contact template that is currently available. In cases like this, encourage members of your staff to improvise with the same type of language in the current contact templates or create their own contact templates if the issue arises with some frequency. You can then edit the templates to your liking and eventually add them to the first post.

One simple way to display contact templates is as a sticky thread in your staff forums. All your moderators have to do is respond to that thread. Regardless of your setup, you should encourage submissions and reorganize the thread or area as necessary.

Keep in mind that as violations become more serious or repetitive, you the administrator may need to take yourself away from these templates and become more firm or serious with people. But for the vast majority of violation notifications, your contact templates are going to be exactly what you need.

Responses to Guideline Violation Warnings

You can get all types of responses to these things. If a response is ever hostile or nasty, I ask my staff members not to respond to it. I tell them to document it in a problem user's thread and I will take care of it. I want to be the one who deals with idiots and the one who takes the brunt of any criticism.

Here are some common responses and how you should handle them.

(No response).

No worries. I like these just fine. As long as the person read your message, that is what counts.

"Sorry. I didn't know. Won't happen again."

The very best thing that you can hope for. I'll usually just respond to these with a "Thanks, I appreciate it" or something of that nature.

"But, but . . . the other guy! You allow this guy to do this, but you contact me . . ."

When cited, some people like to point their fingers in all directions or to other posts on your site, as if it somehow lessens what they did. I tell these people that if they see a violation of our guidelines, please report it. We want their help. Otherwise, it doesn't mean a heck of a lot for them to point it out now. Besides, it doesn't affect what they did. Hold people accountable for their actions.

"Whatever, man."

Not the best response, but not mass murder, either. I like to tell these people that although they are welcome to disagree with how we enforce our user guidelines, if they wish to participate, they must abide by them. I consider this response a little condescending and if it keeps up, there might be repercussions.

"We're all adults here."

And adults don't need guidelines, right? I was in my mid-teens when I started managing communities, so to imply indirectly that kids need user guidelines and adults don't is not going to get you any gold stars from me. With people like this, simply explain that you have specific goals for this community, that your user guidelines help you to accomplish them, and that is why they must be respected and followed by everyone, including adults.

"Uh . . . are you an idiot?"

People can get really nasty. We treat violations in private messages the same as violations elsewhere. And, of course, violations directed at members of your staff (including you) are very serious because your staff is to be respected at all times—not agreed with, just treated with respect. So, if a user sends a nasty message in response to a guideline-violation warning, he or she is written up and dealt with (the message contains something like, "Please do not speak to a staff member in a condescending fashion again.") or they are banned, if appropriate.

"Well, I'm out of here then. Bye."

As I've said, communities have goals. What you want out of your community and what certain people want out of your community may be two different things. Communities are not for everyone, especially when they are run professionally. Even a community for everyone really isn't for everyone, as not everyone wants a community that is for everyone. People leave, people go elsewhere. Don't get me wrong, users matter a great deal and you should take their feedback into account at every turn, but you should make the final call. That final call should be made for the betterment of the community as a whole in line with your goals. Some people won't like it and some people will leave. Handle it like any normal message. Don't make a fuss and don't try to convince them not to go. Just let them go.

"Your time is limited, so don't waste it living someone else's life. Don't be trapped by dogma—which is living with the results of other people's thinking. Don't let the noise of others' opinions drown out your own inner voice."

—Steve Jobs

Process Summary

Let's review.

1. Recognize a violation.

2. Remove the violation.

3. Document the violation and the action taken.

4. Contact the user who made the violation.

The reason step three comes before step four is that it makes it less likely that two staff members will act on the same violation.

It might seem like a bit much, but once you get the hang of the system, it's really a piece of cake and is absolutely worthwhile and necessary.

Old Violations

Sometimes you or your staff will find violations long after they have been made. More than a week ago, weeks ago—even months ago. How did it happen? Who knows? When you have a large site with tons of posts, sometimes not every post gets the look it deserves. That doesn't mean that it should just be left—it should still be removed and documented. But you usually should not contact users on old violations, especially if you feel that it has already been covered or that it will do more harm than good to bring up an old and now possibly dead situation.

For instance, if you have already warned the user about his behavior and the old violation that you found was made before the warning, then it's kind of redundant and annoying to send out another warning a week or weeks or months later when the problem has already been addressed. As I said, you should still document these as you would document others, but instead of saying "PM sent," say something like, "Too old for PM."

Staff Guidelines

The responsibilities that a staff member has are 100 percent up to you. In general, your moderators should have the power to move and close any thread and to contact users about violations. As I've discussed, don't allow your staff members to delete posts outright with no record of those posts remaining. This makes moderator action very hard to track.

You also have to decide if you want to give your moderators power in all (or most) of your public forums or just a certain one or two, etc. In other words, you can have individual forum moderators or what are commonly referred to as "Super Moderators." You may want "specialists" presiding over the forums that require a certain level of expertise. But, generally speaking, giving your moderators power in most (if not all) of your public forums doesn't cause any harm. It makes it easier for them to take care of a violation when they see it instead of waiting for someone else to get to it. Do not allow staff members to have moderator power in private staff forums. Just as a safety precaution. They really have no reason to have such powers, anyway.

You train your new staff members through your guidelines and documentation and by allowing them to watch you and your current staff in action. You must also have an additional set of guidelines that detail their duties and what you expect of them. Again, you should send potential staff members these guidelines before they accept the position, so that they know what is expected of them. This ensures that everyone is clear on the duties from the get-go and helps to get new staff members going on the right track as soon as possible.

Staff Guideline Ideas

In addition to what we have already covered, I am going to list some ideas for staff member guidelines that may be useful for crafting your own. Please keep in mind that these are general guideline ideas. Create the guidelines you need.

Job Duties   You need to make sure that you are all on the same page when it comes to staff member responsibilities and what is expected of them. What qualities do they need to have? Do they need to have a solid understanding of your community software? Do they need to be able to work in a team environment? Do they need to have any specific knowledge (for a support community, for example)? How often should they visit your community at the bare minimum?

This includes staff members' basic moderation responsibilities, but it will usually go beyond that. What other responsibilities do they have? Do they need to post and/or contribute in some way? Do they have to each write one article for your articles section per a certain period of time? Do you want them to greet newcomers? In your community, there are most likely some responsibilities other than just using moderator powers, and you will have to detail them.

Behavior   You expect users to act respectfully. You should expect more out of your staff members. Your staff members represent your community and you to your visitors and others. You should detail how you expect them to act. You should want your moderators to act with kindness and respect and to avoid heated arguments. Part of their job is to cool arguments down—not heat them up. Again, they are the example.

This includes how they communicate about moderator and administrator actions. You should handle your business privately. You don't want your staff members posting things like "Do that again and you'll be in trouble," "I have removed posts of yours before," "I removed Joe's posts because they were full of vulgarities" and that sort of thing. They should not talk publicly about specific actions taken against specific members. It just isn't professional and it will only anger and alienate people, which will make matters worse.

Use of "Powers"   Tell your staff members how to use the powers you give them. If your staff members have moderator powers (typically, the ability to edit, move, or lock posts and threads in your community), you should explain how these are to be used, when they are to be used, where they can be found, and what the process is for handling violations of your guidelines.

When is it time to close a thread? The most common (and acceptable) scenario is when a thread has "run its course." Everyone has had a say and now the topic is going in circles and being talked about to death. The thread is effectively "over," and you put an end to it by closing it. You will find other viable reasons, I am sure.

However, avoid closing threads as much as you can. If a thread or post violates your user guidelines, remove it—don't close it. Even if you close a thread, you should still remove the violations from it, document them, and take the appropriate action. Leaving violations out there allows people to keep doing damage, and if the individuals who violated your guidelines are not contacted, there will have been no repercussions. Closing a thread just because someone violates your user guidelines doesn't really teach much of a lesson or give much of a warning—the user may not even be aware that he did anything wrong. It also shows troublemakers that they can get you to close a thread just by making a little mess.

You may want to detail how you want your staff to handle duplicate threads and posts. A duplicate thread is a thread posted in the same forum within a short period of time. A duplicate post is a post placed on the same thread within a short period of time. If the post appears in two separate forums (cross-posting) or is posted more than five minutes after the first, it is usually not a duplicate.

Duplicates should be looked at as accidents and no action should be taken, other than moving them to your trash bin or wherever you house posts that were violations. You and your staff should make a note on the thread (either in the subject line or as a reply) in your trash bin that it's a duplicate so that you can quickly remember why it was removed.

Documenting Violations and Related Issues and Notifying Members   Outline how you want your staff members to document member violations and how you want them to notify your members of those violations. I covered this in great detail in the "Moderation: The Process" section in this chapter. By creating a problem users forum and using contact templates, you can keep track of what has happened and keep communication with members consistent from staff member to staff member.

Discussing Site-Related Issues with Members   When a community member approaches a member of your staff with a site-related issue, what should she do? What sort of questions should she answer? What sort of questions shouldn't she answer? When should she refer people to you?

When someone contacts a staff member outside of your site (i.e., through e-mail or an instant messenger), those conversations are hard to officially document because you have no firsthand knowledge of them or a digital paper trail. To remedy this, have your staff members bring those sensitive site-related conversations back into the private message system at your site. They can ask community members to discuss issues with them there. That way if something happens that requires action (the member makes a disrespectful comment, for example), you have the documentation you need to take action.

Avoiding Controversial Discussions   It is the nature of some people (myself included) to, at times, avoid controversial discussions or hot-button issues. But you and your staff members simply cannot do this. These types of threads will generally bring about the most violations, so you and the staff should watch them more than pretty much any other type of topic. Don't ignore them because you don't like the discussion or you are not taking part.

Staff Forums   You should talk about your private staff member-only forums. What are they for? Make it clear that the discussions in these forums stay in these forums and among current staff members only, unless you say otherwise.

Interacting with Other Levels of Staff   If you have multiple levels of staff, how does each level interact with one another? Should one level be helping out another level? In what way? By reporting posts in a specific forum or through a "report posts" feature? You want your entire team to be working together, so make sure that you discuss their relationships.

Choosing New Staff Members   Some communities allow current staff members to pick new staff members. If your community is of this nature, describe the process either in your staff member guidelines or in a separate document. Describe how staff members should recommend potential staff members; how a staff member is invited and promoted, and whether they need to have approval from a higher-level staff member before doing so.

Saying Thanks and Being Available   Finally, as I have said a few times already, be sure to thank your staff members for their contributions to your community right there in your guidelines. Also, make sure that you mention that if they have any questions about anything at any time, that they can feel free to contact you. You can never hope to cover everything, and maybe it is best to leave some things vague. Remember that if a staff member wants clarification about something, that shows a distinct interest in learning what it is that you want to see from your staff. So, make sure that your door is open.

Example Staff Guidelines

To help you draft your own staff guidelines, here are a few real-life examples. The first one is from SportsForums.net, a sports discussion community with one level of staff members (moderators) whose primary duty is to ensure that users are abiding by the user guidelines.

LOG IN

SportsForums.net Moderators must work within these guidelines.

Qualities

You must possess leadership capabilities, a good attitude, kind demeanor, good speaking and grammar skills (you must be able to communicate clearly in English), basic understanding of the features of the community software, the ability to stimulate discussion, distinguish a violation of our User Guidelines and aggressively moderate this community, work in a team environment and, finally, have pride in your work and be dedicated to the success of SportsForums.net.

It's required that staff members provide me with their real name for display on our staff page as well as a current mailing address, at all times (it can be work, P.O. Box, home, etc. just as long as it reaches you).

Participation

SportsForums.net Moderators are expected to visit the forums at a minimum of 5 days per week and/or 2 hours per week.

Although you are encouraged to start topics and reply to topics where you see fit, your main function is to make sure that the users of this community are abiding by our User Guidelines.

On your routine visit to this site, you should read a variety of topics—but above all, do not avoid hot button issues just because you are not taking part. Controversial and debatable issues will generally spawn the most violations. So, those are the topics you will want to hit hardest on your visits. Carefully consider each post, but be aggressive in your approach. We can always fix mistakes, but the mistake of leaving a violation in public is one that we want to avoid.

If a user does violate our guidelines, they must be contacted via private message using our Contact Templates.

You should remove any threads and posts that are in violation of our guidelines. You do so by moving them and all of their direct replies to the Trash Bin.

Your moderation tools can be found at the bottom right of the view forum and view topic pages. When moving a topic, you must select the forum that you want to move it to and decide whether or not to leave a shadow topic. If you are moving the topic to the Trash Bin, do not leave a shadow. If you are moving the topic from a public forum to another public forum, leave a shadow. If you spot a topic that is not posted in the most appropriate forum, please move it to the forum. When splitting a topic, check the checkmarks next to the posts you wish to split, choose the forum you wish to split to, give it a title and click "Split selected posts."

If a user makes a reply that violates our guidelines and the thread that they replied to would normally be alright, just remove that post using the split function in the community software. Be sure to remove any posts that reference or were in reply to the post that violated the guidelines. Move it to the Trash Bin. Again, they must be contacted via private message using our Contact Templates. Please note that we do not ever permanently delete posts. Any post that is removed or deleted from public view is moved to the Trash Bin.

If a contact template doesn't exist for the type of violation that you are dealing with, feel free to make one and post it on the Contact Templates thread.

If, during a single visit of yours to the community, you have spotted a user who has violated our guidelines in more than one post or instance, please combine all of the violations into one notification private message. Please do not send private messages one after another for individual violations wherever you can help it. You can help minimize this by completing your routine look throughout the forums and splitting off any violations while you do so, leaving them open individually in a separate window or tab and then coming back to them once you have had a complete look through the forums. Then, you can document and handle them as needed. Feel free to combine contact templates to achieve the desired effect of covering various types of violations inside of a single message.

For all violations, be sure to start or respond to the appropriate thread in the Problem Users forum. Every user who violates our User Guidelines has a thread in this forum with their username as the title.

To check if a thread has already been created for a given user, you can use the search function by searching for their exact username and limiting your search to the Problem Users forum. Or, you can just try to start a topic. If you start a topic for a user who already has one, the software will automatically stop you and direct you to the proper thread. If the person's username has less than 3 characters or any characters that are not letters or numbers and your initial search comes up empty, try substituting the number 1 until the username is at least 3 characters and/or all of the non alphanumeric characters have been replaced. For example, for the username be, you would search for be1. For b&e&, you would search for b1e1.

If a user responds to your private message, help them in the most polite and kind way possible. However, if their message is disrespectful or further violates our User Guidelines—do not respond to the message. Post the entire message in their Problem Users thread and I will handle it.

If a user contacts you via e-mail, instant messenger, etc. in regard to a violation or other sensitive site-related matter, please document it in Problem Users (if appropriate) and then respond to them through the private message system, asking them to correspond with you through private messages instead of e-mail, instant messenger, etc. This allows the conversation to be officially documented and tracked, should something come out of it that requires action.

If a thread is going in circles or getting repetitive (the issue has been talked to death and is at its end), you can close it.

Wherever possible, you should try to keep a thread open and in public. Closing a thread is not an appropriate response to a violation or dispute. Split violations off, take care of them and leave the thread. Do not close a thread and leave the violations in public where they can continue to do harm. They still need to be removed and handled.

Duplicate threads posted in the same forum within a short period of time and duplicate posts posted on the same thread within a short period of time are not considered violations. They are to be considered accidents. Simply move the thread(s)/split the post(s) off into the Trash Bin and reply to the newly created thread in the Trash Bin noting that it was a duplicate or make "Duplicate" the subject of the thread when splitting. There is no need to document in Problem Users or send a private message.

If a user repeatedly violates our guidelines and shows a disregard for the staff of the site, it is a possibility that they will be banned. However, it is I alone that will make this distinction and until I do, just handle all violations as business as usual. Please do not make assertions as to who should be banned and who shouldn't.

If, at any time, you have an issue with another staff member or feel that they may have made a serious mistake, please contact me privately and I will handle it. Do not confront your fellow staff members on any serious issues. If you have a post removed, a decision that you made is reversed or you are otherwise corrected, please do not take it personally. Please make a note of it to prevent it from happening again and ask questions to further understand, if necessary.

Please consult our Situations Guide for further, more specific information on the handling and distinguishing of certain types of violations.

You Are an Example

It is important that you realize that you are an example of this community and should carry yourself as such at all times. You should always act in a responsible and polite manner. Do not allow yourself to appear abusive, rude or inappropriate. It is your job to cool down threads—not heat them up.

Our User Guidelines apply to you and then some. You are held to a higher standard than regular members. You should not approach, let alone push, the limitations of our User Guidelines.

To that end, do not publicly discuss action taken against any user. Do not post "I have removed Joe's posts as they were full of vulgarities" or "You have been warned" or "Keep this up and I'll remove your posts" or anything of the sort. We handle all of our business privately. If someone violates our User Guidelines, their posts are removed and we handle it. We do not post about specific actions taken against specific users publicly.

Staff Forums

The staff forums are for current staff members to privately discuss issues relevant to the community. What is said in these forums is to be kept between current staff members only.

If you have any questions about anything at any time, please feel free to contact me via private message or via e-mail at patrick@ifroggy.com.

Thank you for your contributions to SportsForums.net.

Now, we'll look at a little more complex pair of guidelines. These are from KarateForums.com, a community with two levels of staff—pretty much exactly like what was discussed earlier in this chapter. This site has a few more requirements than the last one, including a requirement that each staff member write one article for the articles section per calendar year. Shown first are the Guide (Sempai) guidelines, followed by the Moderator (Sensei) guidelines.

LOG IN

KarateForums.com Sempais must work within these guidelines.

Qualities

You must possess leadership capabilities, a good attitude, kind demeanor, good speaking and grammar skills (you must be able to communicate clearly in English), basic understanding of the features of the community software, the ability to stimulate discussion, distinguish possible violations of our User Guidelines and aggressively report them, work in a team environment and, finally, have pride in your work and be dedicated to the success of KarateForums.com.

It's required that staff members provide me with their real name for display on our staff page.

Participation

KarateForums.com Sempais are expected to visit the forums at a minimum of 5 days per week and/or 2 hours per week.

Although you are encouraged to start topics and reply to topics where you see fit as well as welcome new users to this community, your main function is to keep an eye out for any guideline violations that may occur. These can include violations of our User Guidelines, Comparative Styles User Guidelines or Photo Album User Guidelines. So, be sure to keep an eye on the Photo Album, in addition to posts.

On your routine visit to this site, you should read a variety of topics—but above all, do not avoid hot button issues just because you are not taking part. Controversial and debatable issues will generally spawn the most violations. So, those are the topics you will want to hit hardest on your visits. Carefully consider each post, but be aggressive in your approach. If you feel there is any chance that it could be a violation, please report it and a Sensei or myself will decide. There is absolutely nothing wrong with reporting something that doesn't prove to be a violation—the mistake of leaving a violation in public is one that we want to avoid.

Whenever you spot a violation, please click the report post icon (it is the button with an exclamation point (!)) in the upper right part of the post where the violation is located. If the thread has numerous violations in it, you need not report each post, simply report one post and note, in your report, that you spotted other violations in the thread.

What if a violation is not on a specific post or thread? Well, for instance, if it's in a signature, just report the post that you saw the signature on. That'll tie it to the user and, in your report, make reference to the fact that it's the signature that you are reporting.

If you spot a violation elsewhere, such as our Photo Album, you can just find a post by that user (you can search for all posts by a user through their profile) and click the report link on one of their posts and then give the details of the problem in your report (including a link to the violation) or you can send a private message to me or a Sensei.

Not everything that can be reported will be a violation, either. If, for any reason, you feel that a post requires the attention of a Sensei or myself, you can report it. For example, if you feel that a thread is not posted in the most appropriate forum, you can report it, calling attention to this fact.

Whenever you report a post, do not draw public attention to it. For instance, don't post "I've reported your post"—just report it and don't make reference to the post (act like it isn't there). After you have submitted your report, we will handle the issue appropriately. Please do not take matters into your own hands or confront a user in any way.

If someone contacts you with a sensitive site-related issue, please forward their message on to me or a Sensei and we will handle it. You are able to help with simple questions like ''How do I upload an avatar?'' or ''How do I change my rank?'' but when a user is looking for an explanation as to a post removal or our guidelines or anything of that nature, it should be directed at myself or a Sensei.

If a user repeatedly violates our guidelines and shows a disregard for the staff of the site, it is a possibility that they will be banned. However, it is I alone that will make this distinction and until I do, just handle all violations as business as usual. Please do not make assertions as to who should be banned and who shouldn't.

If, at any time, you have an issue with another staff member or feel that they may have made a serious mistake, please contact me privately and I will handle it. Do not confront your fellow staff members on any serious issues. If you have a post removed or you are otherwise corrected, please do not take it personally. Please make a note of it to prevent it from happening again and ask questions to further understand, if necessary.

Please consult our Situations Guide for further, more specific information on the handling and distinguishing of certain types of violations.

Article Writing

KarateForums.com Sempais are required to write at least one article for the Karate-Forums.com Articles section per calendar year. You may write more than one. Please refer to the Article Posting Guidelines for more information on writing and submitting an article.

Senseis

While it is true that Senseis are the ones with the power to actually move topics and take action, Sempais are an important part of the team. The two levels are to work together with each level playing its position. We need as many people as we can get out there looking for and finding violations to maintain the high level of quality that this community is known for.

You Are an Example

It is important that you realize that you are an example of this community and should carry yourself as such at all times. You should always act in a responsible and polite manner. Do not allow yourself to appear abusive, rude or inappropriate. It is your job to cool down threads—not heat them up.

Our User Guidelines apply to you and then some. You are held to a higher standard than regular members. You should not approach, let alone push, the limitations of our User Guidelines.

To that end, do not publicly discuss action taken against any user. Do not post "I am going to report you for that" or "Everyone ignore him" or "I know you have already had posts removed" or anything of the sort. We handle all of our business privately. If someone violates our User Guidelines, their posts are removed and we handle it. We do not post about specific actions taken against specific users publicly.

Staff Forums

The staff forums are for current staff members to privately discuss issues relevant to the community. What is said in these forums is to be kept between current staff members only.

If you have any questions about anything at any time, please feel free to contact me via private message or via e-mail at patrick@ifroggy.com.

Thank you for your contributions to KarateForums.com.

And now, the guidelines for the upper level of staff—the Senseis (moderators).

LOG IN

KarateForums.com Senseis must work within these guidelines.

Qualities

You must possess leadership capabilities, a good attitude, kind demeanor, good speaking and grammar skills (you must be able to communicate clearly in English), basic understanding of the features of the community software, the ability to stimulate discussion, distinguish a violation of our User Guidelines and aggressively moderate this community, work in a team environment and, finally, have pride in your work and be dedicated to the success of KarateForums.com.

It's required that staff members provide me with their real name for display on our staff page as well as a current mailing address, at all times (it can be work, P.O. Box, home, etc. just as long as it reaches you).

Participation

KarateForums.com Senseis are expected to visit the forums at a minimum of 5 days per week and/or 3 hours per week.

Although you are encouraged to start topics and reply to topics where you see fit, your main function is to make sure that the users of this community are abiding by our User Guidelines.

On your routine visit to this site, you should read a variety of topics—but above all, do not avoid hot button issues just because you are not taking part. Controversial and debatable issues will generally spawn the most violations. So, those are the topics you will want to hit hardest on your visits. Carefully consider each post, but be aggressive in your approach. We can always fix mistakes, but the mistake of leaving a violation in public is one that we want to avoid.

If a user does violate our guidelines, they must be contacted via private message using our Contact Templates.

You should remove any threads and posts that are in violation of our guidelines. You do so by moving them and all of their direct replies to the Trash Bin.

Your moderation tools can be found at the bottom right of the view forum and view topic pages. When moving a topic, you must select the forum that you want to move it to and decide whether or not to leave a shadow topic. If you are moving the topic to the Trash Bin, do not leave a shadow. If you are moving the topic from a public forum to another public forum, leave a shadow. If you spot a topic that is not posted in the most appropriate forum, please move it to the forum. When splitting a topic, check the checkmarks next to the posts you wish to split, choose the forum you wish to split to, give it a title and click "Split selected posts."

If a user makes a reply that violates our guidelines and the thread that they replied to would normally be alright, just remove that post using the split function in the community software. Be sure to remove any posts that reference or were in reply to the post that violated the guidelines. Move it to the Trash Bin. Again, they must be contacted via private message using our Contact Templates. Please note that we do not ever permanently delete posts. Any post that is removed or deleted from public view is moved to the Trash Bin.

If a contact template doesn't exist for the type of violation that you are dealing with, feel free to make one and post it on the Contact Templates thread.

If, during a single visit of yours to the community, you have spotted a user who has violated our guidelines in more than one post or instance, please combine all of the violations into one notification private message. Please do not send private messages one after another for individual violations wherever you can help it. You can help minimize this by completing your routine look throughout the forums and splitting off any violations while you do so, leaving them open individually in a separate window or tab and then coming back to them once you have had a complete look through the forums. Then, you can document and handle them as needed. Feel free to combine contact templates to achieve the desired effect of covering various types of violations inside of a single message.

For all violations, be sure to start or respond to the appropriate thread in the Problem Users forum. Every user who violates our User Guidelines has a thread in this forum with their username as the title.

To check if a thread has already been created for a given user, you can use the search function by searching for their exact username and limiting your search to the Problem Users forum. Or, you can just try to start a topic. If you start a topic for a user who already has one, the software will automatically stop you and direct you to the proper thread. If the person's username has less than 3 characters or any characters that are not letters or numbers and your initial search comes up empty, try substituting the number 1 until the username is at least 3 characters and/or all of the non alphanumeric characters have been replaced. For example, for the username be, you would search for be1. For b&e&, you would search for b1e1.

You should also keep an eye on all posts made in the Problem Users forum in order to keep yourself up to date on the standing of all users.

If a user responds to your private message, help them in the most polite and kind way possible. However, if their message is disrespectful or further violates our User Guidelines—do not respond to the message. Post the entire message in their Problem Users thread and I will handle it.

If a user contacts you via e-mail, instant messenger, etc. in regard to a violation or other sensitive site-related matter, please document it in Problem Users (if appropriate) and then respond to them through the private message system, asking them to correspond with you through private messages instead of e-mail, instant messenger, etc. This allows the conversation to be officially documented and tracked, should something come out of it that requires action.

If a thread is going in circles or getting repetitive (the issue has been talked to death and is at its end), you can close it.

Wherever possible, you should try to keep a thread open and in public. Closing a thread is not an appropriate response to a violation or dispute. Split violations off, take care of them and leave the thread. Do not close a thread and leave the violations in public where they can continue to do harm. They still need to be removed and handled.

Duplicate threads posted in the same forum within a short period of time and duplicate posts posted on the same thread within a short period of time are not considered violations. They are to be considered accidents. Simply move the thread(s)/split the post(s) off into the Trash Bin and reply to the newly created thread in the Trash Bin noting that it was a duplicate or make "Duplicate" the subject of the thread when splitting. There is no need to document in Problem Users or send a private message.

Senseis are also responsible for making sure that users abide by our Photo Album User Guidelines when posting in our Photo Album. These violations are to be handled like any other. Remove any images that violate our Photo Album User Guidelines by moving them to the Photo Album Trash Bin. Document the violation in Problem Users and contact the user using our Contact Templates as you would with any other violation. The same goes for the Comparative Styles User Guidelines in the Comparative Styles forum.

If a user repeatedly violates our guidelines and shows a disregard for the staff of the site, it is a possibility that they will be banned. However, it is I alone that will make this distinction and until I do, just handle all violations as business as usual. Please do not make assertions as to who should be banned and who shouldn't.

If, at any time, you have an issue with another staff member or feel that they may have made a serious mistake, please contact me privately and I will handle it. Do not confront your fellow staff members on any serious issues. If you have a post removed, a decision that you made is reversed or you are otherwise corrected, please do not take it personally. Please make a note of it to prevent it from happening again and ask questions to further understand, if necessary.

Please consult our Situations Guide for further, more specific information on the handling and distinguishing of certain types of violations.

Reports

Every time you visit KarateForums.com, you should glance into the header toward the "X New Reports" link. We employ a report posts feature that regular users and Sempais use to report posts that they feel may be in violation of our User Guidelines.

If there is a new report, handle it. This may not always mean action. It is possible that people will report something that we view as harmless. Don't act simply because something was reported. Once handled, click the red "not cleared" link to mark the report as "cleared." If you are unable to handle it or require some sort of clarification on how to handle it, leave it as "not cleared" for the time being. In no case should a report be deleted.

Just because there is this report feature does not mean that you should not patrol the community with your eyes open for violations. That should be a constant and you should take care of any and all violations that you see. Do not rely on reports. This feature is an extra that helps us to run more efficiently.

Article Writing

KarateForums.com Senseis are required to write at least one article for the KarateForums.com Articles section per calendar year. You may write more than one. Please refer to the Article Posting Guidelines for more information on writing and submitting an article.

Sempais

While it is true that Senseis are the ones with the power to actually move topics and take action, Sempais are an important part of the team. The two levels are to work together with each level playing its position. We need as many people as we can get out there looking for and finding violations to maintain the high level of quality that this community is known for.

You Are an Example

It is important that you realize that you are an example of this community and should carry yourself as such at all times. You should always act in a responsible and polite manner. Do not allow yourself to appear abusive, rude or inappropriate. It is your job to cool down threads—not heat them up.

Our User Guidelines apply to you and then some. You are held to a higher standard than regular members. You should not approach, let alone push, the limitations of our User Guidelines.

To that end, do not publicly discuss action taken against any user. Do not post "I have removed Joe's posts as they were full of vulgarities" or "You have been warned" or "Keep this up and I'll remove your posts" or anything of the sort. We handle all of our business privately. If someone violates our User Guidelines, their posts are removed and we handle it. We do not post about specific actions taken against specific users publicly.

Staff Forums

The staff forums are for current staff members to privately discuss issues relevant to the community. What is said in these forums is to be kept between current staff members only. What is said in the KarateForums.com Senseis forum is to be kept between current Senseis and the administrator only.

If you have any questions about anything at any time, please feel free to contact me via private message or via e-mail at patrick@ifroggy.com.

Thank you for your contributions to KarateForums.com.

Note that, in all of these guidelines, there are links that cannot be represented in a book. For instance, all mentions of specific guidelines, forums, and contact templates are linked to the actual guidelines, forums, and contact templates on the first mention of each. This saves everyone a bit of time by making them not have to locate all of the pages and areas that you are talking about (even though that is easy enough).

From these examples, you can see how a single-tier staff works and how a multitier staff works together. At the book website, there is a downloadable archive that includes a general set of staff guidelines with blanks that you can fill in. This is also included in appendix B. Although you should craft your own guidelines, the templates can get you on your way.

Situations Guide

The situations guide is a supplement to your staff guidelines. In it, you describe how your moderators should act in certain situations, including interpreting guidelines that may not be immediately clear. Here is a real-life example (from the KarateForums.com community) of what a situations guide contains.

The Situations Guide is a supplement to our Sensei Guidelines. Where the guidelines detail how you go about doing your job, this guide will help you to deal with more specific situations and assist you in distinguishing what is and isn't a violation.

Accidents, Duplicates, and Cross-Posting

Accidental duplicates are identical posts posted on the same thread or identical threads started within the same forum within a short period of time. In these cases, please remove the post(s) or thread(s) and reply to the thread(s) (once inside of the Trash Bin), noting that it is a duplicate.

If the time period between the posting of the identical posts in the same thread or identical threads in the same forum exceeds a short period of time (longer than 5 minutes or so), it is not considered an accident. It is considered a duplicate post that is a violation of our User Guidelines and is documented and handled like any other violation.

Cross-posting is when the same thread or post is posted in two or more locations. Either the same post posted on two or more threads or the same thread posted in two or more forums. It is a violation of our User Guidelines and should be handled as such. The time span between the posts is unimportant.

Banned User Contacts You

If a banned user contacts you with a site-related matter, do not respond (if you must respond, you can simply refer them to me). Simply document their message to you in its entirety in their Problem Users thread and I will take care of it.

Banned User Signs Up for a New Account

When a banned user signs up for a new account (and it becomes plainly apparent to us that it is, in fact, the user we had previous banned), that account must be banned. Their posts should be removed, but do not make contact with them. Simply remove them and document that you removed them in Problem Users. If they attempt to contact you, do not respond to them. Document their private messages in Problem Users and disregard them. I will ban them upon my next visit to the site.

Creating New Topics from Existing Topics

There are times when an existing topic will take a turn off topic in a way that would be deserving of its own topic. To create a new topic from these posts from an existing thread, you can use the split function. Simply select the initial post that brought the new topic up and all of the posts in reply and split them off into their own topic. Another example of this in action would be when someone posts their introduction on someone else's introduction thread. You could split their introduction off, giving them their own thread.

Hotlinking

Hotlinking is when you link directly to a graphic (.jpg, .jpeg, .gif, .png, etc.), video (.avi, .mov, .mpg, .mpeg, .wmv, etc.), audio clip (.mp3, .wav, etc.), archive (.zip, .rar, etc.), or otherwise downloadable or streamable file instead of linking to the page where that item can be found.

Generally, people place this content on their websites as a means to bring people to those websites. When you link directly to the file, the person clicking the link does not visit the site, while using the site owner's bandwidth, which costs money and/or resources.

Instead, we require that users link to the page where this content can be found, rather than directly to the content itself. This is unless they have permission to link directly to the content or the site owner has posted on their site that it is allowed. If you can easily verify that this is the case (i.e., by visiting the site and looking around), then an attempt should be made. Otherwise, we ask that they provide us with information that allows us to verify it.

Here is an example of a link that might be bandwidth theft: http://www.ifroggy .com/funnypicture.jpg

Now, when considering whether or not a link is probably bandwidth theft, look at the domain name portion of the link. In this case, it's "ifroggy.com." Now, I own ifroggy.com, so if it's me using that link, it's not bandwidth theft. But, if someone else is using it without my permission, then it is and it should be removed.

Does the domain name match a domain name listed in the user's signature or as their profile homepage? If so, it might be their site, as well. If this is the case, it is alright.

If the domain name appears to belong to an image or file host (free or otherwise), check out their site and see if they say anything in their policies, terms, etc. about hotlinking or linking directly to files. Often times, file or image hosts allow hotlinking or direct linking.

If the link passes those tests and is otherwise allowable under our User Guidelines, it is most likely alright.

Inappropriate Links/Banned Links

A link is inappropriate when the content displayed at the site is determined to be inappropriate for our userbase. The site does not have to be quite as clean as us, but if a site features excessive vulgarities, nudity, illegal content, etc., the post or link must be removed.

From time to time, we will ban a link from being mentioned on our community. When users try to post a URL to this site, they will not be able to. Posts that previously featured this link will now see the link replaced by an asterisk (such as http://www.*.com). Any post like this must be removed as featuring an inappropriate link. Attempts to circumvent a link ban are treated the same and must be removed.

Inflammatory Comments

An inflammatory comment is generally an unnecessary remark made on a thread that usually doesn't serve much purpose other than angering people or inciting a negative emotion. Often times, people say something that the thought behind would normally be alright, but they say it in a way that is inflammatory. Examples of inflammatory comments would be:

- "You don't know what you're talking about."

- "You're crazy!"

- "Don't talk about things you clearly don't know about."

- "Well, if you actually did any research . . ."

- "Karate sucks."

- "All doctors are stupid."

- "Only an idiot listens to rap music."

- "Micro$oft." (inflammatory name substitution)

This is just a handful of examples of mostly lower-level inflammatory comments, to illustrate what they look like. They get a lot worse. An insulting comment is an inflammatory comment. We don't want people to say something "sucks," we want them to say why. Similarly, we want people to attack the point, not the person making the point.

Short, negative statements can also be inflammatory. For example, one person posts their view on a subject. And then someone else posts something like "That's wrong." or, "Uh, no." And that's all they say. If people are going to disagree with someone and say that something is incorrect, we require that they describe why the person is incorrect, that they elaborate, not simply say that it's incorrect. Otherwise, it adds nothing to the thread outside of hostility.

Links in Introductions

Links in introductions are perfectly fine (as long as they follow our User Guidelines). This is the one time where someone is allowed to link to their website for no apparent reason. However, the whole purpose of the introduction cannot be to send someone to another website. They can mention their personal ventures and links as part of their introduction, but there must be more. If they beg for users to go to their site/register at their site, that must be removed as advertising, as well.

New User Asks if Anyone Has Heard of a Site/What They Think of It

If a new user, or a user with a few posts or less, creates a thread to ask our users if they have heard of a website/what they think of a website (even if they don't appear to be affiliated with it), their post must be removed as advertising. When a user becomes an established member of our community and they post similar remarks, and appear to not be affiliated with the site, we give them the benefit of the doubt. But, new users are not given that benefit until they establish themselves.

For the very same reason, anyone who joins up and immediately starts posting links to outside sites may require similar attention as well.

Referencing Administrative Decisions

Most typically, posts are removed for referencing administrative decisions when they comment on administrative decisions/activities or potential administrative decisions/activities. Here are some common examples:

- "My thread was removed."
- "Well, I had already tried to post this once, but it was removed . . ."
- "They banned Jerry."
- "Why did you remove my thread?"
- "Why was Paul banned?"
- "I was going to post, but I'm afraid they'll remove it on me . . ."

These sorts of comments must be removed. Sometimes, as with comments like "Why was Paul banned?" a post can be considered both referencing administrative decisions and site-related (more on that below) and should be treated as such.

Report, Don't Respond

When someone directly responds to a serious or obvious violation of our User Guidelines, we send them a report, don't respond private message and document it in their Problem Users thread. We do this to encourage them to help us by reporting these posts instead of responding to them and to make it clear to them that this stuff is not permitted here. We don't do it whenever someone responds directly to a violation—just when they respond directly to a serious or obvious one. Here are some examples of cases where we'd send a PM:

- Disrespectful comments directed at them (i.e., "You're an idiot!")
- Racist comments
- Illegal activities

- Advertisements that are so obviously junk (i.e., ''Check out my Vicodin site!'')
- Excessive use of vulgar language

And here are some cases where we wouldn't:

- Simple site-related questions (i.e., ''How do I change my avatar?'')
- Posting of personal, real-life information
- Posting in a language other than English
- Advertisements that are sneaky where it's not really clear that it's an advertisement
- Duplicate posts or cross-posting

However, if the person mentions in their post that something is a violation of our User Guidelines, they are always sent a report, don't respond private message, no matter how serious the violation, even if there is no violation, because we do not want regular members attempting to enforce our guidelines.

Reported Posts

When users report posts to you, you should always consider the reports with a discerning eye. If the report was made through private message, you should always thank them for reporting it and assure them that we will handle it appropriately. Appropriately does not mean that you will do anything. If action needs to be taken, take it. But, if it doesn't, don't. Don't do something simply because it was reported.

Similar Threads

There will be times when users will start threads to cover a subject that is similar or exact to the same subject covered in another recent thread. In these cases, you should close the new thread and, in a reply to the thread you are closing, politely send the person to the other thread that had already existed, by linking to it. Do this only if the topics are identical or near identical. For instance, ''Why is the sky blue?'' and ''What makes the sky blue?'' are similar whereas ''Who likes apples?'' and ''How much fiber is there in apples?'' are not.

If there is an exact or near-exact thread, but it is not recently active (the last reply is more than 4 months old), allow the new thread to proceed. Topics need to be revisited through new threads as our userbase welcomes new faces—do not close a topic because there is an old thread covering the same subject.

Site-Related

Site-related means anything to do with this website itself. We do not allow comments related to the site—whether it be how it works, how it's run, etc. Some examples would be:

- "How do I upload an avatar?"
- "Why was my post removed?"
- "Would it be alright if I post this?"
- "I would like to suggest a new feature."
- "I think the site should have different colors."
- "Why was Larry banned?"
- "I think this site should have such and such—who's with me?"

These should be removed, documented in Problem Users with a private message sent using our Contact Templates. If you are able to answer a question, please do so in the space provided in the contact template. Make a note that you answered the question when you document it in Problem Users. The types of questions you can answer include things like how do I upload an avatar, what are the post-count based rank titles, how do I change my signature, etc. Any questions related to new features, why people were banned, etc. must be left for me. If you cannot answer the question or do not feel comfortable answering the question, please feel free to leave it for me. If you don't mention that you answered it in the Problem Users thread, I will assume that you did not and will take care of it.

If someone makes a duplicate topic and then edits it to say "duplicate, please remove" or something to that extent, it is not a violation. Simply remove the post, mark it as a duplicate and you are done.

As was mentioned before, certain questions, such as "Why was Larry banned?" are considered as both site related and referencing administrative decisions and should be handled as such.

Spamming and Trolling

We don't ever tell people that they are spamming or trolling. These terms, while probably accurate, give a negative connotation that we do not need to use. Instead of spamming, they are violating our User Guidelines as advertising. Instead of trolling, they are violating our User Guidelines as being inflammatory or disrespectful or they are making remarks that are not relevant to the thread or . . . you get the idea. We don't use those terms.

Staff Member Violates Our Guidelines

If you feel that one of your fellow staff members has violated our guidelines, please send me a private message or e-mail at patrick@ifroggy.com. Do not remove it or do anything else. I will take care of it.

Current staff members do not get documented in Problem Users and should not be contacted by other staff members in regard to violations.

User Wants Copy of Removed Post

Sometimes users will ask for a copy of the removed post. If it was a post that made valuable contributions to the community but had to be removed because of a small thing or two, feel free to do so. If it was more serious and much of the post was a mess, tell them that it would probably be better if they started from scratch.

Violations in Private Messages

If a violation in private messages is reported to you, please document it in Problem Users and I will investigate it and act appropriately.

Vulgarities

We allow people to say damn, hell, crap, freaking and anything as or less severe. We do not allow as* (LMAO and similar variants being the single exception), ars*, shi*, bastar* or anything as or more severe.

This goes for abbreviations, as well. For example, WTF (typically short for "what the fuc*") and a-hole are both violations. Self-censoring (such as "f***") and attempts to circumvent our word censoring feature are violations, as well.

What Is Too Religious?

In the case of signatures and the like, we allow for the use of some basic religious terms or related items. This is not the easiest thing to define, but here are some examples of things we allow and don't allow, to give you an idea.

Allowed:

- A cross as an avatar
- Most types of quoted scripture
- "Yours in Christ," (and similar sign-offs)

Not allowed:

- He died for YOU.
- You need God.

When Are Videos or Audio Appropriate?

Videos and audio are generally appropriate when they are linked to in a fashion that allows them to be viewed, but not downloaded. This, of course, excludes sites that simply shout out "illegal." If a user links directly to the video or audio file itself (sometimes, this means that the link will end in .avi, .mov, .mpg, .mpeg, .wmv, .mp3 or .wav, but that is not a be all or end all by any means) and it appears that the user may not have permission to link directly to videos or audio on that site, that post should removed as hotlinking—they should link to a page on that site that features links to the video(s) or audio in question.

If a video or audio file is downloadable (such as links to third-party file upload sites) and the copyright is not clear or cannot be reasonably verified, that post must be removed. Likewise, any posts that specifically request that videos or audio be sent to them or that the user be PMed are inappropriate. Threads that ask where a video or audio clip of such and such can be found are appropriate, but those threads must be monitored for links that violate our User Guidelines.

As with anything, if you are ever not sure about something, please feel free to contact me and I will give you a definitive answer. If you have a suggestion for a situation that could be outlined here, please let me know.

Thank you for your contributions to KarateForums.com.

Make Your Staff Stand Out

You should make your staff members stand out from regular users. Whether it be a special rank image, rank title, username color, or some other decoration, it is good for people to be able to identify them from other users within the community. You may also want to have a staff page that displays all of your staff members' names/usernames (and optionally, some information about them).

Your staff members are an example of your community and you. They should be visible. If your community software has a "hidden" mode, where users do not appear "online" to regular users, your staff members should not utilize it. Staff members need to be visible, approachable examples. Not hidden.

With this increased exposure comes even more expectation of proper behavior at virtually all times. But that is not a bad thing. Your staff members should naturally be good examples. If you didn't think they would be, you wouldn't have brought them on board, right?

Staff Member Benefits

What benefits can you afford to give your staff members? It is rare, although not unheard of, to pay the staff (especially when it comes to moderators). I am going to assume that you aren't going this route—most people don't and with the level of commitment expected at virtually all communities, that makes sense.

Consider your unique position and what you can possibly offer to staff members. If your company develops a product of some kind, it may be a good idea to offer your staff members free or discounted products from your company.

This idea has benefits that are not immediately apparent. If you stand behind your products as much as you should and you allow your staff to be well-acquainted with them, then when people in your community ask about your products, your staff will be well-equipped to give them an opinion or an answer. Plus, if your staff takes pride in the community that it contributes to, staff members will probably recommend your site and your products to other people.

Everything, even small things or perceived small things, are benefits. For example, if your staff page features links to their personal sites in their profiles, that's a benefit (this sort of thing doesn't really make sense for most sites, generally speaking). If your site is established in your niche, being a staff member results in raised visibility. That's a benefit, as well.

I realize that for a majority of people there may not be much to offer or much that you can justify offering. The good thing is that pretty much anyone worth adding to your team in a typical community environment will not really be concerned with that. In a lot of cases, working on staff is a way of "giving back"—users have taken from the community as a resource and now they are giving back by helping to maintain a resource that they still get something out of. Even if you offer free products and things like that, it is still imperative that you be very vocally appreciative of their contributions to your community. You can never say thank you enough. You can't buy or sell appreciation. It's priceless.

Even if you can't afford to have any regular, "normal" benefits, being thoughtful, sporadic, and maybe surprising your staff members with some sort of token of your appreciation can be a cool way to continue to let them know that you appreciate their work.

For instance, you may know CafePress (http://www.cafepress.com). It's a free service that allows you to set up your own merchandise shop. It offers an array of goods that you can put your logo on. After we launched a CafePress-powered merchandise shop for one of my communities, I sent each of my moderators a mouse pad with our logo on it. It was out of the blue and unexpected. They appreciated it and I was happy to do it.

Whatever you send a given level of staff, send it to all the staff members at that level, no matter how active/inactive they are at the time or how long they have been on the staff. If they are on the staff, they are on the staff. Wherever possible, send them all the same thing. This helps to ensure that no one feels that he is less important than anyone else.

When my two largest communities, KarateForums.com and phpBBHacks.com, reached five years online, I sent six of my biggest contributing staff members on each site a framed print commemorating the occasion. On the print, I handwrote a personal message to them, expressing my feelings and gratitude for their contributions. This wasn't just a staff member gift—some of the recipients had since left the staff.

Something much smaller, but often overlooked, is sending a card during the holiday season (early December). You don't want the card to be holiday specific. Just a general "Happy Holidays" card. Don't just sign the card and send it off, however. Sit down and spend time on the cards. I told you to be thoughtful. Write a personal and honest message to the person to whom you are sending the card. This gives the card a sentimental and real value, instead of just a dumb "I sent you a card just to send you a card" feeling.

Keep your staff members in mind for opportunities that you are offered or that you may have available. It's not unusual for a company to hire a qualified individual from their community staff to work for them on a full time basis. If you get a book or product to review, but don't want to review it for whatever reason, consider passing it on to one of your staff members to review (he or she can post the review on your site).

You can use your imagination to come up with other ways to be thoughtful. It isn't that difficult, and you should want to express your appreciation to your staff members whenever you can.

Choosing Your Staff

Selecting new staff members is usually a pretty simple and straightforward task. It's the stuff that happens after that (when people show their true colors, in some cases) that complicates matters.

If your site is new, ask people whom you know share an interest in the subject matter of your community if they are interested in helping or know anyone who would be interested. If your site is established, be on the lookout for the most helpful, kind, and dedicated users in your community. An active community can usually pull staff members right out of the member base. Knowledge is good to have, yes, but kindness is infinitely more important. These people will represent your community and you. In some communities knowledge can be a requirement (such as support forums), but knowledge without kindness isn't any good to you.

Keep in mind that an invitation to join your staff is not some sort of reward for posting a lot. You need to invite people whom you feel will represent you and your community well and can help you execute your goals for the community. In other words, they will need to set an example and be ready to work.

You shouldn't invite people just because you think you need someone. You shouldn't have any user-to-moderator ratio in mind. Don't worry about filling any quotas. Simply promote good people. If that's one or if that's ten, it doesn't matter. You may want to stop inviting people because you are over-staffed, but you should never invite people just to fill spots. Never feel like you have to promote someone. If you look over your pool of candidates and you're thinking, "Well, I have to invite someone because I need this many moderators . . ." that's not the proper frame of mind. Does that mean that you'll have to pick up the slack? Probably. But promoting people you don't care for is a mistake and will only lead to problems later.

"'Tis better to be alone than in bad company."

—GEORGE WASHINGTON

Almost always, I will ask my current staff members what they think about so-and-so or if they have any nominations for a new staff member. In the end, I do make all of the final decisions, but I always carefully consider what my staff says. For instance, if a staff member says that so-and-so has this issue or that issue, and the issues are serious (and well-founded in my eyes), I will most likely not invite the user. It is very possible that a staff member has seen something that you may have missed. If a few staff members (or even one, depending on the size of your staff and the specific complaint) voice serious displeasure over promoting a particular user and you feel their comments are valid, don't invite the user. You should, hopefully, be able to trust all of your staff members, so why not trust their descriptions of a person? Don't forget, it is important that the new person fit into your existing team.

Depending on the size of your community and staff, it may make sense to have a selection process that requires more involvement from the staff. Maybe you want to have the staff (including you) make nominations that everyone can discuss. Then, from those, you can craft a list of people who qualify or meet with your approval.

Make sure that the process does not turn into a campaign or a political process. Everyone must feel comfortable to share their thoughts without fear of attack. Your staff members should be accountable to you—not to one another. For this reason, I don't like to see staff members of the same level grilling one another about things like this. Be clear in that there is no majority rule. If people are openly voicing displeasure over the person, chances are the candidate shouldn't be invited.

I don't like to hold yes or no polls with my staff members for new appointments. The problem with polls is that they are intimidating. If someone sees fifteen "yes" votes and zero "no" votes for a person, it's natural for a person to feel intimidated and to simply abstain or maybe even vote yes. It can be difficult to balance this, but this is a reason I try to avoid such polls. Make sure people understand that you reserve final judgment on everyone. So, getting approved by most or all staff members doesn't mean someone is a given.

When I'm contemplating whether to invite someone onto the staff, I take into account what my staff says as well as what I know of the person, the person's documented history at the site (any violations, especially), their recent posts and activity, and anything else that I can think of. It gives me a complete picture and usually points me to either yes or no fairly clearly.

When you invite a user, be sure to tell her why she is being invited (i.e., for her outstanding attitude and contributions, etc.) and send her a copy of your staff member guidelines for her to agree to before you add her to your staff officially and update her privileges. Be upbeat and complimentary—being invited to join your staff is a compliment to her and vote of confidence in her.

When you add a new staff member, be sure to post a welcome thread in the staff forum. It helps to break the ice, so to speak, and alleviates some of the awkward feelings that can exist when entering a new group.

Finally, if you are thinking about allowing regular users to choose or "elect" who is on your staff—don't. That's insanity. I've heard of (very few) sites that have attempted this and it always make me wonder. You need to be able to work with your staff to execute your vision for the community. It's not a game or a popularity contest—it's important and should be treated with the utmost respect and seriousness. The most popular members can make the worst moderators. It is up to you (and, in some cases, your staff) to choose and it should always be that way. You know how you want your community to be represented, more than anyone else.

When Is It Time for a Staff Member to Move On?

Unfortunately, all good things must eventually come to an end. It is an inevitable truth that pretty much every staff member (good or bad) that you have will resign or have to be removed from staff if your site is around long enough. These instances can end on a very good note, can end in hatred, or can end somewhere in between. Let's run over the four most common scenarios.

Inactive Staff Members

If you have a staff member who goes inactive for a while, you should contact the person, casually ask him how he is doing, and ask him if and when he plans to return to the community. Don't make it sound like some sort of ultimatum or threat. Emphasize more of an honest, personal sentiment. Here is an example of a bad message.

> Hey Randy,
>
> I haven't seen you on the site at all lately. You really need to get there every day or I am going to take you off the staff.
>
> Thanks,
>
> Patrick

And here is an example of a good message.

> Hey Derek,
>
> I haven't seen you on the site at all in recent months, and I wanted to make sure that you were OK and just see how things were going for you. I was curious as to when we could expect you back, as well. Looking forward to it.
>
> Talk to you soon.
>
> Thanks,
>
> Patrick

If you thought enough of this person to bring him on board, you should have genuine concern if the person disappears without contact. If he responds to you with an explanation and an acceptable approximation of his return, that should usually be good enough for you. Await his return. Some people will take your message as an opportunity to ask you to take them off of the staff if they feel that their away time will be extended.

If this is a persistent thing or your e-mail goes without response, it might be time to remove the person from your staff. If this is a person whom you don't really feel has done a good job or has been a disappointment, you may want to tell him that he seems to be very busy and not able to get to the site, thus it is probably best for everyone that he be taken off of the staff so that his responsibilities within your community are no longer a burden. Be sure to thank him for his contributions and say that you hope to see him around. All of this should be true. If it's not true, don't say it. Even though the person may have been a disappointment, he still did something and you need to recognize that.

Now, if the person is someone that you really like and wouldn't mind having back if he were to be active, you can say all of what I just said and then add that if he wants to rejoin the staff in the future, he would be welcome to do so. Great people are not easy to find. If you find someone like this who has to leave because he is busy right now, be sure to make him feel welcome to come back, should he want and be able to.

Resignation in Good Standing

It can be tough to see a good staff member go, but when it happens, you need to remember what she did for your community and the time she spent. Don't mince words. Tell her how much you appreciated her and her contributions. Wish her well. Depending on how long the person was on staff and how much she contributed, you might consider sending her a retirement present, of sorts.

If the person is in good standing, chances are you'd gladly take her back on if she ever wanted to return. If that's the case, say it. Your door should always be open to truly good people. They are hard to find.

Resignation After Disagreement

It isn't uncommon that a staff member will resign after a disagreement with one of your moves or policies. Try as you might to please as many people as you can, it is rare that a person will agree with every decision that you make, and different people have different ways of dealing with things.

Even if a person resigns after a disagreement about one of your actions or policies, you should still remember what this person did for your community and thank him for it.

However, it is not always possible for a moderator who is demoted back to a regular user to continue to be a valuable contributor to the site. Some people are more mature than others, and some of them just develop into big-time pains in the neck.

Some of them go through what I would term "the correction stage," where they go around correcting your staff members, annoying your staff members, or making snide little remarks like, "Well, if I was on staff, I would have removed this." You cannot have someone antagonizing you or your staff. It is unfortunate, but eventually, the person may just force you to ban him. This leads us to the fourth circumstance under which a person might leave your staff.

Wow, I Let This Person onto My Staff?

Hey, it happens. You bring on someone who looks really great, and maybe she is for a few weeks, a few months, or a few years. Then, all of a sudden, she turns into psycho staff member! I have had this happen a few times, which is pretty lucky, considering all of the staff members that I have had. I have been fortunate and blessed to have a lot of truly good people.

Basically, if someone turns out to be an idiot who just strives to make situations more difficult, turns disagreements with you into personal attacks, and/or will not obey your requests, it is time for her to leave. People have bad days, so you can allow for that. People cannot be allowed to have bad weeks or bad months, however.

I had a staff member who had been with me for almost the entire existence of the site. He had contributed quite a bit and he had played a role in some major community changes. But, over time, his work in the community deteriorated and so did his attitude. He started to lack the attention to detail and kind demeanor that I expect from members of my staff. He actually started to act a tad nasty to some of our users. He may have let the position get to his head, he may have been trying to anger me, or he may have thought he had some sort of free pass because of seniority and was untouchable. Whatever it was, it was a mistake.

So, over this period of time, I made him aware of the various issues and things that had happened and how he could improve. He did not take this as well as I would have hoped and proved to be incapable of correction. An argument of sorts did ensue, and I am not one for arguing with staff members, so I was not very pleased with that. All of this culminated in him resigning. I felt this was a good move, because things obviously were not working out and once again, I thanked him and wished him well. Even though he had disappointed me, he still had made some solid contributions, for which I was appreciative.

But then a short while later, he sent me a private message asking if he could come back on staff. I didn't want this person on my staff, and remember, you don't want someone on your staff who really doesn't want to be there. If he had wanted to be on my staff, he wouldn't have resigned in the first place. It was only a game now—a knee-jerk reaction to the instant realization that he was no longer on my staff. This was all about status and that he had blown it, perhaps. Seeing only bad coming out of this, I decided that it was time that we move on. So I did not invite him back. Again, he did not take kindly to this.

I expected him to contact his "friends" and tell them how I had wronged him and what have you. I expected to have some sort of fallout, but this person had a lot of free time. He was a popular member of the staff and reminded me of it by telling me once or twice about his "following" and how he could use it (against me). He contacted user upon user, giving each his distorted and inaccurate account of events with the goal of making me out to be some sort of evil person. This is going to happen, so get ready for it.

The way that you can prevent such a person from affecting the culture of your staff is to be completely open and honest with your staff. Until the person left the staff, no one knew what I had to deal with, except me. Most of our conversations were via private message, and I kept them to myself as you should when you are dealing with a current staff member. But when this particular situation broke, I posted a detailed explanation of what had happened in the private staff forums. This included why it had happened and why this person was such an incredible detriment. I posted all of our messages back and forth in their entirety and invited questions. For the most part, my staff was with me, which was a very good feeling. Even though this person later contacted staff members and tried to manipulate them against me in some way, he failed. In the end, this issue actually made our staff closer, I found out who was really in my corner, and it was the direct result of my openness.

I have a personal policy of doing my best to avoid making nasty personal details about other people public information in my communities. So when we have to ban a user and someone asks about it, I tell her about this policy and describe what happened in vague details. I try to stick to it as much as I can, and I was able to stick to it in my case, for the most part. Many people didn't even want to hear what I had to say. They were all sold on the lies they had been told. Some of these people I had known for quite a while. This really disappointed me. I suppose you could say it is human nature to take the supposed "average working man's" position over the "evil authority figure." But people who buy everything they are told get what they deserve.

"A lie cannot live."

—Martin Luther King, Jr.

In the end, the ex-staffer continued to be nasty publicly. A lot of the nastiness was directed at my staff, and that I simply cannot tolerate. We gave him a great many chances, but he just continued to criticize and annoy the staff and try to make them feel bad. So I banned him.

In doing so, I started a new wave of him contacting people again to make them all aware that I had banned him. He would go to another site of similar content and make his way onto their staff and continue to raid my user base, which I and others had worked hard to build. We lost some users. But, I found out that I would only lose users who weren't really worth having anyway.

Most of the time you will end up having to ban a person like this. He or she will continually violate your guidelines in the forum with snide or bitter remarks. The person will push the limit and test you to see just how much you will allow because, after all, he or she has a "following." It is never fun, but has to be dealt with.

I give people a lot of chances and I am not quick to ban, especially in cases like this, but you have to have the guts to cut someone off—to make the unpopular move that will benefit your community in the long term—regardless of the immediate and short-term effect. You have to have vision and have the long-term growth and attitude of your community in mind. I was thinking long term. In the short term, sure, we suffered a bit. But we survived. In the long term, this community was much better for making the decision I made. We continued to grow and improve and we are a better community.

"If you just set out to be liked, you would be prepared to compromise on anything at any time and you would achieve nothing."

—Margaret Thatcher

Conclusion

In this chapter, I talked all about managing your staff. I talked about selecting new staff members, developing your staff member guidelines, dealing with problems that come up within your staff, making your team feel appreciated, dealing with staff member exits and resignations, and more.

I can't say it enough—your staff is incredibly vital. I would even go as far as to say that your community isn't much of a community without a solid staff. Recruit good people, treat them with respect, and work together for the success of your site or you will probably not be a success. It is that simple.

CHAPTER 6

Banning Users and Dealing with Chaos

"There comes a time when one must take the position that is neither safe nor politic nor popular, but he must do it because conscience tells him it is right."

—MARTIN LUTHER KING, JR.

There are times when you ban users and it is no big deal. They came to spam, they did it, and they expected it. They go away. But, there will also be times when you will have a certified psycho on your hands. Someone who will register a half a dozen accounts. Someone who will keep coming back. Someone who will try to turn other users against you. In this chapter, I'll talk about how to deal with all of this and more as I give an overview of some of the most common situations that I have dealt with.

You will find that your leadership—the type of administrator that you are—is defined in these crucial moments of chaos. It is important that you remain calm, or at the very least, visibly calm for the sake of your staff and your community. Regardless of how much of an idiot the person or persons may be, you have to inspire calmness and confidence in your work and in your actions. At the end of the day, you have to be more dedicated to your cause (your community) than the crazy people are to theirs (hurting your community, directly or indirectly). I know that my level of commitment to protect my community is higher than anyone else's commitment to harm it, and that is one of the reasons that I am successful.

Real People, Real Cases

"Thinking is the hardest work there is, which is the probable reason why so few engage in it."

—HENRY FORD

A great way to learn is to witness actual, real-life experiences and situations. That is what I speak from in this book and is why I have dedicated this section to detailing some noteworthy situations that I have had to deal with. Some are very specific and some are generic in nature.

The Bad

Let's start with some of the less lethal variety.

Forum Spam Bots There are people out there who have created software (or are using software created by other people) to sign up for tons of accounts and/or make loads of junk posts on unsuspecting forums everywhere. It's a very disrespectful practice. But even worse, it can create quite a mess and can include links that would otherwise be inappropriate for your community.

Perhaps the main reason people register accounts in this fashion is to add links in the account's website or homepage field and in turn get that link displayed on a profile or in the member list of your community. The spammer's hope is that search engines will spider those pages, count the links as backlinks, and improve that particular site's search engine ranking.

Although sometimes people set up accounts by hand to accomplish this, most of the time they use software that does it automatically. It isn't always about advertising, however. Sometimes people will do it just because they can—in other words, just to be a pain and stuff up your member list with their junk.

Although there are a limitless number of methods for dealing with this type of thing, perhaps the most popular way to combat them is through a visual confirmation (or CAPTCHA) system. These take different forms. A user might have to type in a randomly generated sequence of letters and/or numbers that are displayed on screen (in a graphic) in order to complete the registration. Or they might have to type a response to a logical or mathematical question such as, "How do you spell blue?" or "What is four plus four?" You can show a series of pictures and ask the person to pick out every picture with something particular in it. For example, the person might see twelve to twenty images randomly. Some of them have animals in them, some don't. The user has to select the ones that have animals. Generally speaking, logic based CAPTCHAs are more user friendly.

Of course, you also want to have e-mail confirmation turned on, forcing your users to activate their accounts by clicking a link that is sent to them via e-mail. Besides adding an extra step that many bots fail at because they do not have valid e-mail addresses associated with them or cannot check them, it also helps to ensure that all of your members keep valid e-mail addresses associated with their accounts, which makes it easier for you to contact them and hold them accountable.

If you are able to do so, it's definitely useful for you to have a link on your site where visitors can have their validation e-mails sent again. These e-mails can get lost, for whatever reason, and users will contact you or go away when they need this.

You should periodically delete any accounts that have no posts and have not been confirmed via e-mail. In my communities, I automatically e-mail those accounts, just explaining that the account was deleted for this reason and encouraging the person to register again if he or she wishes to do so. This reminds the person of the existence of the forum.

If an account is not active, it can't post junk in your community. However, if it somehow got past that requirement (maybe the person registered some accounts by hand, confirmed them, and then turned them over to his software), you could have hundreds, thousands, or more junk posts littering your forums within a very short period of time. Imagine every thread on your site bumped with one spam reply. I have had to deal with this before. A simple, effective way to clean it up is to get the username of each user who made one of these spam posts. Then delete all posts by each of those users.

You use flood controls to slow it down. By requiring your users to wait a short period of time between the creation of posts, you can slow the effects of such an attack and hopefully catch it before it gets too bad.

But if it becomes a huge, consistent problem, you may have to do something else—something more drastic. Here are a couple of general ideas. Make it so that every user who makes a certain number of posts within a given time period is automatically banned. Let's say you have your flood control set to twenty seconds. Well, the most posts that a user can make in two minutes is six (if they catch it just right, which is pretty much impossible). You could make it so that any user who makes four or five posts within two minutes is automatically banned. This won't stop them from making any posts (that is relatively impossible to do while not hurting your users in a very noticeable way), but it will prevent them and/or noticeably slow them from making a large number of posts.

Although I recommend using a visual confirmation system on your registration form, another possible solution is to require visual confirmation on a user's first post or posts within a specified period of time. Having visual confirmation on every post is way too much and will only displease your users. But, let us use the example I gave earlier. In this case, if a user made four or five posts in two minutes, before she makes her next post, she would be asked to pass a visual confirmation test or she would not be able to post again. This would quite possibly put a stop to accounts made specifically for bots (although, if they have 100 accounts and they make five posts each, that is still 500 posts, of course—but the chances of that with the checks on account registration are hopefully slim).

It's a constant battle for community administrators. "Professional" spammers are becoming more and more a part of our daily lives. The technology that they use gets better, smarter, and then the safeguards that we use get better and smarter. Then maybe they find a way to defeat those and we have to come up with new ones. It is always changing and the technology is always getting better.

Whatever you do, when you are dealing with bots like this, it can be easy to get flustered and frustrated. However, don't give up. Be tough and find solutions. Check the resource sites for your given community software. Don't give in.

That Doesn't Look Like Spam . . .   Spammers get cleverer everyday, so you always have to have your eyes open. An example of this is smilie and period spammers. These are bots (or people) who create posts that look fine but that actually contain a potentially hard-to-find embedded link. They might add a smilie or a set of smilies somewhere in their post, and then one of those smilies is linked to the spammer's site. Or they may have a long post and then have a single period in that post linked. It can be easy to miss these. You can help prevent it by doing things like making your links stand out with a different color and placing a border of an unmistakable color around any linked images.

Introtisements and Adverquestions   Not what I would call terribly "chaotic" but still annoying and worth watching out for are what I like to call introtisements and adverquestions.

An introtisement is an introduction posted in your community that appears to exist solely for the purpose of promoting something and/or sending users to another site. I have no problem with users mentioning their sites, jobs, affiliations, etc. in their introductions, but there has to be more and there cannot be redundant "join my site" comments, etc. Of course, that assumes that the person is creative. Some aren't—their introductions are simply marketing messages.

Adverquestions come from people who (seemingly) ask a question in your community (sometimes on support communities) but include some sort of link or thinly veiled marketing message that promotes or mentions something or other that may not even be related to the question they are asking. The more clever ones are things like, "Have you heard of xyz.com? I just visited the site and I'm really enjoying it." Some of the more obvious and stupid ones might sound like this: "Before I ask my question, I wanted to say that I got a great deal on these tires from xyz.com. If you are having a tough time affording a set of these babies, check them out. Now, my question is where should I go to have these tires put on my car?" Lame. But it happens. Don't let people get away with it.

Violations in Private Messages   It's not uncommon for users to abuse your private message system to violate your user guidelines or to mass PM your users with whatever message they want to get across (whether it be advertising a website or calling you an idiot). To look into these matters and verify that it is happening, you need to be able to view the private messages that your members send in your community.

In my communities, the only person who has the power to view the private messages of all users is me. If at all possible, this is the recommended method of handling these sensitive matters. Limit it to as few people as possible. Absolutely do not go looking for violations through private messages. These are "private messages." You should only view this data if you have received a report or you have a serious suspicion about a certain user. Even then, limit yourself to viewing as few messages as possible.

Some people do have a problem with this policy and they may say something like, "What happened to the 'private' in private message?" That's nonsense. The messages stay private. You should almost never post a private message that you have had to read in a public forum. I would say *never*, but the fact is, if you have a spammer who signs up and sends a million PMs out, does it really matter if you quote his spam publicly? No, it's not sensitive information. Beyond that, you don't quote private messages publicly. So, they are still private. There is a certain (if misplaced) expectation of privacy and you should respect that—the exact content of these messages should not be shared with anyone outside of your staff, and even then, try to limit it to just the applicable messages. Doing otherwise may alienate people.

I have had users send private messages to hundreds of users in my communities, spamming some website or asking my users to join their community. These people have no respect for the hard work of others and no respect for their fellow community administrators. The point is: People will abuse this feature and you need to be able to handle it when they do.

Again, some people feel that private messages should remain private in the sense that no one should ever view them except for the sender and the recipient. In a perfect world, that'd be the way to do it. Unfortunately, that's just not realistic in this world. People will abuse your private message system and you need to be equipped to combat it. You cannot allow people to spam or abuse your members via private message. I've had people spam via PM manually, electing to contact active users only to try to recruit them to their site or their forums. I've had people sign up and use some sort of bot to attempt to send PMs to every single user that I have. When this happens, you need to be able to act and to act fast.

If a user contacts me and tells me that so-and-so is sending nasty, harassing private messages, do you think that, "Sorry, I can't do anything about private messages," is an appropriate response? No, it implies that your guidelines have no meaning and that you don't have very much control over what is happening on your very own website because people can very easily circumvent the guidelines through private messages. If an administrator sends me a response like that, there is a chance that I'm no longer going to visit that site or, at least, that I am going to reduce my activity. I don't visit a community to be abused, publicly or privately. As an administrator, I cannot bring myself to tell a user to ignore it. It's not professional and I'd feel like a doofus telling someone to ignore something bad happening on my own website.

So, when I say act, what do I mean? I mean that you need to be able to view private messages quickly and easily, who they are from and to, and when they were sent. You need to be able to limit the search to just private messages sent from or to a specific user. And you need to be able to "mass delete" PMs. However you accomplish this setup, it's the ideal method because it allows you to find what you need to find quickly—and only what you need—and to act right away.

Do not view private messages without any sort of discrimination. That's not what I do. Almost all the private messages sent in my communities are never seen by anyone other than the sender and recipient. So, when do I view? When someone reports something to me or when I have a solid suspicion. Even then, I limit myself to as few private messages as possible. This is where being able to limit your searches comes in. What's a solid suspicion? Well, on my communities you need to have twenty-five posts to initiate conversations via private message. If someone makes twenty-five junk posts and stops at twenty-five, I have good reason to believe she did it so that she could send junk PMs. I can quickly see if she's sent any PMs and how many she's sent without actually viewing the PMs, and I can take it from there. Being able to act and act quickly saves you and your users aggravation.

If you do nothing, every user on your site could be spammed. Think about it. Some idiot uses your member list as his personal mailing list. Is that what you want? Is that what your hard work is for? Think about your users having to read the private messages. What if they had e-mail notification turned on? That's a lot of e-mails going out! It may or may not be a big deal, but it's definitely an annoyance. And it's a waste of your server's resources. And then, when members report it to you, are you going to say, "Well, I can't do anything"? That would be embarrassing. Act as soon as you can on the first report. If the user is mass spamming, delete every PM she has sent and ban her.

Flood controls help (i.e., making it so that a set period of time must pass between sending private messages), but they can only do so much. You can't set them very high because they affect your users' experience. Twenty seconds is a good number—they can safely send at least two PMs a minute (technically three, but that's probably impossible). If they're diligent, that's at least 240 PMs in two hours. Usually a person won't send that many so quickly (although I've had people hit sixty or more), but if he is using a bot of some sort, it can easily get that high—and much higher.

A lot of the time users will spam your site after you ban them. They'll sign up for another account and try to mass PM your users, telling them that you banned them and that they're on a new forum (link included in the PM, of course). There is only so much that you can do, but one solution is requiring that users have a certain number of posts before being able to initiate conversations through your private message system. Twenty-five seems like a good number. Usually, spammers won't want to make twenty-five "good" posts, so they'll either not bother or will make twenty-five junk posts, in which case that'll set off a red flag with you (especially if they post twenty-five and exactly twenty-five) to check their private messages and make sure they aren't abusing the privilege.

Moderating private messages in this fashion is not unethical, inappropriate, illegal, etc. It's a good idea, it's appropriate, and it's the way it has to be. Again, limit yourself to just what you have to view. You should also do what you can to keep private the private messages that you do have to read. You have to quote violations in the problem users forum, but try to limit it to just the bad messages and make sure that your staff members know they are not to divulge specific details of these matters to the public. Again, limit who can view private messages to as few people as possible.

In this day and age, being able to deal with private message abuse is not optional, it is required. Nothing in your community can be fair game to those who wish to harm you and your community. Allowing users to abuse your PM system will turn users off to your site and will harm the atmosphere of your community. You have to fight for what is yours.

I'm Locked out of My Account!   This isn't all that chaotic, but I wanted to cover it, nonetheless. From time to time, you will encounter someone who is helplessly locked out of his account. He may or may not know his username, he has forgotten his password, or he no longer has access to the e-mail address that is associated with his account. All is not lost, however, because he has you.

If the user doesn't have access to his e-mail address, how can you be sure that it's really him? The first place to go is his profile. Look at all of the data he's listed. Does he have any instant messengers listed? If so, get him on an instant messenger to confirm. Does he have a website listed? Have him add a page to that website that displays a key phrase that you give him. Failing that, take a look at his posts. Have they mentioned anything at all that would help to identify the user? Maybe the posts list the user's IMs, a website, a MySpace page, or something like that. Is there a question that you could ask him about a private, site-related matter that you addressed with him? For example, if you had to remove one of his posts, you can ask him to recount what post that was and what it was about.

Now, if he doesn't have any of that and you really have no way to verify that it's him, this is where it gets difficult. You see, you don't want to let anyone into an account that is not his. If the account has had little or no activity and nothing at all seemed suspicious, perhaps, maybe, I would let him in. But, if it is an established account in any way, I'm not going to let anyone into it without some sort of verification.

If we can't verify the user in some way and I opt not to let the person in, I give him permission to sign up for a new account and document the entire episode in the problem users forum.

Why Use of "Microoft/M" Is Bad   You've seen it. Someone is talking about Microsoft, but instead of typing *Microsoft* or *MS*, they type *Micro$oft* or *M$* with the dollar sign.

This particular remark is what I would call an inflammatory name substitution, but in a more general sense, it is a rather tame example of an unnecessary, inflammatory comment. These get much worse and add nothing to the discussion. They are not good-natured—they only seek to anger people, which is harmful to the community as a whole.

Inflammatory comments take many forms. People say things that would normally be OK if they hadn't said them in an inflammatory way. People add snide little remarks to their posts (such as, "You don't know what you're talking about," "Are you crazy?" and the like). What is considered inflammatory depends on the subject matter of the community. For instance, on a sports community, someone saying, "I hate ," would qualify. What I would call inflammatory comments some would call trolling. I don't tell people they are trolling as that is too accusatory. I tell them they have posted an inflammatory comment. Witness this exchange:

Poster 1: I think Green Day is a great band.

Poster 2: I don't care for them.

Poster 3: Green Day sucks!!!

Poster 3 has made an inflammatory comment. These types of comments make discussions personal and send them in a negative, unproductive direction.

Content Thieves and Scrapers   Content thieves are everywhere, searching for content that they can copy and use for their own means. When unauthorized, scraping is little more than content theft, but the term implies that it is done in an automated fashion.

You need to be able to protect your content and take down those that steal from your site. Besides the obvious matter of principle, part of what is appealing about your community is the unique voices within it. You don't want to build up your community only to allow someone to steal your posts. If I were a member of a community where this happened and I knew that the people behind it were doing what they could to pursue the scraper, I would think more highly of them than if they just allowed it to happen openly and didn't attempt to do anything. On top of that, duplicate content can hurt your search engine rankings.

Sometimes, the first step is contacting the organization or individual who copied your content. It's important to be able to identify how blatant the theft is. For example, if a member of another community copied a post or two from your site, that isn't going to be that big a deal. Try shooting off a quick e-mail or report to that site's administrator or staff, just letting them know that this person is copying posts from your community. You don't need to make any claims as far as copyright because, unless it's your post, you probably don't have any to make. A simple report is often enough. Community managers don't want people ripping their content, usually, so they might not want to allow people to rip content from other communities. It may very well be a violation of their policies.

One problem that can arise while you are trying to protect your content is that, with virtually all communities, the copyright to all submitted posts remains with the person who posted them. So, if you have 20,000 members who have made posts, you have 20,000 copyright holders. How are you ever going to get them all together to fight? Well, the good news is that you don't have to. Usually, assembling a few people will suffice. You should approach people who have contributed actively to your site and people that you feel comfortable approaching with such a matter. Perhaps you could just approach members of your staff, if that is possible.

Basically, you should explain that someone is stealing posts from the site and, as the copyright holder, they have the ability to get the content removed from this other site. You need them to either give you permission to act on their behalf or to sign a letter that you will then send to the appropriate individuals. This is a good reason to participate in your community yourself. If you post actively, you are a party to the copyright infringement and can appropriately demand the removal of your posts.

Even with just a few people from your site, the combined post count of the group could amount to a significant number or a significant portion of the work and should be more than enough because, at the very least, the removed posts from key contributors on the offending site will help cripple the rest of the stolen content and may even cause the offender to remove the site entirely. Seeing the extent of the theft, a web host may see what is going on—that the offender is scraping—and simply pull the site itself.

Once you have your assembled parties, contact the person who is ripping your content. If it's someone who appears to be mass scraping your content through a bot and doesn't appear to run a respectable operation (often, the difference is pretty clear), this may not even be worth doing. But, if it looks like someone is home and just may not be aware, it's a good idea to contact the person first.

After that, the next step is to contact the person hosting the content. This can be a web hosting company or a service provider. For example, infringement on a MySpace page would be sent to MySpace, infringement on Yahoo! Answers would be sent to Yahoo!, etc. You will want to locate the host's abuse contact or its Digital Millennium Copyright Act (DMCA) contact. Many providers list their DMCA contact information with the U.S. Copyright Office (http://www.copyright.gov/onlinesp/list/a_agents.html). But you may also want to check on the host's or provider's website for the most up-to-date info.

If you are unsure of who is hosting a site, you can use a site like DomainTools (http://www.domaintools.com) to find out who owns a particular IP address. And then you can look up the site's abuse/DMCA contact info. If you can't locate the site's contact information here or on the U.S. Copyright Office site, contact the company directly and ask how such reports should be filed.

Once you know whom to contact, you will want to send that person a DMCA notice. Your DMCA notice should include, at least, a handful of things. It should include your name and contact information (not just an e-mail address, but also a mailing address and phone number, if possible), links to the pages where the infringement is occurring, links to the pages on your site where these works appear (if this is a mass infringement, just cite ten or twenty of them and explain that these are examples of a mass scraping), a pair of statements (one saying that you're telling the truth and that you are the copyright holder or that you represent the copyright holder, the other stating that you have a "good faith belief" that the material that you are reporting is being used in an unauthorized manner), and your signature. If you're sending the notice via e-mail, you can simply say, "Signed: First Name Last Name." For ready-made templates and to see what a DMCA notice looks like when it comes together, check out PlagiarismToday's stock letters (http://www.plagiarismtoday.com/stock-letters).

You can also file DMCA notices with the major search engines. Most of the world's search engine traffic flows through a few key players, and those players have some sort of basis in the United States, so the DMCA applies to them. Copyright-infringing sites may be pulled out of their search engine results through the filing of a properly formatted DMCA letter. The same can be done for ad networks, as well. Many ad networks will stop allowing ads to be shown on a given site in these cases.

Keep in mind that the DMCA is for hosts, providers, and entities based in the United States. Some other countries have their own DMCA-like laws, so all is not lost if the provider is outside of the United States.

The Reply-to-Every-Post Guy   This is the user who sets himself up as some sort of opinion judge (and jury). When a thread piques his interest, he'll reply to each and every post (for the most part), telling the person behind each post whether he or she agrees, whether the poster has a valid point/opinion, and so on.

This type of user is exceedingly annoying to most everyone. He acts as if an opinion is not valid unless he says it is. He doesn't truly allow people to have opinions; he more or less interrupts the thread after each opinion to give his opinion about the opinion (did you get all that?).

As much as you may love to see the post totals in your community rise, it has to stop, assuming that you don't have a militant debate club mentality. You have to tell the user to post less, which may seem a little funny but really is the truth. He needs to allow people to discuss the topic without him interrupting between each post.

"Freedom of Speech"   The belief that freedom of speech entitles people to say whatever they wish, whenever they wish, wherever they wish is one of the most common misconceptions and problem issues for community administrators. The scenario is predictable: Your community has guidelines, a user violated those guidelines, you removed the post or comment and contacted the user, and the user doesn't like it. She feels she is entitled to "freedom of speech," and who are you to limit her "right" to it? First of all—there is no such thing as "freedom of speech" on a professional, well-run Internet community. It doesn't exist. This is hard for some people to understand, but to quote the United States Constitution, Amendment I:

Congress shall make no law respecting an establishment of religion, or prohibiting the free exercise thereof; or abridging the freedom of speech, or of the press; or the right of the people peaceably to assemble, and to petition the government for a redress of grievances.

Key word: *Congress*. Congress must not make any laws that abridge freedom of speech. You are not Congress. Your privately owned community writes its own guidelines—within reason, of course; they must be written with the law in mind (i.e., planning a murder in your community isn't OK just because you say it is in your user guidelines). It is your right and responsibility to enforce them in order to make your community as good as it can be in line with your goals.

Me vs. You   Sometimes, there will be two users who just do not get along. They may hate one another. Although that is bound to happen, it becomes a problem when it spills into public threads and posts that violate your guidelines.

When two users violate your user guidelines when talking to one another and you are really reaching your limit with them (even though they are otherwise pretty solid contributors), I have found that an effective solution can be to tell both of them simply to not speak to or make reference to each other on your community, publicly or privately in even the slightest way, or else. And by "or else," I mean that they will be banned. No warnings.

If one of them then sends a private message to the other guy, or one of them makes an unhelpful public comment directed at the other person, such as, "Well, someone told me I didn't know what I was talking about when it came to such and such," they are banned. Your words need to have meaning, and when you warn two guys over and over again when they are basically just talking to one another, wasting your moderation time, you need to bring it to some sort of final conclusion when enough becomes enough. This can be a good way to do it.

"You Are So Biased"   Some users, after having their posts or some bit of content removed, will attack you or your staff as being biased, playing favorites, removing posts because you don't like what they said, etc. This is never acceptable. In fact, this should be treated as a very serious violation, especially when directed at your staff. Those users, depending on the wording of their claims and their histories, may be or may soon be on their way off of the site.

Accusations of bias levied against me are not only bogus, but often humorous. A great example of this is when a user at KarateForums.com was causing a great deal of trouble and eventually was banned. He sent me an e-mail that said something like:

Every time I say something negative about Karate, you remove my post and you tell
me that have I violated the guidelines. Well, that's funny . . . it might have
something to do with the fact that you do Karate.

These are the priceless moments of community administration. The reason
that this is funny is because I don't participate in any martial arts. I have never
participated in any martial arts. I may very well never participate in any martial arts. And I have never said, implied, and/or acted otherwise. It's not that
I don't like the martial arts; it's just not my "thing." There are no martial arts
that I "like." There are no martial arts that I "dislike." There are no martial
arts that I even really know about (save what I may have read on the site, of
course), now that I think about it. To have real bias, you have to have some
sort of knowledge; even misguided knowledge. To have bias, you have to
know something or like something or dislike something. I don't. I don't know
Karate from Tai Chi. By definition, I can't be biased.

I've had people say all sorts of things. I've had people say that I banned
them because I loved Firefox. But, in reality, I'm actually an Internet Explorer
user. Not that browser selection affects how I manage my community, of
course. These are the types of insane assumptions that you will almost certainly have to deal with. People lie; they come up with things to somehow
excuse their own actions and make it your fault. When they are users in your
community, it's unacceptable. But, after they're banned, most of the time, you
should simply smile and move forward.

Not that it would matter if I did know something more, of course. At
SportsForums.net, I have to moderate threads where people say something
about various sports teams and they violate our user guidelines. Sometimes
these statements are directed at my favorite teams—the New York Yankees
and the Miami Dolphins. Once in a while (usually someone who is new to the
site) will imply that I am operating in a biased way when I deal with violations
that mention the Yankees or Dolphins. Again, someone like this, depending
on what he's done in the past and how he is presenting himself, may no longer
be welcome on the site or, at the very least, will be warned not to do it again.

When people talk about things that they really don't know about, they
make themselves vulnerable to repercussion. They don't have behind-the-
scenes access. They don't see how many posts I've removed that say the very
same thing (and worse) about another team, about their favorite teams, or

about the rivals of my favorite teams. The staff knows what I'm about, of course, and that's important. But I will simply not tolerate users saying that my staff or I are operating in a biased manner, and neither should you.

So what can you do to minimize such accusations? First, don't be biased. I know that seems like common sense, but when you make decisions, make sure that you are making them with a clear head. When you aren't biased, it's a lot easier for you to sound like you're not biased, right?

When users report issues to you that are worthy of consideration, don't tell the user it affects who reported them. Don't say, "Joe told me that you were doing this, and I'd have to agree." Say, "You are violating our user guidelines by posting inflammatory comments." In other words, keep Joe out of it—don't make it sound like someone tattled and you agreed with him. It's not about who reported it, it's about what actually happened. There really isn't any reason to mention that it was reported at all—it's unimportant.

Sometimes, in response to a violation notification, a member will say, "Who reported it?" or "Did someone actually report that?" I tell the member that whether someone reported it isn't important, the important thing is that it's a violation and the member should keep it in mind to ensure that it doesn't happen again.

When you make decisions, try to put yourself in the shoes of the person whom it concerns. For instance, the Boston Red Sox and New York Yankees are fierce rivals, so I am, naturally, not a fan of the Red Sox. This doesn't affect my management of that community, however. Whenever someone makes a comment about the Red Sox that I feel is questionable, I think about it like this: How would I feel if this person were talking about my favorite team or my favorite player? What would my feelings be? And I make my decision based on that. Relate what people are saying to yourself and how you would feel. It can help you to make the most appropriate decision.

Regardless, know that no matter what you do, you will be called biased. The more you grow, the more it happens.

"I'm Creating My Own YourSite.com _____!" Some users take it upon themselves to create a site or feature that is some sort of "home" to users of your community. It's something that you may not have been asked about, may not have approved, or may not want at all. For example, if you had an active community and some users wanted a chat room but you didn't want to or couldn't host one at that time, someone might take matters into their own hands and create a chat room somewhere off of your server without your knowledge or approval.

You should treat these just like you treat any other outside website. If someone creates a thread or post to mention this site or send people to it, it would violate your user guidelines as advertising. Remove it if that is how you normally handle advertisements or self-promotion. Do not allow people to use your community as a way to jump start their chat rooms, even if it's just for users of your site, according to them.

You should also ask the person responsible to make sure that if they use your site's name at all, they put the word *unofficial* before the name of the site, at the very least. So, for instance: "YourSite.com Chat Room" would not be acceptable, but "Unofficial YourSite.com Chat Room" might be. You don't want people to think that your sites are affiliated, and depending on how you feel and what your name is, you may not even want the other site to use your name at all. As I have said before, this book cannot be misconstrued as legal advice, so please seek the services of qualified professionals in that arena, if so required.

When Users Say Good-Bye   When a user leaves your community of her own freewill (rather than just disappearing or being too busy), a lot of the time it will not be on the best of terms. It may be because she is unhappy with something related to the site—most likely something you are doing or not doing. Obviously, you cannot change policies specifically because of threats of leaving, so this type of thing is inevitable.

If the person is not at all established in your community and is a relative nobody who doesn't have a lot of posts, you should usually just remove any farewell thread as being inappropriate because it makes no sense for a user no one knows to make some grand exit. Now, if a user is established in your community and has made a number of posts, then you should allow her to have a single farewell thread. But it should definitely be scrutinized. Obviously, it cannot violate your user guidelines. No negative or disrespectful remarks about the staff or administrative decisions. No advertising (or very little, if you feel it is appropriate—for instance, for a personal home page). No storytelling—no attempts to drum up public "support" for her "cause" (particularly in regard to something you may have done—possibly why she is leaving?). Just let her have a plain, respectful, farewell message. Dedicated users earn that, and you should give it to them. If this is a person you like and whom you are sorry to see go, be sure to post in the thread and say so.

When someone says farewell, don't automatically close her account or ban her. People do come back, as annoying as that may be. If they do, treat any future farewell threads with great suspicion and consider not allowing the person a second one. A farewell thread is different from someone posting that he is going away for a while or that he is going to be busy for a certain period of time; a farewell thread is him saying that he is gone—for good.

Threats (. . . or I'm Leaving!)   When users threaten you or a member of your staff, this could be grounds for an immediate ban. Some examples of threats would be:

> *If you remove another one of my posts, I am going to leave.*

> *I will tell everyone I know about your heavy-handed moderation tactics if you remove that again.*

> *"If you ban me, I'll just sign up for another account."*

And so on and so forth. You should not tolerate threats from anyone. If someone threatens to leave—he's probably already sealed the deal by making that comment, because you will most likely want to help him leave. Don't allow yourself or your staff to be threatened.

. . . And the Worst

And now, those special, special ones. I thought that it might be interesting if I recounted some of my more memorable experiences with "chaos" and psychos and the like. Some details have been changed to protect these . . . fine people.

"Remove All of My Posts and Delete My Account!"   When some people find that they are unable to act however they want in your community and they want to leave, they may ask you to remove their posts and/or delete their accounts.

You should not do this. If someone wants her e-mail address taken off her profile, fine. If someone wants his signature removed, his profile cleared, and his username changed so that he is not identified with his posts/your community any longer, fine. That is what you should offer him. But do not delete accounts and posts at someone else's whim. This information should also be included in your guidelines.

When people create a thread, it becomes part of a community, if it is allowed to exist, and should not be removed unless there is a valid reason for doing so. That said, you may be pressured, asked, or forced by your web host or data center to remove the posts. If you come to the conclusion that you must remove them and it is not feasible for you to fight, just send them all to your trash bin forum, delete all the profile information for that person, change the username to something general, and that is the end of the story.

I am not going to speak about the law, necessarily, but not everyone who e-mails a host in regard to a copyright or intellectual property violation has the right or grounds to do so. Sadly, it doesn't always matter if the person is right or wrong. That's life.

"Hate Him, My Minions! Hate Him!"   Let's say you run a community that is related to a certain subject matter. A person whom you really do not know that well is an authority of sorts in that subject matter and runs a site of his own. He becomes jealous of you and abuses his position of authority to manipulate his user base (and possibly the users of the overall online community for the subject matter) by coming up with damaging lies about you or your site. He might say that you stole something from him or his site, that you are a liar, that you can't be trusted, and so on and so forth.

It can be tough to overcome an issue like this because he is an authority. Most current and new users on his site will believe him right off the bat just because he is who he is. How do you beat that? You beat it with honesty, integrity, and hard work. Where he has things handed to him, you have to work for what you get. You have to win people over and show them who you are and how good you are.

You can try to respond at his site. But it probably won't accomplish much. Your posts may be removed and you will probably be vilified, but those who have the chance to read your posts may become enlightened. As long as you are (generally) polite and stick to the facts, it may win some people over. At the same time, if he bans your account, do not continue to sign up for accounts. One is enough. Try to keep your responses from getting too nasty. Stick to the facts of the matter and respond to the areas in which he has attacked you. Keep attacks on him to a minimum. Throwing hostility at hostility generally won't win people over. If you are facing this scenario but the person is not an "authority" (a nobody or at your level), forget responding on his site at all—it is a waste of time.

You may feel the desire to address his posts at your own site. If someone brings it up, do so directly to the user who brought it up. If it becomes a huge issue (if the site attacking you is very large, for example), you may want to start a topic on the subject to set the record straight. Then, close that topic. Besides that, avoid starting public threads about it or allowing discussions related to it. Don't let the issue drag on publicly. Feel free to start threads in your staff forums so that your staff knows the truth and can be an asset to you in such a conflict. You should not bring your community into the battle unless someone else does. Even then, minimize it. You don't want your community to be swallowed up by this nonsense. Stay above it and keep your community going forward on a positive note. Stay in pursuit of your goals. Ultimately, this will be the more professional choice.

What is the best way that you can beat him? Simple. By being more successful. Work tirelessly to improve your offering and do it the right way. That's how you will "win." With strong ethics and a dedication to your community and your users, many people will eventually see through this person. He will always have his blind loyalists, but you really shouldn't worry about those people. The popularity of your site will speak volumes.

Admin to Users: "Attack!"   Say that you have another site in your genre, but for some reason, the owners of the other site hate you. I mean, even if you have never even met the owners, they hate you for whatever out-of-whack logic they may have.

> *"Inside of a ring or out, ain't nothing wrong with going down. It's staying down that's wrong."*
>
> —MUHAMMAD ALI

In my case, one particular administrator encouraged users from his site to come over to my community and violate my guidelines. Register multiple accounts, post junk messages, post rude messages, post vulgar messages, anger users, disregard the staff, and violate our user guidelines however they could. That was their objective. Why? Because they didn't like that I allowed people to express opinions that they considered silly. Their community was a place of personal attacks, vulgarities, etc., where mine was based more on respect for one's opinion, even if you disagreed with it. As you can see, contacting the administrator and asking him to knock it off wouldn't have mattered, as the guy didn't have any dignity if he encouraged his users to do this in the first place. So forget that option in this case because it isn't one.

One of the side effects of this type of attack is that it can sometimes make you press your hand—potentially make you go on witch hunts. Don't. This is part of the "game" and part of their aim: to disrupt you and make you act in a way that you normally would not act. Maintain your cool. Treat all users equally until you know otherwise—in other words, don't go on any witch hunts. Allow them to show themselves to you.

Here's how I handled it. They would sign up and post their junk. Their posts would vanish without response and so would their accounts, as they would be banned. Where we saw trends in IPs, we also took the liberty of banning those, as well. They didn't get responses, we didn't contact them, and we ignored any contact they made with us. We did not post in their community. Not once. They got the hint. I mean, we could do this forever if they wanted to. Our will to protect our community is simply greater than their will to harm us. People like this will pop up from time to time (usually not in a big concentrated ball like that, but individually), but take care of them like it's business as usual. Good, strong policies can overcome the poor intent that such activities have.

In the end, it was kind of funny. They would gather around their community bragging about what they had done and talk about how they "owned" us and all that stuff. It didn't happen. They live in a fantasy world. In the end, that's how these types of people usually act—they like to talk about their "victories," but where they talk the talk—you are the one walking the walk. You can claim a silent or private victory through your consistent efforts.

The Grand Delusion   Some folks just don't realize that the way you say something can be as important as what you say. I have banned users *after* they disagreed with me but never *because* they disagreed with me, and that is an importance difference. It's important to realize that these two quotes are not the same:

"I disagree with the policy."

*"That is so f****** wrong and you are an immature little b****. And you should die."*

The first one is fine. Anyone is allowed to disagree with me. People can disagree with my policies all day long, but as long as they follow and abide by them, we will have no issues. But, the second one, you see, that is a violation of our user guidelines because it contains disrespectful comments and vulgarities. And so, having been previously warned, the member is now banned. It is not if you disagree, it is how you disagree. There's a very important difference. But fully expect to see and hear folks mouthing off about how you banned them just for disagreeing with you, regardless of the facts. Those poor, poor dears. This is the grand delusion.

Personal Crusades: What It All Comes Down To   Generally, they are all just baseless personal crusades; that's the summation of most of the lies and unfounded accusations that you will get from disgruntled members. They didn't like your guidelines and they didn't like being told that they have to follow them. Tough.

So when they are finally banned, they automatically fly into a rage, describing how you censored them, how you are too strict, stupid, egotistical, you name it. They try to hurt you and your community. They try to lure users away from you and they try to prevent people from visiting your community. They fill people's heads with half-truths and outright lies. And some actually believe them.

But you should never fall into the trap of going to their website and responding. There is no such thing as "clearing the air" in such a hostile environment. Stick to your website and possibly (if appropriate) third-party websites, if they are already discussing the issue. If you have to explain the situation to people who aren't staff members, try not to get into the gory details unless you absolutely have to. Just explain that your community has guidelines, those guidelines are to be followed, and they are one of the primary reasons that your community is as good as it is. Politely and vaguely clear up any untruths and move on. Handle yourself professionally and use the garbage as motivation for your continued success.

Persistent Idiots

Regardless, in any of these scenarios, it may not end for a long time. We're talking more than a year. I've had people do everything: sign up for multiple accounts; send a dozen or more nasty e-mails to me (I don't respond); try to instant message me from a dozen different accounts; manipulate other users; post inappropriate, concocted rants on their sites; go to rating sites and give us bad ratings while leaving comments as to the idiocy of one Patrick O'Keefe; disappear for three months and then show up again—you name it. Seasoned community administrators will know exactly what I am talking about: "Those people."

People have even sent me messages saying something like, "We're both wrong, but we have the power to take you down and you have the power to take us down, so why don't we just make up?" Um, what? It's nonsense and nothing I'll be responding to.

I won't be responding because I was not wrong. Not that I'm never wrong, but when I am, I correct it and apologize. When it comes to bans, which I take very seriously, I am virtually never wrong. Pretty much nobody gets banned by mistake, because I don't consider a ban until the person forces me to consider it. Second, I would never send anyone to "take you down," because I wouldn't sink to that level (not that I even know how to take someone down). Finally, if someone can "take me down," I may not be able to stop it right away, but whatever happens, I will fix it, I will correct it, and I will move forward. Do not negotiate with people who threaten you like this. You rise above them. People will waste their time being fixated on you while you continue to progress and move forward.

The bottom line is that you have to be ready to weather this "storm" and laugh at it from time to time. The fact that you are on the minds of these folks all the time is either very funny or very strange, depending on your perspective. They're just too busy dreaming about you to worry about accomplishing anything on their own accounts. You are always best not responding except in appropriate venues. Ignore it, make light of it (while being honest) in front of your staff, and focus on the long-term goals that you have for your community. Stick to them.

Solutions

For every problem that you encounter, there is some sort of solution. There are also things that you can do to prevent problems or, at least, spot them as quickly as possible. That is the focus of this section.

Post Reporting System

If your community becomes active and guideline violations seem to be happening regularly (or even if not), you may find it useful to integrate a post reporting system (if you haven't already) where users can report posts that they feel violate your user guidelines. Staff members can then give these reports the attention they deserve.

The best way to accomplish this is to have a "report post" button on every post and then make your site list the reports on a central page that only staff members are able to view. You can have a link in the header that only members of the appropriate level of staff can view. It should display the number of new reports (so that you and your staff don't have to actually view the reports page to see if there are new reports) and link to the reports page, which displays each report along with when it was reported, who reported it, and a link to the post that was reported and the report the user submitted. It should also include a link that allows the staff member to mark the report as "cleared" and "not cleared." This setup allows your staff to see very easily if there are any reports, makes it harder to miss reports, and saves people time when checking on the status of reports.

Be sure to encourage users to use the system by making it a part of your user guidelines and discouraging responses to violations. If you have staff members who do not have moderator powers but are there to spot violations, you can make it part of their responsibilities to report posts according to the staff guidelines highlighted in chapter 3. This is more effective than having a Report Posts forum or something of that nature.

Instruct your moderators not to remove posts because they are reported. Not all reported posts will be violations, but all must receive the necessary attention. If a user makes a report that doesn't lead to any sort of action, treat it like you treat any other report. Do not, in any way, discourage people from reporting posts—including abrasively telling them, "Well, that isn't a violation." If they are at all afraid of being wrong, they may not report anything at all and that would be worse.

Turning Negatives into Positives

There are times when a thread starts to head down a bad road but is not yet violating your guidelines. The thread can be pushed back in the right direction through the involvement of a staff member. It's not something that should be done all the time, but for example, at KarateForums.com, we don't allow general discussions of what martial art is better than others. Yet, we do allow people to seek help in their selection of a martial art under specific circumstances. Sometimes, while members try to help someone pick a martial art, their discussions can degrade away from the topic starter and into the more general realm of what martial art they think is better period. So, in those cases, a reminder on the thread of the user topic starter's request can be helpful.

Helpful Notices

You can help to curb the occurrence of repeat violations through the use of well-placed, helpful notices that remind people to watch what they are doing. Here are two examples.

On the phpBBHacks.com Support Forums, when someone starts a new topic, the word *important* appears right above subject line in red text. Members are then urged to ensure that they are posting in the right forum. A portion of this notice is linked to a special topic that I created that explains where the most popular kinds of topics should be posted.

Another example is in the SitePoint Forums where, when a member attempts to reply to a thread that is older than a certain age, he is reminded, in red text, that the thread is X months old and that he might want to consider creating a new thread instead.

Innovative Tools

When a site gets swamped with moderator work that stretches the limits of your and your staff's available hours, it is easy and understandable to think,

"We need more staff." And that's fine. You should be actively looking for good people. But bringing people in just to bring people in is dangerous.

So instead of just thinking, "We need more staff," also think about what you can do to make better use of your team and how you can use technology to help you do this. Put your community software to work for you. I have a couple of good examples.

At phpBBHacks.com, we have a fairly strict guideline in place in regard to the bumping of support topics. Users are only allowed one noninformative bump (i.e., a post that adds no new information to the thread), and it must come after forty-eight hours after the last activity on the thread in question.

With the site being as active as it is, we had to remove quite a number of posts for bumping. I was thinking about how we could more effectively handle this and I had an idea. I wanted a hack that would check to see if the person adding a reply was the thread starter and had made the last post on the thread. If both of those things were true and the last activity on the thread was within the last forty-eight hours, the post would not go through and this message would display:

> *You have attempted to add a reply to a thread when your last post is not yet forty-eight hours old and has not received a reply. Please edit your last post or wait until forty-eight hours have passed. Please remember that we only allow one noninformative bump per thread, and it must occur after forty-eight hours of the last reply on the thread, regardless of who created that reply.*

A friend of mine, Jeremy Rogers, wrote the hack for me and it turned out great. Because of this hack, we have had to remove fewer posts for "bumping" while not measurably affecting the user experience. I'm not simply for automation. I'm for automation that works, helps you to do your job better, and helps your community.

Another example of an innovative tool is a hack that I have installed on my sites that evaluates whether a post triggers the community software's word censor feature before the message actually posts. We had used the word censor to block out inappropriate language but I was thinking about that system one day and it dawned on me: What if those posts were stopped when the users tried to post them? And what if the community software explained why and even highlighted the sections of the posts where the violation(s) occurred, allowing users to make adjustments without losing their posts? Again, my friend Jeremy came to the rescue, writing a hack and expanding it so that it also checked private messages and profile fields (including signatures). Brilliant! Now, when a member puts a bad word in a post or profile, this sort of message is displayed:

> *Your post has triggered our word censor feature. The portions of the post that triggered the censor are highlighted in the preview below. Please adjust it and attempt to post again. Please note that abbreviating the term/string that was censored or circumventing our word censor feature in any way constitutes a violation of our user guidelines, and your post will be removed. If you require assistance or feel that the censor may be acting in error, please contact us. Thank you.*

This saves us time and it saves the member time—his post doesn't have to be removed and we don't have to document the violation and contact him, because the violation is never made. It does require maintaining a decent word censor list, ensuring that you only add words that are clear-cut violations. This hack is awesome. It saves so much moderation time and allows us to spend our time doing other things.

These are just a couple of examples. As you find real problems in your community, you should try to consider whether there is an innovative solution of sorts that can help you deal with it.

Banning

In a perfect world, you'd never have to ban anyone. Of course, this is far from a perfect world. Idiots and bad people exist and you'll be dealing with them. Some people will do things that will make you ban them without warning. Most others will be worthy of receiving at least one warning, if not many more. But, at the end of the day, your warnings have to have meaning when people defy them. You will have to ban people to protect your community.

Really, I don't ban people—they ban themselves. As an administrator, you are simply reacting to what a member does. The decision to ban a person is made by his own actions and that is the way that it should be approached.

Give Every User a Chance

First and foremost, be sure to give people the opportunity to rehabilitate when it's possible. With rare exceptions (multiple spam posts all at the same time, a post with fifty pharmaceutical links, non-English spam, racial slurs, porn, etc.), you should not ban a user on the first offense, so by making her aware of violations in a respectful tone, you are helping her to get a feel for your community. Everyone makes mistakes, so you should try to be rather forgiving as long as the violations are not of the worst kind and/or too frequent. If a user makes one violation this month and one violation six months from now, she shouldn't be treated the same as a user who does something today and then after you have told her not to, does the same thing tomorrow.

Some users just may not care. They have no vested interest and it could just be a game of hit and run with their only purpose being to act like a fool and agitate your community. However, you don't know whom you are dealing with, so don't assume—treat everyone fairly and act once you have a good reason to do so.

Of course, there are some users who think they have some sort of right to do whatever it is that they want to do, without regard for your guidelines or your staff. These are the types of users that you need to get rid of.

Public Humiliation

When you ban a user, don't fool around. Don't give the user a user title that says "Banned" or something similar, don't have a banned users list, don't advertise the fact that people are banned, etc. I find this type of behavior to be kind of unprofessional. A banned user is not something to celebrate or commemorate (publicly). Public humiliation like this does not have a place in a professionally run community.

When Should You Ban?

The time to ban is not really an exact science and should usually be at your discretion. Generally, you should give a user at least a couple of chances to correct his behavior. The type of violation, the time period between violations, whether a particular violation is being repeated, how long the member has belonged to the community, and how many posts he's made should all be taken into account. Some generic situations where I would look to ban include:

- The user has just registered and posted multiple advertising threads, made a post with fifty links in it, or posted non-English spam right off the bat.

- The user has recently received several warnings and continues to violate our user guidelines, looking as though he doesn't care.

- After being warned, the user responds with a nasty, disrespectful, and/or condescending message to a staff member.

- The user does or says something so terribly offensive that it is beyond warning. An example would be a racial slur or a link to a porn site.

- The user sends out a number of advertising private messages.

- After being warned about doing something, the user does the exact same thing shortly thereafter.

This list is certainly not all-encompassing, and not all circumstances can be completely described on paper. The biggest and most important thing that I do is always to monitor the threads in our problem users forum. I make decisions based on the documentation of violations in each thread. This allows me to make decisions consistently. Develop your own system of discretion.

Responding to Banned Users   A lot of the time, you will never hear from a banned user again. But other times you will receive an e-mail, instant message, or private message through your forums (from another account that the banned user signed up for). If signing up for another account is against your policies, as it should be, it doesn't bode well for this person. Ban the new account and log the activity in the user's previous problem users thread. Depending on the private message the user sent, you may or may not want to respond to the person through e-mail. For example, if they are asking if they have been banned, you can confirm that.

The same goes for e-mails and instant messages. Most of the time, the user will not have been so horrendous that you will never want to speak to her again (it happens, but is rare), so as long as her message was respectful enough and you feel there is a valid reason for you to respond, then you should respond. Don't just respond to confirm that you saw her message or to thank her for sending it. Respond if there is something that you need to respond to. Note that defending yourself is not a valid reason—people are welcome to disagree with you and hate you, even—you shouldn't really care, but do not argue about it. So, if it fits those guidelines, you should respond. Plainly, briefly, but respectfully.

There are two common questions that it is worth your time to respond to. The first sounds something like, "Did you ban me? Why?" or "Why can't I access the site?" or "I suppose you banned me."

A typical response would be:

> Hello,
>
> Yes, you have been banned. After being given several warnings, you have continued to show a lack of respect for our users, staff, and user guidelines.
>
> Sincerely,
>
> Patrick

The second is something like, "So, you banned me. Just delete my account then." Again, here is a typical response.

> Hello,
>
> We do not delete accounts. But, what we can do is close your account, remove all profile details (including your e-mail, signature, etc.), and change your username to something vague and unspecific—thus, your account will be devoid of personal details and will no longer be personally identifiable. Please let me know if this is what you would like. This action cannot be reversed.
>
> Sincerely,
>
> Patrick

Those examples give you the basic tone. Remember, as long as the message was generally respectful, not too hostile, and you have valid reason, reply. Otherwise, you don't need to respond. Don't send multiple replies repeating what you already told him or her. And be sure to document all conversations in Problem Users for your staff to see. When you share all of this information—when your staff members see everything that you see—they are more likely to support you on the ban. Honesty is a great thing.

Lifting a Ban   You don't want to be 100 percent against lifting a ban. It all depends on the situation. If the user was just a total idiot who treated the community, you, and/or your staff like a piece of trash, you probably never want to see him again. If he did something that was very harsh and very serious, it may not be a good idea to lift his ban. Assuming the ban is reversible, the main thing that you need to see from a user is an expression of guilt or remorse and an apology. If he realizes he did something wrong and he's sorry for doing it, it may be worth considering depending on the situation surrounding his ban. On the other hand, if he says something like, "I didn't do anything wrong, unban me," he can go to some other community, because you don't really want him.

I rarely lift a ban, but it has happened. I think, in a majority of cases, I have not had to ban the person again. But when it has happened, I have never lifted the ban. That's not to say it won't ever happen. If someone gets himself banned twice, chances are it is for the best.

Banning Methods

In this section, I talk about the actual banning of a user through your community software and other methods.

Banning Usernames   Banning the username is, of course, a requirement and the most basic type of ban. The member may just sign up again, but the username is her identity on your site and should, as such, be the first thing you ban. Yes, she may be able to create a new account, but that cannot stop you from banning people.

Temporary Bans   Temporary bans expire after a specified amount of time. On communities that utilize this function, it's usually used as a bit of a cooling-off period or a time out. I don't recommend it. I find that, in a lot of people, being banned will just trigger bad blood and won't be used as a time to reflect and change the error of their ways, which is the intended effect. Often they'll just come back bitter. For some, it can make bans a bit of game and you don't want that. Your bans should have a sense of finality—a final-consequence sort of thing. They are serious business.

Banning IPs   Banning by IP address can be effective in some cases. Most dial-up users seem to get a different IP every time they log on to the Internet and, even if they don't, an IP ban can be worked around by those who know how.

Your community software should allow you to check what IPs a user has posted from and how many posts he has made from each address. If the user made all of his posts from one address, it may actually work. If he made most of his posts from IPs that are similar except for the last few digits, you can block an IP range and that also might work. For instance, if he made ten posts from 0.0.0.0, ten posts from 0.0.0.1, and ten posts from 0.0.0.2, you could ban 0.0.0.* (not always an asterisk; check your software's documentation for more information on creating wild cards) and that will prevent any user with an IP that starts with 0.0.0. from accessing your community.

However, there is also some risk involved in banning IPs. Besides not always being effective, it sometimes prevents other users of that same Internet service provider (ISP) from reaching your community. However, if the user has been particularly destructive and the stars align, it might be worth it. It shouldn't be done randomly (you don't want to ban an AOL proxy, for example), but it's a necessary tool to have at your disposal. It may be a good idea to clear out old IP bans from time to time when you are confident that the person has gotten the hint. The longer they go, the more likely it is he'll get a new IP or change his ISP anyway.

Users Who Use the Same IP   It's not wise to ban users simply for using the same IP. Users who have never heard of one another will post on your communities from the same ISP and, often times, the same IP. It is not uncommon, especially with big ISPs such as AOL, where IPs can change every time a user logs on. I've had IPs that a dozen or more users have posted from. It doesn't (and didn't) mean that those users were all the same person. IPs can be used as an indicator for action, but there must be some corroborating evidence. There have to be some surrounding circumstances for you to consider taking action on it. For instance, if you banned Joe on Friday and on Saturday Frank signed up with the same IP, it would be an interesting situation if they are the only two users who have utilized that IP on your site.

If you see two users who are contributing and talking to each other and have the same IP, don't assume that it's the same guy unless it's really, really obvious. For example, if one posts, "Hey, have you heard of xyz.com?" and then shortly thereafter, the other guy posts "Yeah, it's awesome!" and they're both new users, that would be another interesting circumstance. But, if they seem to be contributing in a positive fashion with no other suspicious traits, don't jump the gun. If you feel the need, you can contact one of them and ask about the similarity. It could be a family member, a friend, a school computer, who knows. Ask the user to clear it up. If the answer is believable, you should accept it.

Doesn't That Look Like . . .?   You will have banned users who re-register in your community. Don't go crazy hunting for such things, but definitely keep an eye out for it. If you banned a user and she signed up for a new account, it doesn't make her any less banned—in fact, it makes her more banned (especially if having multiple accounts is against your guidelines) and you should ban her new account. It's like you throwing someone out of your house, only for the person to break in through a window.

There are some times when people will do this and you will never find out. That's just the way it is. That is the nature of the Internet and there is nothing that you can do about it. So don't lose any sleep.

That said, definitely keep an eye out for similarities in banned dates, joined dates, e-mail addresses, IPs, profile data, and so on and so forth. For instance, if you banned someone whose e-mail address was bigfatdoofus666 @ifroggy.com and then you had a new account with a similar IP whose e-mail address is bigfatdoofus666@phpbbhacks.com, you should ban that user.

This can go on for a while. I've had users do it for more than a year. Any posts that the user makes should be ignored by your staff and removed as soon as possible. If the banned user sends e-mails or private messages to your staff members, instruct them to inform you (via the problem users forum) and ignore the user. Basically, you totally ignore the user while documenting every single thing that he does. Don't give him any attention. You may have to repeat this process as the user continues to sign up for new accounts.

The problem with some of these users is that they view an account on your site as some sort of inalienable right. It isn't. An account on your site is a privilege. To maintain this privilege, members must maintain decent reputations, meaning that they must abide by your user guidelines. Otherwise, they lose it. So, a user who seems to operate under this belief should not be unbanned.

Whatever you do, don't let people get away with things. It doesn't matter how long it's taken you to discover that he signed up for another account—ban him.

Get Creative   Creativity never hurts when you're trying to get major-league idiots off of your community. I am sure that you can think of more concepts, but here are a few helpful ones.

➤ **The System Is Down**   You could make it so that a 404 (not found) page displays when a specific IP visits your community. If you have cPanel (http://www.cpanel.net) installed on your server, it may have an IP Deny Manager that will allow you to display a 403 (forbidden) page to certain IPs. This is done with .htaccess, so you can also do this by hand. For an example of how to do this, see the "Comprehensive guide to .htaccess" article at JavaScript Kit (http://www.javascriptkit.com/howto/htaccess5.shtml). You can customize your 403 page to look like a 404 page, which will give the impression that the site is down. The standard 403 page by itself may not be too convincing as it may say "forbidden" on it, which just about equates to "banned."

It can be very effective as long as the user continues to access your site from the IPs that you have specified, which doesn't always happen.

➤ **Make It So That Only They Can See Their Posts (Global Ignore)**
Sometimes referred to as global ignore, you can incorporate a function that lets the banned user log in but then makes this user go unseen to all users of your community. The banned user cannot receive private messages, and if he tries to send them, they don't reach the intended users. He can still make his posts, but only he (and maybe you and your staff) can see the posts—no one else. Basically, in his eyes, the site works as is intended. He will, hopefully,

just think that everyone is ignoring him and go away. You will want to make sure that these posts are flagged in some special way (maybe colored red or something) so that you and/or your staff don't accidentally respond to one of them.

➤ **Simulated Downtime** The idea of simulated downtime has been taken to an impressive level through hacks like "Miserable Users" for vBulletin and the "Troll" hack for phpBB. They combine downtime, slowness, general confusion, and the site actually working. Sometimes the site may just take forever to load, sometimes it may come up as a 404, sometimes it may work, sometimes it may *look* like a post went in or a private message was sent (it wasn't)—the hopeful end result is that it frustrates these troublemakers and drives them away.

Generally, these "creative" methods are not something that you want to do when you first ban someone. I mean, unless someone was a straight-up troll, go with a standard ban first. Give him an opportunity to leave. If he reregisters and shows you that he wishes to circumvent your ban, you can pull out the big guns.

Some may consider these tactics questionable. But the truth is, you have guidelines. When someone violates those guidelines so many times and shows such a disregard for them, your staff, and your community, he is no longer welcome. If a user just continues to register accounts, cause trouble, and waste your time, you need to worry about the environment of your community, first and foremost, and you have the right to block them from your site via these means.

Automated Banning and Point-Based Systems Some communities automatically ban people through a point-based system, sometimes referred to as infractions. Basically, various offenses on your site are worth points. When someone reaches a certain number of points, she is banned.

I don't like these sorts of systems, generally speaking, because they can eliminate discretion, which is a part of running a community. You may have to ban someone because she has X number of points, not because you actually think she should be banned.

That's not to say that they are not without their use. Eliminating discretion can be just what you are after. I find that they make more sense on larger communities where you place the responsibility of banning in the hands of many individuals. Using a point-based system can help to maintain some semblance of consistency.

When using a point system, some points should expire after a given period of time. For example, let's say that you ban at ten points and an inflammatory comment counts as four points. Someone who makes three inflammatory comments within a week should be treated differently than someone who makes one inflammatory comment in 2002, one inflammatory comment in 2005, and one inflammatory comment in 2007, but also made 2,000 other posts along the way. That's where discretion is supposed to come in. So make sure that your system allows for that.

Banning URLs

If a site has spammed you particularly heavily, used your site to boost its own user base, or maybe even been inappropriately and unfairly negative and critical of you, you may want to ban that URL from even being mentioned in your community.

This is not a step that should be taken lightly, however. Only in severe and/or meaningful cases should you exercise this power. For example, if a site's administrators encourage their users to come to your community and disrupt it however they can, that is not a site that you wish to support.

If a site has inappropriate content yet some people keep linking to it, you could ban it. Another case would be a site that has done something wrong to the overall community (maybe not just your community, but to an entire subject matter or group of people on the Internet) in a way that makes you not want to send traffic its way. Here's an illustration of what this might mean. At phpBBHacks.com we treat hack authors with a great deal of respect. There was a project at a third-party site that took their work and treated them disrespectfully. So, we stopped allowing links to that project. Again, you should only do this when it has serious meaning. Don't use it to block competitors.

You can use your word censoring feature to accomplish this, making it so that when the URL to one of these sites is posted, it is displayed as http://www.*.com or similar. Treat these links as inappropriate and remove them in accordance with your user guidelines.

Contacting a User's ISP

If a user has persistently disrupted your community and/or continues to come back and register new accounts, you may feel that he deserves to be reported to his ISP. Usually, this is not something that you want to do when someone is simply banned, because it would be an unnecessary use of your time and it's best to give people an opportunity to accept the ban and leave. It's an option if the user insists on coming back and tries to circumvent your ban over and over again.

You can find out whom to contact by looking at the IP address from which the user last visited your community. For a variety of reasons, the IP you logged may not be a real one for the user. Often that is not the case. So assuming you have an accurate IP address, you can do a reverse lookup at a site like DomainTools (http://www.domaintools.com) and find out who owns it. There might be an abuse contact listed right in the output, but if you are unable to find it or would like the most updated information (as well as guidelines for reporting abuse, which the ISP may have available), you can also visit the ISP's domain name or homepage to find an abuse contact e-mail.

If you have followed my instructions and recommendations throughout this book, you will have all incidents well documented. This is vital because you will need to send them to the ISP. ISPs will not do a thing if you don't have any proof—nor should they. You should send them as much important information as you can, but don't send them duplicates. Send them IP searches (that your community software generates) that document the user's IP addresses and usernames, and provide posts (a sampling, if there is a large number) that violated your user guidelines and so on. Obviously you can't really leave these things out in public and can't really give them administrator access, so the easiest way to give them this information is as an HTML document. So save these documents as static HTML pages, upload them to a "secret" location on your server, and include direct links to all files in your e-mail to the ISP.

In the e-mail, you should also cite your guidelines (link to them and describe which guidelines were broken). The more documentation you can provide, the better off you will be. In your e-mail, don't take your displeasure with the user out on the ISP. Don't threaten, don't issue ultimatums, don't say things like "this idiot," etc. That won't help anything. Be respectful, productive, professional, and concise. Make it clear that you understand that it is not an easy situation and that you are glad to help them in whatever way you can.

You may or may not get a response (or a favorable response), but depending on the situation, it may be worth the effort.

Conclusion

"My philosophy is that not only are you responsible for your life, but doing the best at this moment puts you in the best place for the next moment."

—OPRAH WINFREY

In this chapter, I took a look at much of the chaos and craziness that can and will ensue in your community. But, even so, I cannot hope to cover everything or even a majority of everything that can happen. The bottom line is that stuff happens, you make decisions, you adapt, you persevere, and you move on. You learn and you understand by doing. The greatest communities become great by adapting, facing, and conquering the issues and obstacles that lay before them.

Your leadership and your community will be defined in moments of chaos. If you handle things incorrectly, your community will suffer. If it is bad enough, you or it may even kill your community (or at least put it on life support). However, by making the right moves, these moments will pass, in time, and your community will be stronger for it.

CHAPTER 7

Creating a Good Environment

"A business that makes nothing but money is a poor kind of business."

—HENRY FORD

There is no such thing as a truly good community without a good environment. A good community can mean many things. It can mean that your users usually respect one another, that new users of all ages and groups feel welcome within your community, and that your users generally feel like the administrators care about and consider their feelings and suggestions. You can be proud of a community that has a great environment. It will also be easier for you to find partners, affiliates, and to get publicity when you have a friendly and inviting atmosphere. This chapter will focus on things that you can do to make this happen.

Respect Is Everything

I can't stress this enough. Respect is the cornerstone of a good environment. You create a respectful community by requiring that everyone treat everyone else with the respect that they deserve. You do this by having written policies and by actively enforcing those policies. Don't let people get away with disrespectful comments. All members of your community (regular members and staff members) must treat one another with respect at all times.

You should encourage your members to attack the point and not the person. Address what people say, don't try to attack them as human beings for having a given view. This extends to respect of choice. Like your favorite team or your favorite music. A comment like "Rap sucks!" doesn't help your community; it hurts it by creating an unnecessary divide through hostility. There is no reason for it.

Welcoming New Users

You should welcome new users to your site. If you have an introductions forum, as you usually should, that is perfect. Whenever a user posts an introduction thread, you should reply to the thread welcoming that user to your site. Encourage your staff members to do so—make it one of their responsibilities, especially if your site is large (if it is, you may not be able to welcome everyone). Welcome people even if it is just a one-word post. If something about the user's intro sparks your curiosity, definitely ask a question and engage the person. This will make new users feel more at ease and more inclined to contribute and participate.

If you do not have an introductions forum (why don't you?), you can still welcome a user when you notice someone new post in your community. You can also make it so that all new members receive an automatic "welcome" private message that shows them around a bit and provides a link to your user guidelines. This shouldn't replace introduction threads or the need to welcome people in that form.

Be Human, Be Fun, Be Involved

"I was saving sugar for my wedding night."

—TODD FLANDERS

Don't allow you and/or your staff to act like Mr./Ms. Business all of the time. Joke around with users, if that's your personality, and allow them to get to know you. Participate in discussions. Pull an April Fools' joke on your users.

Have fun and allow people to have fun (within your guidelines, of course). Do not discourage good, clean humor and fun. These things help people bond and in turn make your community a true community. It's good to be human and to be involved—it helps to show people that there is a real person behind the site. You don't want to be regarded as some sort of inanimate object.

Answering Questions

If you run a support community of some kind, most of the posts on your forums are undoubtedly questions, and the guidelines in this section especially apply to you. But regardless of the purpose of your site, you and your staff will be answering a lot of questions. Users are "customers" of your community. So, you often need to take somewhat of a customer-service approach to answering questions.

Don't Have an Attitude of Expected Knowledge

Don't expect users to know things—or anything. Assume that they know nothing, and approach from that position. If you answer their questions but they don't understand, explain in more detail, respectfully. Once you get an idea of the background and experience level of the users, you can more safely make assumptions.

Don't Link Users to General, Unhelpful Sites

For instance, if someone asks for a specific script, don't tell her to go to a site that has lots of scripts and do a search. Try to find a script that fulfills her needs and link her to it directly. If you can't do that, consider not responding at all.

Don't Tell Users to Search

Do not tell users to search or link them to your search page. I cannot stress this enough. Don't do it! Locate the information for them and link them to it directly. Telling users to find it, when you know it is there or suspect that it might be, just shows a lack of effort and care. People ask questions to find solutions, not to be told to go look somewhere else.

If a Question Has Been Asked Before

If a user asks a question that you know has been answered before, you have two options. If it is fairly quick and easy to do so, just answer the question straight away. However, if the question requires a detailed answer and has been answered before, provide a link to the answer and then close the thread (assuming the thread you are linking the user to is still open, ready for replies, and has recently been active). Don't act like the user was supposed to have found it on his own.

Make Your Users Feel Involved

Part of creating a great environment is making your users feel like their feelings and their suggestions are considered and appreciated. When users participate in a community for a while, they will start to feel a sense of ownership in it. Although you may be the true owner, it is important that you try not to make drastic changes without announcing them. If you would like their feedback, try to ask for it before making the change. If you want their help finding problems after a change has been made, ask them as well. Your members are a terrific resource.

If they feel that you don't care what they think, that isn't going to bode well for you. They will either decide not to provide you with any feedback or they will resent you (probably both). It is true that you will make the final decision on all changes. However, when it's feasible, hear people out and thank them for their suggestions even if you don't act on them, which will probably be the case a lot of the time.

Ask Users for Input

If you have an idea for a new feature or a change to your community, you can create a thread to ask your users their opinion. Besides making them feel involved, they may unearth something that you missed. This improves the proposed change or addition. When asking for feedback, it can be helpful to avoid inferring any strong views, so that you don't influence their thoughts too much.

Just because you ask users for input does not mean that you have to go with the majority. Ultimately, you will make the final decision based upon what you think is best for the community, but the opinions of users can some-times help you in this process, whether it be in the final decision or in fine-tuning the idea.

However, there is a limit. For instance, you shouldn't ask users whether a thread should be removed (that is crazy) or whether a user should be banned. These are decisions that should be left up to you and/or your staff. You cannot run an efficient community if you allow your users to make these decisions. It takes too long and it is prone to turn into some political show with people playing favorites. As I said, communities are not—nor should they be—democracies. Should users have an impact on policy? Definitely. But once that policy is set, they cannot be the ones to enforce it.

Announce Changes

When you make major changes (and sometimes, even small and noticeable ones), announce them and, if you can, explain why the change was made. If you have launched a new feature or something else to be excited about, tell everyone what is exciting about it and encourage participation. If you are excited, they are more likely to be excited. This will spark interest if nothing else. It can also be used to encourage people to report any errors that they see, allowing them to help you iron out any bugs.

Share Your Successes

"You can accomplish much if you don't care who gets the credit."

—RONALD REAGAN

When you reach a milestone—for instance, a certain number of posts, threads, members, etc.—make an announcement bringing attention to this fact and thank your users for their contributions and support. You—and many others, I am sure—know that you have (probably) worked harder than anyone else in your community. But without your users, your community would be a ghost town. For this reason, you should try to give a lot of glory to your user base when reaching milestones or receiving awards, etc.

Also, don't forget to credit your staff members, who—like you—toil behind the scenes to keep your community in tip-top shape (and not always getting the credit that they deserve from the general public).

Customer Service

As I said earlier, users are your customers. Their time is their currency. They pay you with time spent at your community (among other things, of course). So although you definitely should not take any abuse from them, it is important to have the proper respect for them. Here are some ways to inject a customer-service attitude into your community administration.

When a Problem Occurs, Apologize and Explain

"Bad news isn't wine. It doesn't improve with age."

—COLIN POWELL

We're all human, we all make mistakes. Technology is flawed. With these two things in mind, it is inevitable that problems will arise within your community. Whether it is downtime, slowness, loss of data, or just your average everyday mental mistake, it is still a problem even if it is out of your control. If it is and you feel you need to make that clear, do so.

If the problem affects all users, such as prolonged downtime, you should create a thread explaining the situation, why it came about, and that you are sorry for the trouble, inconvenience, or whatever you want to call it.

If you have an issue that affects a specific user or group of users, it may be best to contact them individually and privately. If it is something like the accidental removal of a thread, just put the thread back and add a reply saying that we ("we"—not someone in particular; you are a team, remember) made a mistake, that you are sorry, and that's it. I've said this before, but it is very important: You are a team. When people make mistakes, there is no he or she—there are only we or I (you, the administrator).

Responding to Bad or Rude Suggestions

If a suggestion is so rude that it violates your guidelines, obviously you should remove it (assuming you have a feedback-and-suggestions forum, of course) and deal with it as you must—as you would deal with any violation.

If it is just a little rude, try not to read too much into what the user is saying. Respond to what he means without the little extra snide remarks that he may have added in. Try to maintain a positive but honest attitude.

Even if a suggestion is just bad (but politely offered), you had to consider it to determine it was bad, right? Well, then you did consider it, so be sure to get across to the user that you did give it some thought but decided that it was not for the best at this time.

If someone creates a public thread to offer a suggestion that is a definite no, you may want to close the thread after you have responded, because there is not much else to say. This is the truth: You were nice, you thanked the person and were honest, and nothing that can be said in the thread is really going to change your perspective. It is good just to get the thread over with, rather than leaving it out there as a possibility that users will get behind or get excited about—you don't want people to raise their hopes only for you to crush them. Of course, for this reason (among others), I recommend not having a feedback-and-suggestions forum at all.

How to Handle Private Contact with Users

On your community and off of it (e-mail and instant messengers, for instance), you should always act the same toward people. Maintain the same professionalism. Address people in the same way. Same old, same old. When a user contacts you privately with an issue, engage her and treat her like you would in your community—with patience, understanding, and respect—and thank her for contacting you. You should be candid. If users don't feel like you are approachable, they won't approach you at all—and that's not a good thing, even though it may seem like it at times.

Don't Take It Personally

It isn't easy to do, because of the amount of work that you can put into a community; but you must try hard to refrain from taking criticism personally. Try to remember that it is not usually a criticism of you personally—it is a criticism of your website, of your decisions, of a product that you offer, etc. You may work very, very hard on what you offer, only to have someone criticize it in a way that you feel is unfair and tough to swallow. This is understandable, but it's usually not personal. Do your best to keep it in that perspective.

Of course, there are also people who make it personal, who seem to enjoy criticizing you or pointing out some flaw (even though it may not be a flaw) in your operation. Maybe they love to see you make a (perceived) mistake or love to see you in a moment of weakness. Don't let these people bother you.

"It is not the critic who counts: not the man who points out how the strong man stumbles or where the doer of deeds could have done better. The credit belongs to the man who is actually in the arena, whose face is marred by dust and sweat and blood, who strives valiantly, who errs and comes up short again and again, because there is no effort without error or shortcoming, but who knows the great enthusiasms, the great devotions, who spends himself for a worthy cause; who, at the best, knows, in the end, the triumph of high achievement, and who, at the worst, if he fails, at least he fails while daring greatly, so that his place shall never be with those cold and timid souls who knew neither victory nor defeat."

—THEODORE ROOSEVELT

Allow All Wrath to Be Directed at You, Not Your Staff

That sounds fun, doesn't it? Run your community so that if a user is going to hate anyone on your team, it is probably going to be you. You are the top dog, you issue all of the bans (probably), and you correct certain situations as necessary. Your staff should have a certain amount of discretion—they will make a lot of decisions, in other words. Once in a while, a decision will be made that you won't agree with and you will have to reverse it, but that is probably going to be infrequent if all goes as it should. So your moderators make a lot of judgment calls based upon the vision that you have laid out for them to follow.

Even so, if a user contacts a staff member and gives them some garbage about a decision the staff member made, often times I will step up and contact the member directly to reinforce what the staff member said (assuming it's correct). If the user feels a specific member of staff is targeting her or she is being critical of a specific member of staff, I may also remind the member that she is welcome to contact me. My staff members are only following my directions, so I am the one that the user really has an issue with. This has the obvious effect of deflecting criticism from the staff member and onto you. In my communities, that is just how I like it.

One of the worst guideline violations is when a user personally attacks another user or worse, a staff member, via private message or in a thread. If there is one thing you cannot have, it is someone taking potshots at your staff.

Obviously, you should remove such disrespectful posts. But, if such comments are ever directed at a staff member, you need to take serious note. Staff members are definitely to be treated with respect—as much as or even more so than you.

In most cases, your staff will be volunteers. Would you want to volunteer at a community where you had to take garbage from users every day and the administrator didn't seem to care or did nothing about it? Of course you wouldn't.

Your moderators need to be generally liked and respected, and you need to do whatever is in your power to make that a reality. Forget about you—when your moderators are comfortable and respected, your community is a better place to be.

Politics, Religion, and Other Very Controversial Discussions

Discussions on politics, religion, and browsers form what I like to call "The Holy Trinity of Community Atmosphere Wreckers." Of course, there are other types of controversial discussions, but these three seem to pop up a lot.

The truth is that some types of discussions are way more (nastily) opinionated than others. You may want to try to allow these discussions under strict guidelines. Consider giving them their own forum(s), so they are all self-contained. You might even make such discussions available on an opt-in and opt-out basis only (opt-out by default). That may work for some communities.

If your community is based around religion, politics, or something of a similarly controversial nature, good luck. But if your focus is not on politics or religion and you do aim to have a nice, friendly community, I have to ask you: Why allow these discussions at all? Even if they are conducted "respectfully" and are compartmentalized, they often make some users hate other users because of disagreements or membership in different groups, religions, parties, or whatever else.

If the discussions in your forums are getting to this point, it is probably best to ban these discussions from your community entirely. It is just not worth it. Better yet, don't allow them from the start. That's what I've done and it's worked well. Don't allow it to become a problem. For all of the extra posts you will get, the potential for animosity to grow in your community is real. This animosity will spill into your other forums.

Did you see the movie *Ghostbusters 2*? All of the negative and nasty emotions created that slime that flowed through the city? Yeah, that's what could happen to your site. The Ghostbusters are no longer around—so, you need to cut it off before it gets to that point.

It is human nature to be emotionally involved in issues like these. The most responsible and respectful people can be offensive in these situations, depending on how you look at it. It only makes sense to decide to keep your community's environment positive and productive.

Some people feel that controversial topics equal lots of posts. That depends on the situation, but being controversial just to be controversial and doing so without regard to the atmosphere of your community will be damaging. Besides, moderating such discussions can be very tedious and time-consuming, especially if you aren't overrun with great moderators. Why waste your moderator hours on discussions that are that far off topic?

Conclusion

In this chapter, I talked about many different ways that you can encourage a positive, friendly, and inviting atmosphere in your community.

You should always keep an eye out for trends and issues that could have a negative effect on the environment of your community. Cut those things off at the head. Atmosphere can be a pretty fragile thing, and you don't want to mess it up.

CHAPTER 8

Keeping It Interesting

Your community will probably be naturally interesting, in one way or another, but there are some things that you can do to increase and enhance interest, if only for a limited period. It is true that over time some users will just plain lose interest in your community and maybe even forget that it exists. This chapter aims to help you remind people about your community and keep it interesting.

New Features

"Anyone who has never made a mistake has never tried anything new."

—ALBERT EINSTEIN

New features definitely can get people excited and/or make longtime users renew their interest in your community. This is why you should always be on the lookout for new concepts and ideas that you can use to create new features for your user base.

Never add features just to add features, but always keep an eye out for great features that could enhance your community. Keep an eye out for needs. I say it a lot, but the best get better and so should you.

Newsletters and Mailing Lists

If your community is popular enough and has the resources enough to run a good, solid e-mail newsletter, it can definitely add something to your community. Make sure that it has actual value so that people will actually subscribe and won't think of it as just a piece of spam. Timely, content-filled newsletters add value to your community, help you retain members, and remind people that you're still there and want them to participate. It can be easy to lose members; newsletters help you to bring them back. It's hard enough to gain new members, so it's definitely worthwhile to do what you can to keep the ones you already have.

If you can't run a full-fledged newsletter, you can have an opt-in mailing list where users receive an e-mail every time you post in your announcements forum. This helps keep those interested in receiving the e-mails up-to-date on issues within your community.

Some community software lets you e-mail all of your users with a few clicks. You may want to take advantage of this to announce major changes, wish everyone a happy holiday season, or whatever you want. Don't do this frequently or it will be regarded as a nuisance (or even spam), especially if people are unable to easily opt-out. The ability to opt-out is crucial for any newsletter.

Also, be sure that your community software doesn't e-mail banned users. You don't want to remind people whom you have worked hard to get rid of that your site exists. You are better off with them forgetting about you.

Newsletters can be forwarded and, as such, can bring new users to your site and even help you generate revenue. For more detail on the subject, I talked with Ted Sindzinski (whom I interviewed in chapter 2). Ted is a marketing consultant who has helped some big-time communities as well as Inc. 500 companies with their marketing efforts.

Q. *What should a newsletter consist of?*

These days, people get more e-mail than they can deal with and most promotional messaging never makes it past the preview pane, let alone spam filters. To make sure your newsletter makes it to the inbox, it needs to be seen as interesting or important. For that to happen, it needs good content. The best community newsletters go beyond merely providing site updates and offer quality content that is original and targeted to your niche. Even in the most loyal communities, knowing how a website is doing is only important to those who run it; to the vast majority, interest lays in what the community has to offer to them.

You need to decide what content to put into your newsletter. Before you go rushing off to write or acquire fifty articles, consider the long-term strategy of your newsletter. What you do today, people will expect tomorrow. Consistency is key. Over time, a newsletter with valuable content will build up a following and become more and more important to the point that you can market it as a stand-alone feature. But achieving this means sending out a high-quality product every mailing cycle. To ensure that's possible, you need to set a realistic goal.

If you have a lot of well-written content, newsletter length will likely dictate your format. However, if you are like most, getting good content isn't easy. In this case, aim for one or two good articles or lists of tips; these don't have to be long but they do have to be on target. This will serve as the pillar of your newsletter and the true value to readers.

With that foundation, add layers of content based on your forums and other user-contributed features. Take what your visitors are creating to build out the newsletter and make it interactive. Find hot topics, new polls, funny stories or photos—anything that relates to the bulk of your user base, and select five or six useful pieces to add in.

Q. *What about the layout of the newsletter?*

To decide how to make it look, you need to decide what technologies you wish to use. At their most basic level, e-mails are nothing more than text. Of course, using only text poses a major disadvantage—you can't add any formatting and you can't make the newsletter come to life. But, although looks do count, so does compatibility and, with more than half of e-mail being checked through web based clients, HTML poses a challenge.

Additionally, HTML is often considered a negative in spam-scoring systems, especially those of corporate networks, and negatively affects delivery rates.

For these reasons and more, many major sites use only basic text or extremely limited HTML. Although text is likely to be accepted more often than HTML, it seriously lacks in formatting and reporting abilities. Luckily, you don't necessarily have to choose. By using a multipart message, it can be delivered in both formats for the client to interpret as it sees fit. Unfortunately, this delivery option will not address spam-filter concerns. Ultimately, the method you choose is a function of what you feel is most useful for your site and what is read more—it's often a good idea to test both.

If your message uses HTML, you will likely want to create a template that mimics the look of your main website. You not only increase your branding, but users are more likely to identify the e-mail as being from a trusted source and read it. Keep in mind that e-mails should be much smaller in size than web pages so as not to delay while loading. Many e-mail clients disable image viewing when a message is first opened. As such, you'll want to set proper alt tags and have content visible near/at the top to ensure the message is further explored. Keep in mind that clients tend to have much less viewing space than normal browser windows, so it may be necessary to downsize the width or height of your design to accommodate this format. If you need to modify your site layout to fit e-mail limitations, be sure to keep your logo, color scheme, and main navigation constant with that of your main site for improved usability.

With your shell design in hand, create an inner page format that best fits your content. Using the two-article example, you can either divide the page into two main columns or stack it as separate rows. If your articles are longer than a few sentences, post them to your site and provide an excerpt and link in your newsletter. If space allows, consider adding small photos for each article. Based on your alignment, you can place the other pieces of content on the right or left or toward the bottom. Because this content comes directly from your site, you'll want to provide a link back to the specific page (i.e., the thread) and a link to the area (the forum category).

If you do not use HTML, arrange your content in a linear manner in order of importance, using dashes or other special characters to separate elements.

In most cases, your newsletter should not exceed one to one-and-a-half full screen views. Because clients tend to compress the horizontal viewing area, this is about a half to three-quarters of a page of copy plus formatting. Remember, the purpose of the newsletter is to provide interesting bits of content that lead the user back to your site.

Q. *What can you do to keep your newsletter from being regarded as spam?*

At a minimum, all messages should contain clear opt-out instructions such as a link or address to e-mail. You will want to include your physical mailing address at the end of the message. All e-mails should be sent from a valid address that you'll monitor for complaints or opt-out requests. Process these requests in under ten days if possible. Based on your own location and legal jurisdiction, you may need to adhere to different regulations.

For your spam compliance, you may want to review how your system handles opt-out requests. For many popular community applications, a user can either opt to receive all e-mails or none. This is a problem as you may end up losing the chance to communicate with people if they opt-out from your newsletter. Rather than relying on one opt-in/opt-out point, consider a lower-tier subscription option, allowing users to remove themselves from just your newsletter. This way, if they wish to get system e-mails or other messages but not your newsletter, they can.

Q. *How can you go about monetizing your newsletter?*

E-mail sponsorships can be lucrative. But, they should be done gracefully. When you start a newsletter or any regular mailing, limit or skip ads as they can be seen as a nuisance by people who just want content. As your newsletter grows, you may want to include one or two ads in the form of special banners, text links, or sponsored content. Keep these on target with your content and limit their obtrusiveness. By keeping the number of ads to a minimum, you are less likely to offend subscribers and you'll make the newsletter more valuable to advertisers by giving them a level of exclusivity. Be sure to remember to keep content first and ads second.

Q. *How should you handle the actual distribution of the newsletter?*

For small lists reaching only a few hundred people, most community software includes an e-mail sending tool that allows you to select recipient criteria, input a message, and have it delivered. As long as this program sends a command to your server without forcing you to leave your browser open, this will probably work, provided that it has the feature set you need. Check with your ISP before sending out a message—many have special requirements or limits for bulk mailing. Even the most regulated lists get spam complaints at some point and, even if no one reports the message as being bad, many ISPs will close accounts for sending large batches of e-mail regardless of purpose or their own terms of service. Larger e-mail blasts take considerable resources, and small applications tend to be ill-equipped to handle simultaneous requests to get the e-mail out quickly. Perhaps even more important, few, if any, community programs include truly robust delivery programs with reporting, open-rate tracking, or opt-out management. For all these reasons and more, when sending to more than a few hundred people, it's almost always a good idea to use some sort of remotely hosted service.

Luckily, these services do not have to cost a lot. On the cheaper end, providers like Constant Contact (http://www.constantcontact.com) and ResultsMail (http://www.resultsmail.com) will deliver up to 10,000 e-mails for around $75 per month. If your list is substantially larger or if you plan to deliver larger quantities of e-mail beyond a single newsletter, you may want to consider higher-end solutions like Yesmail (http://www.yesmail.com) and Email-Labs (http://www.emaillabs.com), which offer extremely robust features. The benefit to these services is dramatically improved reporting, GUI-based sending tools, bounce and opt-out management, and most important—reduced workload for you.

There are many options when it comes to delivering and, although you should choose the method that works for your site and budget, always remember this golden rule: Don't send an e-mail through a web interface that uses a live connection. This is risky as your connection to the server can be interrupted or duplicated, causing all sorts of delivery issues. However you send an e-mail, you want your system to run the program without you having to be connected to the application.

$Q.$ *How can you monitor the performance of your newsletter?*

The whole point is to better connect to your visitors, providing some level of customer relationship management. You need to monitor the results. At least, you'll want to know how many people received, opened, and clicked a link in your newsletter. If you're using a simple delivery tool or plain text, this sort of reporting may not be available—another reason to consider your format and sending options. If you do have detailed reports, then you're in business.

There are several initial elements to test and monitor. First, the subject line. This makes or breaks your initial impression. Test various types—some with your site name, some that say "newsletter," and some with bold or shocking statements. Another important factor to monitor and test is the delivery day and time. For some, the hour the message is sent can have major impact on read rate. Most perform better at the beginning of the week and in early hours as most e-mail is checked from the office. But, you may find better results on a Tuesday rather than Monday or at 10 a.m. instead of 7 a.m. Your audience is likely to respond differently to these factors. After a few months of testing, you should be able to hone in on what they respond to best.

The other testing options are virtually limitless. Try testing format changes, versions with/without extra images, new calls to action, offers/discounts (if you sell anything), or anything else you can think of. The better you understand who is reading and how they respond, the more you can tailor it to them. As you increase your effectiveness, you'll be able to use this knowledge for other parts of your e-mail marketing, changing how your system messages are delivered, what they say, and how they look.

Always remember that just like with your website, a newsletter should be produced, measured, and adjusted over and over again. You can always optimize more, always test more, and always make it better, and the better it is the more it will help your community grow.

■ ■ ■

RSS Feeds and Syndication

RSS feeds, syndication, etc., are becoming more and more popular everyday. As such, forums across the Internet are now offering RSS feeds that allow people to keep tabs on the community.

Your community already has tools that allow people to stay up-to-date with the latest activity. Part of being a member of a community is participating in (and actually being at) said community. For this reason, you may want to serve up a partial text feed only. This means that they can only see a portion of each post or thread (or just the titles) in their feed readers, rather than the entire thing, and they must visit your site to view it all. This can make them more likely to participate inside of the community because they actually have to be inside of your community to read the content.

Alternatively, you may elect to offer full text feeds, meaning that people can view the entire content of all of your posts in a feed reader. It all depends on your goals, really. If someone really wants to participate, he will visit your site anyway. But offering up a full-text RSS feed can make it a lot easier for content scrapers to accurately rip content from your site, so that is something to keep in mind and a good reason not to do it. And if money is a consideration, it's usually easier to monetize a website than it is to monetize an RSS feed.

Bots

A forum bot is a script that automatically posts content to your community. There are different types of bots. The bots that you can randomly "talk" to are pretty questionable in value. They are there for entertainment purposes, mainly, but the real value of a community is talking to a real person and the connections that you make with real people. Talking to a bot is a bit of a novelty, and although it may be good for some things or perhaps a few laughs, it can eventually get old and tired. You don't really want bots interjecting into actual discussions.

One area that bots can do well in is the posting of news and articles that are relevant to the subject matter of your community. For instance, if you run a sports discussion community, you could have a bot that would post recent sports news, allowing your users to discuss it. You do this by letting the bot post content from RSS feeds that various websites make available. Ensure that it is posting from truncated feeds and that it includes a link to the whole article. You don't want it posting entire articles in your community, even with the link to the article, as that would constitute copyright infringement.

Be sure to keep the bot on a leash—don't let it post too much, in other words. Have it post a few threads or so a day based upon the activity level of your forums. It can add something valuable and get some discussions going, but don't let it take over and be the only thing that people see.

If you have a content section or a content partner that has an RSS feed or something of that nature, a news bot set up like this can act as a sort of poor man's content-site integration, allowing links to your articles to be posted automatically in your community.

Posting Games

Games are fun, and coming up with a game that your community can partake in will definitely help to keep people coming back.

An example of this would be the community version of *Survivor*, based on the hit TV show. Basically, it'll start with a thread inviting people to join and outlining the rules. Once you have enough people (ten or twelve is a pretty good number, but it could be more), the participants are randomly divided into teams. These teams are then allowed to come up with a name. You then hold a series of team events or challenges where the contributions of an entire team are generally valued as more important than the accomplishments of one individual. Whichever team wins an individual event cannot have any of its members voted off of the "island" during the next round of voting.

Participants vote via private message and the results are then revealed publicly. But, the names associated with each vote are not. The person voted off is removed from the game and a new team event is started.

This continues until one team is whittled down to where the team concept makes a bit less sense. In a ten- or twelve-person game, this might mean when a team gets down to two participants. At that point, the teams disband and it becomes an individual game—everyone for himself. Similar to the team version, the individual who wins each event cannot be voted off. As a means of "mixing it up," you can let a person who is voted off remove one of the remaining players. You may not want to do that, however, just because it could create a little animosity, which isn't the point of the game, really.

Regardless, eventually you will get down to two competitors. You then hold a final event to determine the winner. There are different ways to handle this. You could declare the winner of the last event the winner of the competition if it's a cut-and-dried victory based on hard data and statistics. Another way to do it is to come up with a judged event. Often this will mean that both people must create something unique: an article, a design, an image, a photograph, an idea, a concept related to your community, etc. You could allow all of the people who have been voted off to vote on who should win the game. You can give the winner some sort of prize if you are able (one of our winners got a t-shirt with our logo on it), or there can be no prize besides maybe a special user title for a limited time and recognition on a side page of some kind on your site.

During "Survivor," try to keep the challenges as varied as possible. No one likes doing the same thing over and over again. Some challenge ideas include seeing who can make the most posts during a specific time period, score the highest on a multiple-choice quiz (about your site, about the subject matter of your site, off-topic, etc.), win a scavenger hunt (where players have to find objects around your community), complete some sort of creative assignment, or help a certain aspect of your community. For instance, if you have an articles section, one challenge can consist of submissions to this section that you can then judge based upon whatever metrics that you come up with. You should constantly ask for challenge ideas from your users, because they are easy to run out of.

Pulling another one from TV, you can host your own "Millionaire" game based on *Who Wants to be a Millionaire?* This one is different because it can be ongoing as long as you have someone who is dedicated to the game and to coming up with questions.

To find out who should play next, you can have a "fastest-finger round" just like the show. Have the contestants put a series of answers in the right order, and the person who gets the correct order fastest is the person who gets to play. You may want to limit the number of answers someone can give in the same fastest finger round to one per twenty-four hours or something like that so that the same person doesn't just guess every combination. Whenever you need a new player, you just hold a new fastest-finger round.

For example, in my sports community, users are asked sports questions as users climb up the money ladder. They have lifelines that are adapted from the show. A contestant can use the "phone a friend" lifeline to ask another user for the answer to the current question in the Millionaire thread. The "ask the audience" lifeline allows the contestant to ask all users viewing the thread to send a private message to the person running the game, who then shows the results to the contestant within a certain period of time. This could also be accomplished through the use of a poll as long as the votes remain anonymous and users cannot reply to the thread to say how they voted. The "50/50 lifeline" works as you might expect: Two incorrect answers are removed, leaving the participant with one correct answer and one incorrect answer to choose from. The participant can stop at any time (just like the TV show), and you can have a nice page that displays the scores of past contestants. It is very popular and very fun.

These are just a couple of examples of some of the larger and more immersive types of games that you can play in an Internet community. There are also smaller, ongoing games that users might start up on your site. These often include a word-association game, a movie quotes game (where people try to name which movie a specific quote came from), and so on. Depending on how active this type of thing is in your community, you might want to start a game-threads forum so that these threads are self-contained and do not overpower other forums. This would also include threads like, "What song are you listening to right now?" and similar.

Be careful not to run the big, time-consuming games too often (although a game like Millionaire go on and on) or they will lose some of their attraction and get old.

Arcade Games

Arcade games are generally Flash, Java, etc. games that integrate into your community software. These can include popular games (or versions of them) like Asteroids and Snake or more obscure games. They track high scores and make results available to all. In addition to other features, sometimes they will give the top scorers for each game a champion badge or distinction in their profiles, posts, or somewhere else in the community. They often allow users to challenge other users to matches and keep detailed challenge histories for each member.

Although they may generally make the most sense on gaming-related communities, arcade games can be fun on communities covering any topic. However, they can suck up bandwidth. So before adding one, you should take your limitations into consideration because once you add it in, it will not be fun to take it out.

Contests and Giveaways

In addition to the affects they can have on bringing users to your community (as described in the "Contests and Giveaways" section of chapter 4), contests and giveaways can create a temporary infusion of excitement that brings past users back to your site and gives active members something else to do.

If you end up having a contest that can be abused (such as a referral contest, where you are awarding people who refer the most new members), be sure to stress that you expect users to act appropriately and ethically. No violating the guidelines of other communities or doing anything shady, such as contacting people that they do not really know. You definitely do not want to ignore bad behavior, because there will be consequences. It makes your community look bad.

One such example that comes to mind is a site that held a membership drive of sorts, where it encouraged its users to take users from my site by spamming (making posts, sending private messages, etc.) and violating our user guidelines. The efforts weren't particularly successful; I banned the site's users, and I banned the site from ever being mentioned on my site again. As I said, the site's administrators actually encouraged this behavior, which is completely unacceptable. To add to the absurdity, on their site, they didn't even allow people to link to other sites in their own signatures without permission, let alone post about other sites. If you don't show other people respect, you simply cannot expect respect in return.

Member of the Month

Member-of-the-month programs allow you to reward members who very positively contribute to your community and are, as such, deserving of recognition.

I've found that the most efficient way of selecting members of the month is to work with the staff to choose one. Having the most posts should not be one of the criteria, but having a lot of useful, helpful, or thought-provoking posts should be. If you can afford a prize (or prizes), that's cool, but if not, you will be fine. People will be pleased to receive the recognition from you and/or your staff and will be happy with a special user title for a month, recognition on a subpage of your site, and congratulations through an announcement in your community. You are rewarding your best members without prizes being a major motivation. This is very good for your atmosphere and, as such, your site.

Articles and Content

Whether you have a content partner or you have your own active content section, having access to editorials, articles, news pieces, etc. can constantly give your community something new to discuss. Many users would love to read articles that relate to your subject matter, and they might even like to comment on them. It is yet another way to continue the infusion of valid discussion topics into your community.

You can use your community to encourage your users and staff members to contribute to your content area.

Chat Rooms

If your community is large enough to justify it, you could have a chat room and you could schedule a periodic chat event. You should try to have a moderator or two on hand to make sure that things remain cool. Feel free to create a set of guidelines or say that your current community guidelines apply to the chat room, as well. Logging all chat messages is a good way to ensure that people are abiding by your guidelines, allowing you concrete evidence to consider when you receive a report of chat room abuse. There are two very beneficial things that you can do to make your chat room more engaging.

First, make it so that your chat room can use the username and password combos from your community so that there is no impersonation, etc. Second, if there is some way that you can display that there are "Five users in chat" or something of that nature on your main site, that is also very, very, enticing for people who are considering checking out your chat room. One of the biggest problems with chat rooms is that people fear that there is no one in there. If you show them who is in there at that moment, you will improve your chances of them logging in.

If you ever have the opportunity to get some sort of celebrity in your area of interest to chat with your users, get a chat script that lets only certain people ask questions so that you can have a moderator choose which questions the person of interest receives. Such events can bring many people on your site at one time, so be sure your web host can handle it.

You can also schedule chat events in line with events happening in the outside world, such as a sporting event, an awards show, a TV program, etc. For instance, if you ran a fan community for the *American Idol* TV show, you could run chat events while the show is on so that you and your users can chat about what is transpiring on the show at that moment.

The decision to have a chat room should be considered carefully. Most communities do not have them because they add to the work load and often offer limited value to the actual community. When someone adds a post in your community, it's there forever. But when someone posts a message in a chat room, generally, only the people who are in the room at that time are going to see it.

Chat rooms also make your site more vulnerable to inappropriate content, simply because it is pretty difficult to have a moderator reading the chat room twenty-four hours a day. So unless you have people poring over your logs, you are going to be relying on member reports and people are going to be more likely to get away with things.

Awards Programs

The Emmys, the Oscars, the ESPYs, the Golden Globes, the VMAs . . . how about the YourSite.com awards? These sorts of events can be really big hits with your members. When you feel you can hold a meaningful, enjoyable event with enough nominees and voters, hold one.

Basically, you can kick off the process (publicly, anyway) by creating a thread to ask users to make suggestions for award categories (or for anything else related to the program). Do this especially if it's the first year, but, even if it's not, if you are looking to expand your categories, asking for suggestions can be a great way to do so. In one of my communities, categories included Member of the Year, Funniest Member of the Year, Staff Member of the Year, and Thread of the Year. This is just a general example.

You can expand on the categories as you need to. For instance, if you have an articles section, you can have an Article of the Year award. If you have a web-development community that is large enough to support such categories, you can have a Web Designer of the Year, PHP Guru of the Year, Server Guru of the Year, etc., as SitePoint Forums (http://www.sitepoint.com/forums) has done.

Once you have your categories nailed down, start a thread to ask people to privately send nominations (via private message in your community is probably the best, so that a username is associated with each nomination— this helps to deter abuse) for as many categories as they want. In other words, people do not have to nominate for every category, but they can only make one nomination per category and no one can nominate themselves or anything that they had anything to do with (i.e., a thread they created, an article they submitted, etc.). As an additional deterrent to abuse, you could choose not to accept nominations from users who do not have at least a certain number of posts before your call for nominations. This shuts down anyone who tries to create new accounts to submit additional nominations. After the deadline has passed, tally the nominations and put the people and threads (or whatever) with the most nominations in each category on the ballots. Usually three to five choices are good, but if you have six people who tie for the lead in nominations, all six people should be on the ballot. Although it is unlikely, be sure that no banned users make any ballot.

After you have all of the ballots settled, create a poll thread for each award category. The poll results should be kept private (even if the user has voted), so that no one knows where the votes stand and no one will have any idea who wins until you announce it. This is important because if people know the current results, it really ruins a lot of the surprise and may sway their votes, as well. Be sure to keep an eye on abuse in voting also. You can apply the same sort of antiabuse deterrents for voting as you can for nominating: no votes from people who didn't have a certain number of posts before the awards process began, no encouraging people to blindly stuff the ballot, etc.

Once the voting deadline passes, announce the winners for each category, congratulate them and the nominees, and thank everyone who participated in the process. Create a special page that displays current and past winners. You can use your imagination to come up with what each winner might get. On a web development or programming-related community (where someone is likely to have a website of her own), you could give each winner a special image/badge to display on her own site. You can give winners a special user title (and/or badge) on their profiles and next to all of their posts. If you have the resources, you can even have prizes although that's not really needed. The main thing to give is appreciation and gratitude for contributions made in your community. It creates a very nice feeling.

Besides that, these types of things can be very fun and most users that win will be very humble and appreciative. If anyone gets out of line, be sure to explain to them and stress that it is for fun and although it does have meaning and importance, it should also be kept in perspective.

Conclusion

In this chapter, I discussed methods with which you can generate and maintain interest in your community.

I want to conclude by saying that you should always be trying to think of and listen to ideas for events, programs, or anything that could increase your users' interest and/or enjoyment in the community. It is this tireless search for improvement that will set you apart from other sites in your genre.

CHAPTER 9

Making Money

I can hear you thinking: "What?! Making money only gets a small section at the end of the book?! That's stupid!"

Sorry. Making money is definitely not a focal point of this book—managing and cultivating a community is the focus. But I thought I'd go over some of the main ways that you can make money from your community, which is probably one of your goals. Without money, it will be tough for you to continue operating your site. No one wants just to keep spending money—it would be nice to pay for your costs at the very least, right? But hopefully you can do more than that. Some of you may even be trying to make this your job and/or a bigger part of your life.

When it comes to monetizing a site, there are really only so many truly original ideas. From them, many other ideas are derived. Most of them center around advertising of some sort. In this chapter, I'll take a look at some of the more popular ones.

Advertising

Advertising is the main source of income for the vast majority of communities on the web. To state the obvious, the best way to get people to click on or look at the advertisements on your site is to make them as attractive as possible in both placement and appearance.

This is true for all advertisements—but especially for ads people need to click on for you to make money. If the ads are displayed in relation to content people might click on them more frequently and, as such, make you more money. As a general rule of thumb, the closer an ad is to content, the better it will perform. That's not always the case, and you can, of course, over do it. If an ad is in an odd area, such as far away from your content and your layout, it is harder for people to notice. You can place ads in the middle of articles, next to posts, below forum content, above forum content, and so on and so forth.

You need to decide what ad placements are appropriate. Having too many ads can get annoying, so be careful. For instance, displaying an ad after the first post on a thread is OK, but displaying an ad after the first three posts (an ad after each one) is probably overkill. Advertisements on the first screen tend to do best, but ads after posts, on the sides, and at the bottom (below the thread but above anything else) can also do well and earn you additional revenue.

Having multiple ads on a page is not a bad thing. It's not really the number of ads on a page that matters but the percentage of the page that the ads take up. You should integrate ads in a way that is both tasteful and not too excessive. You can have half a dozen or more sizable ads on a given page (depending on the size of the ads and the width and length of the page) and still keep them appropriate. One of the things that can be your guide is simply to look at your content. Does it look strange with the ads around it? Is it squished? Oddly shapen? Shoving ads in your users' face, at the expense of making your site look atrocious, won't make them click more; it'll just make them angry, which may make them leave.

You should also consider your audience. For example, in my experience, I have often found that people who do a lot of work online (like web designers and programmers) tend to be more sensitive to advertising than those who use the Internet more casually. So, the average ad tolerance may be higher on say, a sports community, as opposed to a web development community.

When we're talking about ads served by a network like Google AdSense (http://www.google.com/adsense) and Yahoo! Publisher Network (http://ypn .yahoo.com), where you can customize the colors and appearance of the ads, it's generally a good idea to make them blend into your site by giving the links and text the same color as the links and text on your site, matching the background colors, and removing the borders (making the borders the same color as the background on which they will be displayed). For some sites, such as a site that receives a lot of page views per visitor, it may make sense to randomize the appearance of ads, making it so that different colors display on each page view, to help combat advertisement blindness. Some people experience better performance when they set the link color to the default blue link color (#0000FF) that people are used to seeing.

At the end of the day, the best way to find your ideal setting is to experiment. Make changes, make adjustments, track performance, and see what works best.

Displaying (Some) Ads to Guests Only

Generally speaking, members of your community are less likely to click on or pay attention to advertisements because they visit your community frequently and are used to seeing your ads where they are. They can develop a sort of blindness to them. For this reason, you may want to serve fewer ads to logged-in members. This can enhance their experience and create a benefit of registration.

I'm not saying that you shouldn't serve any ads to members, but consider serving fewer. Members still count as traffic, and they still generate ad revenue (especially with cost-per-thousand ads). That is not something to give up lightly. If you think you might ever want to serve ads to them, you don't want them to think of your site as ad-free. So, keep the ads in the main areas. For example, you could place ads around the top and bottom of your pages for all users, but have ads in between posts in a topic for guests only. Below these ads, you might place a link that says that users can register and log in to remove that advertisement (be sure to include links to the registration and log-in pages).

Start with Ads

When I started developing websites and communities, I used to think that I would add advertisements to the site when it had traffic. I thought that adding them when there was little traffic made little sense because it would generate little money.

I don't do that any longer. I believe that you should start with advertisements or, at least, placeholders, so that people will be used to your ads from day one. It is not usually easy to add advertisements—or even to add additional advertisements—once the site is large. You have to do what you have to do, but why not make it a little easier for yourself right off the bat?

Advertising Networks

For many, advertising networks represent a bulk of their income. This is because they are a great starting point for those looking to generate revenue from advertising in their community. They aren't just a starting point, though—many highly trafficked sites rely on them as well. You give the company your information, it (hopefully) approves your site, you put the code on your site, and you start earning money. The network finds the advertisers, bills the advertisers, collects the payments, handles customer support (for the people advertising on your site), takes its cut, and pays you.

Most of the time, the system also allows you to serve ads for many advertisers all at once with the same ad code, making it easier for you to serve more advertisements and allowing you to make more money. The downside? The network provides a service to you and it is not a charity—it is a business, it is working hard, and it must generate its own revenue. Still, for many, advertising networks represent the easiest way to generate revenue from your available ad space.

There are many ad networks out there: graphical (static images, rich media, etc.), text-based (often times contextual), cost-per-thousand (CPM), cost-per-click (CPC), cost-per-action (CPA), affiliate networks, and so on and so forth. Some ad networks (especially CPM ads) do not accept forums. Some do. You should check network policies and contact the networks themselves to make sure.

Regardless of whom you use, be sure to read the policies and terms-of-use pages before you submit your site for membership (so that you can know if you even qualify and will know just what you can and cannot do). This will improve your chances of being accepted and continuing your membership in the program.

CPM and CPC Networks   Some advertising networks (with varying models) that openly accept forums include Tribal Fusion (http://www.tribalfusion.com), BurstMedia (http://www.burstmedia.com), Casale Media (http://www

.casalemedia.com), Specific Media (http://www.specificmedia.com), Google AdSense (http://www.google.com/adsense), Yahoo! Publisher Network (http://ypn.yahoo.com), and Chitika (http://www.chitika.com). There are more and the list is always growing and changing.

Work with networks that have customizable defaults. What's a default? Well, often ad networks run out of paying ads. When they run out of paying ads, they will serve a default ad of sorts, often a public service announcement (PSA) or something that may not make you much, or any, money. But if the network allows you to set your own defaults, you can make it so that when the network runs out of paying ads, your site will execute the code and display the image of your choosing. A very popular use of this is to be a member of multiple advertising networks and to default one network to the next and from that network to the next and so on. This helps to maximize your revenue across the networks that you are a member of. If a network allows you to set a floor CPM, that is something worth experimenting with, as well, to see how it affects your income. Basically, "floor CPM" means that if the network doesn't have an ad that pays at least a certain amount, it will then serve your defaults.

CPA Networks and Affiliate Programs

Don't limit yourself to just the CPM and CPC models, though. CPA networks and affiliate programs can do well, depending on your subject and the CPA ads that are available to you. There are many CPA networks out there.

CPA stands for cost-per-action, which is what a traditional affiliate program usually is. In an affiliate program, it means that the network or company is paying you when people from your site buy something from them, register at their site, etc.—i.e., they are paying you for actions.

Affiliate programs often allow you to create links on your website that will earn you a percentage of or a flat fee for any sales generated from those links. These can have many uses. You can sign up with merchants that sell goods related to the content of your site and then have a link to the merchant's site. Hopefully your users will click on the links and make purchases that you will be credited for. You can integrate these links into your design and around your content, just as you would for other forms of advertisement. The idea is to get people to click—to entice them. The more enticing your integration, the easier it will be to make money.

You can use affiliate programs to create "stores" on your site, where users can view different products and click a "buy" link that takes them to the affiliated merchants to make their purchases. Amazon.com has an insanely popular affiliate program that allows you to sell an incredible array of products. If you know how to use Amazon.com Web Services (http://www.amazon.com/gp/aws/landing.html), you can probably create a really cool store that is not only integrated into your website, but targets products that relate to your community.

For instance, in my martial arts discussion community, you might sell martial arts DVDs, books, VHS tapes, equipment, uniforms, and so on and so forth. You could put the store on the same domain name as your community or place it on its own domain, linking it to your community (and from your community) as your website's official shop. There is also an assortment of pay scripts and free scripts available that allow you to create your own Amazon.com stores easily. If that is not your cup of tea, you can still use Amazon.com's link generators to create links that you can use on your site for whatever you need. They're not nearly as good, but they're better than nothing.

Amazon.com is just one affiliate program. Its product offering is very diverse, however, so it will likely work for you. But there are tons of companies out there that offer their own affiliate programs and products, many of them through CPA/affiliate networks like Commission Junction (http://www.cj.com), LinkShare (http://www.linkshare.com), ClickBank (http://www.clickbank.com), AzoogleAds (http://www.azoogleads.com), and shareasale.com (http://www.shareasale.com). Do a search and you are likely to find one that will relate to your site's subject matter in one way or another.

There are a limitless number of creative ways that you can use these programs to engage users. For instance, you could ask your users to recommend products (related to your subject matter in one way or another, of course) that you will then display on a separate "user-recommended products" page. In my martial arts community, I could ask users to tell me what their favorite martial arts books are. I can then link these books to a site with an affiliate program (of which I am a member) so people can buy the books and I will earn a commission on any sales. I could also ask members to review products and include a "buy" link in the review.

You can make it so that whenever a user posts a link to Amazon.com (or any other affiliate program that would work with such a system), the link is amended to include your affiliate code so you get credited if sales are generated from the posted link. This type of adjustment, although probably requiring custom programming, has great potential.

These are just a few of the ways that you can integrate affiliate programs into your community. Like I said, the more enticing the link, the easier the sale. So be creative and come up with something enticing—something that people will notice.

Selling Advertising

With or without ad networks, you can also sell your own advertising. You can sell ads in whatever placements you want to make available. Communities with a niche (depending on what that niche is) may stand a better chance of selling advertisements than a general chat community.

Be careful who you sell to. You shouldn't sell advertisements to sites that are not appropriate for your user base. It may be common sense, but avoid selling to sites that you notice are doing something shady in one way or another (with their promotions, business, or otherwise) and/or have been blocked from search engines. Although not everyone who is blocked from search engines deserves it (I know because I have been), it can be a good indicator of underhandedness.

If you are seriously exploring selling advertising yourself, it would be a good idea to put together a media kit or advertising-information page of some kind. Often times, this will include information about the site, the ad locations available, user demographics, and other details that potential advertisers may find interesting. Do some research and check out the media kits of other websites to see what they usually contain.

It's usually in the best interest of your community to avoid nasty popup advertisements (i.e., you try to close it and it spawns two more!) or ads that are highly obtrusive and annoying. I don't really mean advertisements that have animation, movies, etc., I'm speaking more about ads that take over your browser, try to make you download a file, are very noisy, etc. If you have to display popups, interstitials, etc., try to limit their occurrence (such as having only one display per user per twenty-four hours or something like that). Although you have to do what you have to do, users are your most important commodity and it is not in your best interest to anger them with annoying and/or excessive advertising methods.

Other Ads

There are all sorts of advertisements that you can sell—you are mainly limited by your imagination and what is appropriate. Let's take a look at some additional forms of advertising besides typical banner ads.

Ad Threads   Advertising threads are an unobtrusive method of advertising that I have sold, and they are worthy of consideration.

They are basically advertisements that are posted threads in your community. An ad thread contains an advertising message that you approve of (that is appropriate for your community). You can post these under your account (or under a separate account dedicated to such things) and use a "sticky" topic function to put it at the top of the forum that it is posted in. The thread is then closed. You should minimize the number of ad threads per forum (one is a good number because it also helps to give advertisers some value). Clearly denote it as an advertisement by putting "This is a paid advertisement" below the ad message and making the thread title "Advertisement: Advertising Message Here" for when it appears in searches and on the forum. This allows people interested in the ad to view it and those with no interest in viewing an ad to skip it. It works well.

After the advertiser's time is up (and/or if it chooses not to renew the ad), you simply move the thread to your Trash Bin. If you are unable to bump the thread to give it the "new post" benefits (such as showing up in the new posts search, etc.), you may want to give the advertiser a small discount on renewal or charge the full price to repost the thread.

Classifieds   Depending on the subject matter of (and level of activity on) your community, a paid classifieds section or forum where people can sell things and/or advertise their services may be a terrific way for you to generate some revenue. Providing people with a quick, easy, and affordable way to reach your audience and keeping it all in a section or an organized group of sections is a win for you, your advertisers, and your users. Although a dedicated classifieds script that's integrated into your community may work best for some, it's easier to simply create a forum and charge a certain amount of money per thread posted. Be sure to set clear rules for the usage of such a forum.

One incredible example of a classified ads section is the SitePoint Marketplace (http://www.sitepoint.com/marketplace). Ranging in price from $1 to $40 per listing (with add-on features available) to start a thread, it works very well. It represents a terrific value to the people who purchase ads, it accommodates those who wanted the opportunity to post ads, and it creates revenue.

Sponsorships   Sponsorships can take many forms. They can be very simple with just a text link, or they can be quite elaborate with a great deal of integration throughout the community.

One example of a sponsorship deal would be the SitePoint Forums (http://www.sitepoint.com/forums), which sells advertisements for each category in its community. These advertisers can be thought of as category sponsors as there is only one per category. Their ads appear on the index page (on alternating days), at the top of each forum, and within each topic in their sponsored categories.

What Else . . . ?   Who knows? There are so many different ways that you can earn money from advertising on your site. At the end of the day, be creative and keep an open mind. Look for the opportunities that make sense for you, your operation, and your audience.

Merchandise

Being part of a community often means being loyal to it and being proud of your involvement, just like being a fan of a sports team, actor, or something else of that nature. As such, it makes sense that people would want to buy merchandise that features some sort of content from your community—whether it be your logo, slogan, URL, or something else.

Through the use of free, print-on-demand services like CafePress (http://www.cafepress.com), Zazzle (http://www.zazzle.com), and Spreadshirt (http://www.spreadshirt.com), you can create your own merchandise shop easily with little investment and risk. They handle customer service, payment, and host the shop and shopping carts on their servers.

Keep in mind that, with services like these, it can be hard to charge what some would consider a decent price and make much of a profit. The great thing about merchandise is that if people think enough of your community to buy merchandise, they are going to think enough of it to use that merchandise (or at least show their friends). When they use the stuff, other people will see it and maybe those people will check out your community. You can also utilize this merchandise in giveaways and contests—its a very cool prize to offer your users (either a specific product or a gift certificate to pick out what they want). In this way, merchandise is also a useful promotion tool.

If your user base is big enough (you can take polls to make sure that people are interested in it) and you feel pretty good about your prospects, you might want to make a small investment, take on some added responsibility, and move away from print-on-demand services and into small-stock merchandising in order to have more flexibility and turn more of a profit. For more information, I did one final interview with Ted Sindzinski, a marketing consultant who has worked with large communities in their merchandising efforts.

Q. *What products should you start out with?*

The first trick in small-stock merchandising is identifying a set of core products that you will stock and sell. For cost reasons, you should probably start with a single t-shirt design, mugs, and either stickers or mouse pads (key chains, license plate holders, and plastic drinkware items are also acceptable). T-shirts serve as the staple item of any store—users flock to purchase them and will often pay $15 or more on a product with a cost of $7 or less. Mugs are another popular purchase that complements t-shirts and also have a low cost of around $5 and high resale value. There are thousands more promotional items you can consider selling—all of which have great promotional benefits and are much less expensive than you might think.

Q. *Where can you find a supplier?*

There are thousands of companies that sell t-shirts, mugs, and more. Odds are there's one that's local to you. If you don't know a local print shop, check your phonebook or Google. Remember, you want your users to talk your products up, not down, so don't sacrifice quality for price.

Q. *How many should you buy at first?*

Because the goal of small-stock merchandising is to keep costs low in order to minimize initial risk, purchase 24–36 t-shirts ($175–$225), 15–20 mugs ($75–$100), and a small variety of other items under the $5 price point as determined by your individual users. Depending on your audience, you may find you want to increase volume or move up to nicer products like polo shirts. For most sites, t-shirts will do. If your traffic is high enough and your wallet can afford the extra pinch, purchasing higher bulks will net lower prices. Keep in mind that while running out of product when you have pending orders is a pain, having fifty shirts that you can't sell is not a better alternative. Most sites will find that one percent or fewer visitors will end up purchasing from them, so act accordingly and don't be afraid to ask for preorders to estimate your necessary volume.

To save more on big orders, look for price-tier breaks. Every manufacturer will price at preset volume levels and by ordering just a few more units, you may make it to a lower price level. Sometimes the discount can be strong enough that you end up paying just a little more for a lot more quantity. As your price per unit goes down, your profit return will be even higher. Keep it smart and start small, moving up as your demand grows. Don't jump the gun looking to save on huge bulk discounts. But, do shop around to find the best deal. The idea is to keep limited supplies on hand and a good rate of return, not open a warehouse—at least not yet.

Q. *How much should you charge?*

The cost dilemma affects sites of all sizes. You can't overcharge or no one will buy. At the same time, you want to make the most profit. As a general rule, do as others do; if a t-shirt on a similar site goes for $19.95, don't sell yours for $29.95. But, if the market allows it, aim for a 2.5–3x profit ratio turning a $6.40 wholesale shirt into a $15–$20 retail item. If you use this model, you'll see a serious return on even the smallest number of sales (100 shirts over a year would yield you between \$860 and \$1,360 in net profit). Remember to gauge your user base and your product types; cheap t-shirts for college students should go for less than high-quality shirts or a polo. As you start selling more expensive items, you may find that your margin decreases as a percentage but you end up making more money on each item—this is acceptable, just be sure you're making enough to justify the time of collecting, packaging, and shipping those orders.

Q. *How should you take the payments?*

Because small merchandise like this isn't a big-ticket item, there's no reason not to setup a basic merchant account and shopping cart or a third-party payment system like PayPal (http://www.paypal.com). If you want a more robust but simple-to-use system for a larger store, consider something like MonsterCommerce (http://www.monstercommerce.com) or Yahoo! Merchant Solutions (http://smallbusiness.yahoo.com/ecommerce)—both offer remotely hosted e-commerce solutions and can handle accepting payments for a relatively low monthly fee. Whatever solution you find, be sure to match your store's design to look like the rest of your site. Users will feel more comfortable with the process and trust you enough to make the order. If things grow or if you really want to look the part, opening a true merchant account and upgrading your store to a full-fledged shopping system will help boost your sales rate and conversions. However, you need to start making enough profit to justify the added expense of e-commerce software, merchant fees, and a secure transaction system.

Q. *How can you bring attention to the store?*

Getting the initial word out is the hardest part for most. Instead of watching users trickle in from a small link, welcome them all in with a campaign no one can miss. The rule for getting the word out is very similar to a physical store: Discounts and sales work—just building the site isn't enough. The day you launch, announce a contest to get exposure (give away a few items) and discount the prices on everything for that day or week for "early adopters."

You can try preselling items two to three weeks before you plan to have them. This can help provide funds to cover the costs upfront.

Your store link and welcome message should be prominent and bold (remember, you are selling your store to users as a part of your site, not as an ad). After you've been running for a few days, settle things down to a standard link in your main navigation and consider adding a rotating banner to promote your products. Be sure to utilize the power of your existing community by encouraging viral promotion. Having users submit photos of themselves with your products is a great way to create hype and if you have people who meet for local events, be sure they have a few of your shirts or other items handy to add to those photos as well.

Q. *How should you handle shipping?*

One of the biggest challenges faced by small-stock sellers is delivering the product. This may seem simple—put the item in the box, take the box to the mail, and off it goes—but when you think about shipping dozens of orders, possibly every day, it can be a challenge. But, getting your orders out is really just a matter of setting a schedule. Start by going to a local office supply store and picking up enough small boxes and padded envelopes to get you through most of your inventory—when you purchase these items directly they are much cheaper than having someone else package for you. Pick one or two days a week and every week on that day take all your orders, verify payment, print packaging slips with your site logo and contact information, and pack the item. That day or the next day, take the items to your mailing location and ship them.

Many find it easier to use a private shipping company like Mail Boxes Etc. (http://www.mbe.com) and have it handle labeling and mailing the boxes. If you're doing enough volume, you may consider purchasing a shipping-label system to save on time and potentially lower your rates. Be sure to inform your users of your shipping cycles on your site so their expectations are met. There's nothing wrong with telling customers that orders ship weekly or to allow seven to fourteen days for delivery. Being upfront about this may cost an order or two but will save you a lot of headache from customer-service inquiries.

Q. *How do you grow the business?*

Like most businesses, merchandising is best accomplished when you create a cycle of growth. Your initial investment should easily be something you can double, which if put back into products, can grow more. As long as you can drive demand to your store, there is reason to grow. Putting revenue back into more products allows you to order larger bulk quantities and lower the per-unit price and increase your profit. Putting your profit back into the store also means you can expand your product line and with more variation comes larger orders.

With growth comes the opportunity to create a product line rather than just self-promotional items. Many successful shops hire artists (or find volunteers) to create interesting designs, cartoons, or other drawings for their shirts. Sometimes the best option is to pair a small logo and a great image, other times the logo itself is the image. The more variety you offer, the more people can buy and the more opportunity exists. If you're finding you can sell enough to your base users to grow, try adding more product styles and designs to create a secondary market in gifts. With the right products, your users won't be the only people who want to wear one of your shirts!

As you continue to fuel the cycle, your net profit will rise until it reaches a level where you can begin to keep a portion for yourself while comfortably covering the costs of your store and future growth. Assuming you follow the cycle, your orders will naturally grow in size as customers find more to buy. But in small or closed sites, you may discover your order frequency diminishing. There are several ways to revitalize a store without requiring much effort.

Check the promotion of your store. On many sites, webmasters place a link on an obscure toolbar, which is never noticed. Rotating a banner or direct linking from a prominent part of your site should help business. Specials such as "buy one, get one half off" can bring in sales (remember, people purchase things when they feel they are getting a good deal).

If linking and discount promotions aren't enough, consider finding some matching niche manufacturers and offering their products as a dropshipped solution. This is where the real power play comes in for merchandising—any store can offer shirts and mugs for loyal users, but if your site is about Anime

DVDs, actually selling DVDs through your trusted store can be a serious profit boost. Unlike affiliate systems, harnessing an existing store in conjunction with a dropshipping partner allows your users to trust that they are purchasing from a site they know without requiring you to spend thousands on serious product inventory.

Q. *What sort of expectations should you have for your store?*

Merchandising a store rarely makes anyone rich, but when you think about a community with 5,000 active users, it only takes one percent (fifty users) buying a t-shirt at $20 to bring in enough profit to cover most sites' hosting and software costs for long into the future, and if you can double or triple your orders, as many sites do, the take-home profit is even higher. Keep in mind, however, that not all sites are ready for merchandise; only those niche sites with existing, loyal users (and lots of them) convert into sales—so think before you buy!

■ ■ ■

Paid Memberships

Although they don't always make sense and can add to the burden of managing your site, some communities offer paid-membership programs where paid members enjoy more benefits than regular members. People should almost never have to pay to post; paying should generally be more of an "I want to support the community and here are some nice, worthwhile side benefits for doing so" type of thing.

Tangible benefits can include such things as a badge and/or user title next to the user's posts, a badge or title in his profile, special recognition on a subpage, extra private message storage space, no advertisements or a reduced number of advertisements, the ability to use and view basic profile functions (such as being able to add a signature, avatar, etc.), access to a special private forum, exclusive offers and deals (in your merchandise shop or out of it), and more.

If you do have a merchandise shop, you can bundle it with your paid-memberships offering. For example, you could have varying levels of paid membership, including a level where a t-shirt is bundled in at a discounted rate, so that people get both the membership and the shirt for less than they would if they had purchased the two separately.

You probably should not start such a program until after you are well established and very active. It's going to be harder to get people to pay for an upgraded account in an inactive community.

One downside to having paid members is that they may be tougher to ban and they may feel a sense of entitlement. You need to treat your paid members just like your regular members and stick to your guidelines. Develop clear and concise policies regarding what paid members are entitled to (including a refund policy), ensure that all members are treated equally, and make sure there is no divide between paid members and regular members.

Donations

I hesitate to put this in here at all, but depending on the nature of your user base, you might be able to make some money off of donations if you really, really want to avoid advertisements and especially if you are very desperate (for instance, if you need a new server or something of that nature because the traffic load is extreme). But really it should never get to that point.

Sure, it isn't a bad thing to have a small text link in your footer or a link on a subpage, but constantly placing donation links in highly visible areas will eventually end up annoying some users and will make others question the stability of your operation. It can get annoying. So, keep any donation pleas direct and to the point, if at all necessary. Don't beg for donations or pressure people.

Conclusion

In this chapter, I took a look at some of the more popular ways that you can earn revenue from your community. With these ideas in mind, you should have a base of knowledge that will allow you to come up with more creative ways to make money.

I will end this chapter with what I have said time and time again—be creative. Keep your eyes open for opportunities that allow you to make money without unnecessarily annoying your users.

End Note

The book is now at its end. I've tackled the issues that community managers face. With this knowledge, no matter what happens tomorrow, you'll be better prepared to not only deal with it, but to handle it well. As your own management experience grows, you will become a better and better community administrator every single day. No matter how much you know, no matter how experienced you are—if you are any good, you are always improving.

Remember to read the appendices. They contain helpful related links, blank guidelines and contact templates, and a glossary of various terms that I've used in the book.

Thank you for reading. Please check out the book's website (http://www.managingonlineforums.com) for more and, if you have any thoughts you'd like to share with me, please don't hesitate to contact me directly at patrick@ifroggy.com.

Good luck in your community management endeavors!

Online Resources

In this section, you will find an assortment of useful community management resources.

Big Boards (http://www.big-boards.com)
This is a directory showcasing the largest communities on the Internet. It includes other features such as articles and resources.

Common Craft Blog (http://www.commoncraft.com/blog)
This is a blog covering community-related issues in a very insightful way.

Community Answers (http://www.communityanswers.com)
Community Answers features a lot of community-related content and advice. It's definitely a good site to read—very thought provoking.

CommunityAdmins.com (http://www.communityadmins.com)
This is a community where you can discuss community management, marketing, monetization, and more with other community administrators. Get advice and ideas, discuss strategy, etc. I own it, so you can talk about the book and find me there.

CommunityPromotion.com (http://www.communitypromotion.com)
This is a database of community promotion tips that I run. Stop by to share and/or get ideas for your own community.

DeveloperCube (http://www.developercube.com)
This is my web development community and a place where you can start discussions related to this book.

DomainTools (http://www.domaintools.com)
DomainTools is a handy site where you can find out who owns or hosts a domain name or IP, which is helpful if you are looking to report abuse or take down a content thief.

Managing Online Forums Book Website (http://www.managingonlineforums.com)
This is the book's website. It features many resources related to the book, such as a downloadable set of blank, general templates for guidelines and contact templates (also featured in appendix B); an example community setup; book information; updates; links; and more.

ManagingCommunities.com (http://www.managingcommunities.com)
This blog, written by me, features random community-management-related posts and information.

PlagiarismToday (http://www.plagiarismtoday.com)
Written by Jonathan Bailey, PlagiarismToday is an extremely useful blog dedicated to plagiarism, content theft, and copyright online.

ProBlogger (http://www.problogger.net)
Written by Darren Rowse, ProBlogger is a blog dedicated to helping bloggers earn money. However, many of the strategies that are discussed can be applied to community forums, as well.

SitePoint (http://www.sitepoint.com)
SitePoint is one of the most popular web development and design-related content sites and communities on the Internet. There is an abundance of related topics here as well as many useful articles. Their community is also a great place to ask questions. I'm an active contributor.

Blank General Templates

In this section, you will find a series of blank, general templates for user guidelines, staff member guidelines, and contact templates. These are also available in a downloadable archive from the book's website (http://www.managingon lineforums.com). Although you should craft your own for your specific needs, you are welcome to use these. The parts that you need to fill in, at the bare minimum, are in bold, capital letters and in angle brackets.

When referring to a page or section of your website, you should link to that page or section on your first mention (or in the place that it makes the most sense) in that particular document. For instance, when you say "contact us," link "contact us" to your e-mail address or a page where users can contact you. This saves everyone time.

These examples are written from the perspective of being inside of a post or message from or by the administrator. Depending on your needs, you may need to change "me" or "I" to "the administrator" or something similar.

User Guidelines

This is a set of user guidelines that cover participation in your community.

Participation in the <**YOUR SITE'S NAME**> website constitutes agreement to the following guidelines, which apply to posts, profile information, avatars, signatures, any other content on this site and participation in general. This includes private messages, which we have the ability to read, but only do so when a violation is reported to us or we have a legitimate reason. Although rare, it does happen.

Because of the live nature of the discussions on this community, it is not possible for us to review and/or confirm the accuracy or validity of a message before it is posted. If you believe that someone has violated our User Guidelines or you have spotted content that may otherwise require attention, please send a private message to me or a staff member with a link to the content and a brief description of what you believe is wrong. Notification is voluntary and anonymous, but in no case should a user respond to a situation personally, thereby aggravating the situation further. Responding to a violation in an inflammatory manner is a violation in itself and will result in appropriate action.

This is a for profit website that will attempt to generate revenue through avenues that we deem appropriate. Any content that violates our User Guidelines will be removed. Interpretation of our guidelines is at the discretion of the staff.

1. Cross-posting is not allowed and will result in the removal of one or more posts. Cross-posting is defined as posting the same information in two or more locations. When posting your topic, please try to post it in the most appropriate place within the organizational structure of our community. Identical topics posted in the same or different forums will be removed.

2. While member post count has meaning, it should not be taken too seriously. Attempts to artificially increase your post count are prohibited. This includes the mass creation of short or meaningless posts. When participating in game threads such as ''Word Association Game'' or ''What song are you listening to right now?'' please do not post consecutive replies within a short period of time.

3. Advertisements are not allowed. Generally speaking, posts made specifically for the promotion of a website, product or service are considered advertising or, at least, posts made that unnecessarily send people to a website that you are in some way affiliated with. It does not matter if it is a commercial website, a personal website, a non profit website, etc. We do authorize and/or sell adver-

tisements on a case-by-case basis. If you are interested in utilizing this option, please contact us.

All signature links must be kept in your signature in your profile. Anyone found to be posting excessive links to their websites or suspected of using "sneaky" advertising methods is in violation of this guideline. You may only post a link to your site/a site that you are in some way affiliated with if the link specifically answers the question that is being asked and the answer cannot be simply posted without the link. Even then, link directly to the page where the information can be found. General and unnecessary links will be tagged as advertising. If you are found to be excessively posting links to your site (or you appear to be seeking out threads where your link may be relevant, so that you can post it), you may lose the ability to post links to your site.

4. You are not allowed to post an affiliate URL that leads to you earning cash, banner impressions, credits, points, etc. Such links are only allowed in signatures and profiles, but may not be referred to in posts.

5. Do not post personal, real-life information such as home addresses and home phone numbers.

6. As this is an English-speaking community, we require that posted content be in the English language, so that it can be well received and properly monitored.

7. Vulgar language and inappropriate material is not allowed and will be removed. Abbreviations, self censoring, and attempts to circumvent the word censoring feature of the community software also violate this guideline. If your post contains a word that is censored by the software, you must remove that word or the post will be removed. If you feel that the censor is acting in error, please contact us.

We try to maintain a family friendly atmosphere whenever it is possible within the main subject matter of this community. Please keep this in mind when participating.

8. When linking to outside websites, you must ensure that the content of the link is appropriate for our community, in line with the guidelines laid out here. This includes mentioning or referencing a site, even if the mention is not hyperlinked. If you post a link and that link is automatically censored, it is considered to be an inappropriate link and you should remove it from your post immediately. If left, all posts that feature inappropriate links will be removed.

9. Posts that discuss illegal activities, transactions, or websites such as warez, cracks, etc. will be removed. This includes the posting of information that you have obtained illegally.

10. Political and religious discussions are not allowed on this website. If it is believed that the end result of a discussion will be political or religious, the post may be removed. Likewise, strong political and religious sentiments should be kept out of profiles, signatures, and other content.

11. Do not post copyrighted materials (articles, videos, audio, etc.) that you do not have permission to reproduce or distribute. For text articles, most of the time you may quote a small portion of the article (usually no more than 1/5 or 1/6) and you must link to the source (if online) or provide the source (if offline). Posting the entire article, even with the source, constitutes copyright infringement. This is not the place to illegally trade or distribute copyrighted (or those with questionable copyright status) video or audio clips.

12. When posting and linking to images, videos, files, etc., please refrain from hotlinking. This is the direct linking to images (.jpg, .jpeg, .gif, .png, etc.), video (.avi, .mov, .mpg, .mpeg, .wmv, etc.), audio (.mp3, .wav, etc.), archives (.zip, .rar, etc.) or otherwise downloadable or streamable files, on servers that you do not have permission to link to, instead of linking to the page where the item can be found. This includes providing a direct link to the file, even if that file is not embedded into your post. This practice costs the server owner money and resources.

13. Respect is the name of the game. You must respect your fellow members. Please refrain from inflammatory and defamatory comments as well as flaming, taunting, and general disrespect. Do not simply put down the opinion or advice given by others. If you don't agree with it, say why—respectfully. Don't just tell them they're wrong. Do not make uninvited remarks about typos, duplicate posts, posting styles, etc.

    When an opinion-based discussion is being had, do not state things like "there is no argument" as if your opinion is the only one or the only one that matters. When someone has clearly stated their opinion, do not say things like "Are you serious?" and "Are you kidding me?" Remember, this is not a debate club. This is a friendly discussion community. Allow people to have their opinion. No one is to act as some sort of opinion judge, responding to each one to say whether they agree with it or not or whether or not it is a valid, well thought out opinion.

    We do not allow threads to be started to discuss who or what is the most overrated, who or what is your least favorite, etc.

14. Signatures are limited to <**NUMBER**> lines of text. This includes blank lines. No images. The text in the signature may be customized by the BBCode in use on the forums. It is recommended that you stick with readable fonts and colors and

that the size is not too large. You may mention websites and ventures that you are in some way related to, as long as they are otherwise appropriate for this community. Focus on things that you like, not things that you don't.

15. Each user is allowed to create one account. If you would like to change your username, please contact us and, most likely, we can do it for you while you can keep all of your profile data, posts, and other content.

16. Automated account creation, participation, and content scraping is not permitted.

17. We know that people will have to leave our community (of their own free will or otherwise) from time to time and to that end, we do not delete accounts, posts, or other content posted on our community. All content is granted to us with perpetual electronic publishing rights because any content posted on this community becomes a part of the community, even if you no longer are. You may request an item to be removed at any time, but we will decide when and if to remove content from our community. If you wish to no longer be identified with our community, we will be glad to close your account and alter your profile information to remove all identifying characteristics. After account closure, you will no longer be able to participate in this community and this action is not reversible.

18. Moderators and myself have the final say on anything. If you have a problem, you may make a complaint to them directly and not publicly on the website. Creating threads or posts that question or reference administrative decisions or potential administrative decisions, such as post removals and thread closures, is not permitted. We are not perfect and if you feel that we have made a mistake, please privately contact a staff member and we will review the situation. If you would like a copy of your removed post so that you can adjust it and repost, please contact us. As long as we wouldn't prefer you to simply start over, we'll be glad to send you a copy.

19. Whenever you are participating in this community, please keep in mind that we strive to create a fun, friendly and inviting atmosphere. So, please have fun and enjoy the forums!

Freedom of speech rights do not extend to privately owned websites, such as this one. These guidelines detail the types of behavior and activities that are allowed here.

If a user violates our guidelines and shows a disregard for them, our staff and our community, they run the risk of losing their account. We reserve the right to deactivate any account and to edit or remove any content without warning. These guidelines are subject to change at any time without notice.

Do you have a question about our User Guidelines or anything else? Do you have a suggestion? Do you want to offer some feedback? Or are you experiencing some trouble with the site? Well, no matter what it is, please do not hesitate to contact us and we will be glad to help in any way that we can.

Thank you for visiting <**YOUR SITE'S NAME**>.

Staff Member Guidelines

This is a set of guidelines that detail the responsibilities of your staff members as well as your expectations of them.

<**YOUR SITE'S NAME**> moderators must work within these guidelines.

Qualities

You must possess leadership capabilities, a good attitude, kind demeanor, good speaking and grammar skills (you must be able to communicate clearly in English), basic understanding of the features of the community software, the ability to stimulate discussion, distinguish a violation of our User Guidelines and aggressively moderate this community, work in a team environment and, finally, have pride in your work and be dedicated to the success of <**YOUR SITE'S NAME**>.

It's required that staff members provide me with their real name for display on our staff page as well as a current mailing address, at all times (it can be work, P.O. Box, home, etc. just as long as it reaches you).

Participation

<**YOUR SITE'S NAME**> moderators are expected to visit the forums at a minimum of <**NUMBER**> days per week and/or <**NUMBER**> hours per week.

Although you are encouraged to start topics and reply to topics where you see fit, your main function is to make sure that the users of this community are abiding by our User Guidelines.

On your routine visit to this site, you should read a variety of topics—but above all, do not avoid hot button issues just because you are not taking part. Controversial and debatable issues will generally spawn the most violations. So, those are the topics you will want to hit hardest on your visits. Carefully consider each post, but be aggressive in your approach. We can always fix mistakes, but the mistake of leaving a violation in public is one that we want to avoid.

If a user does violate our guidelines, they must be contacted via private message using our Contact Templates.

You should remove any threads and posts that are in violation of our guidelines. You do so by moving them and all of their direct replies to the Trash Bin.

Your moderation tools can be found <**WHERE MODERATION TOOLS CAN BE FOUND**>. When moving a topic, you must select the forum that you want to move it to and decide whether or not to leave a shadow topic. If you are moving the topic to the Trash Bin, do not leave a shadow. If you are moving the topic from a public forum to another public forum, leave a shadow. If you spot a topic that is not posted in the most appropriate forum, please move it to the forum. When splitting a topic, <**PROCESS FOR SPLITTING A TOPIC**>.

If a user makes a reply that violates our guidelines and the thread that they replied to would normally be alright, just remove that post using the split function in the community software. Be sure to remove any posts that reference or were in reply to the post that violated the guidelines. Move it to the Trash Bin. Again, they must be contacted via private message using our Contact Templates. Please note that we do not ever permanently delete posts. Any post that is removed or deleted from public view is moved to the Trash Bin.

If a contact template doesn't exist for the type of violation that you are dealing with, feel free to make one and post it on the Contact Templates thread.

If, during a single visit of yours to the community, you have spotted a user who has violated our guidelines in more than one post or instance, please combine all of the violations into one notification private message. Please do not send private messages one after another for individual violations wherever you can help it. You can help minimize this by completing your routine look throughout the forums and split-

ting off any violations while you do so, leaving them open individually in a separate window or tab and then coming back to them once you have had a complete look through the forums. Then, you can document and handle them as needed. Feel free to combine contact templates to achieve the desired effect of covering various types of violations inside of a single message.

For all violations, be sure to start or respond to the appropriate thread in the Problem Users forum. Every user who violates our User Guidelines has a thread in this forum with their username as the title.

To check if a thread has already been created for a given user, you can use the search function by searching for their exact username and limiting your search to the Problem Users forum.

If a user responds to your private message, help them in the most polite and kind way possible. However, if their message is disrespectful or further violates our User Guidelines—do not respond to the message. Post the entire message in their Problem Users thread and I will handle it.

If a user contacts you via e-mail, instant messenger, etc. in regard to a violation or other sensitive site-related matter, please document it in Problem Users (if appropriate) and then respond to them through the private message system, asking them to correspond with you through private messages instead of e-mail, instant messenger, etc. This allows the conversation to be officially documented and tracked, should something come out of it that requires action.

If a thread is going in circles or getting repetitive (the issue has been talked to death and is at its end), you can close it.

Wherever possible, you should try to keep a thread open and in public. Closing a thread is not an appropriate response to a violation or dispute. Split violations off, take care of them and leave the thread. Do not close a thread and leave the violations in public where they can continue to do harm. They still need to be removed and handled.

Duplicate threads posted in the same forum within a short period of time and duplicate posts posted on the same thread within a short period of time are not considered violations. They are to be considered accidents. Simply move the thread(s)/split the post(s) off into the Trash Bin and reply to the newly created thread in the Trash Bin noting that it was a duplicate or make "Duplicate" the subject of the thread when splitting. There is no need to document in Problem Users or send a private message.

If a user repeatedly violates our guidelines and shows a disregard for the staff of

the site, it is a possibility that they will be banned. However, it is I alone that will make this distinction and until I do, just handle all violations as business as usual. Please do not make assertions as to who should be banned and who shouldn't.

If, at any time, you have an issue with another staff member or feel that they may have made a serious mistake, please contact me privately and I will handle it. Do not confront your fellow staff members on any serious issues. If you have a post removed, a decision that you made is reversed or you are otherwise corrected, please do not take it personally. Please make a note of it to prevent it from happening again and ask questions to further understand, if necessary.

Please consult our Situations Guide for further, more specific information on the handling and distinguishing of certain types of violations.

You Are an Example

It is important that you realize that you are an example of this community and should carry yourself as such at all times. You should always act in a responsible and polite manner. Do not allow yourself to appear abusive, rude or inappropriate. It is your job to cool down threads—not heat them up.

Our User Guidelines apply to you and then some. You are held to a higher standard than regular members. You should not approach, let alone push, the limitations of our User Guidelines.

To that end, do not publicly discuss action taken against any user. Do not post "I have removed Joe's posts as they were full of vulgarities" or "You have been warned" or "Keep this up and I'll remove your posts" or anything of the sort. We handle all of our business privately. If someone violates our User Guidelines, their posts are removed and we handle it. We do not post about specific actions taken against specific users publicly.

Staff Forums

The staff forums are for current staff members to privately discuss issues relevant to the community. What is said in these forums is to be kept between current staff members only.

If you have any questions about anything at any time, please feel free to contact me via private message or via e-mail at <**YOUR E-MAIL ADDRESS**>.

Thank you for your contributions to <**YOUR SITE'S NAME**>.

Contact Templates

Contact templates are blank templates that your staff members can use to contact users who violate your user guidelines. This helps to ensure consistent communication from staff member to staff member.

Below you will find an example of a contact templates thread in its entirety. This includes the BBCode that is a part of the templates, such as a URL to your user guidelines, so that your staff members can easily copy and paste everything that they need. This may not be the BBCode in use for your particular community software, however, so you may need to make adjustments.

This thread contains contact templates that you should use to contact users in regard to violations of our User Guidelines.

These templates should give you an idea of the type of verbiage to use when you must contact members in regard to violations. Whenever possible, please use the template in its entirety. However, if the template does not fit the violation perfectly or if you are contacting a user in regard to more than one violation, please feel free to combine templates and add additional, consistent wording that follows the usage and tone expressed in the templates posted here. Don't forget to change "post quoted below as it" to "posts quoted below as they" if you are quoting from more than one post.

If a template does not exist for a violation and you feel one would be valuable, please feel free to make one and post it as a reply to this thread. I will take a look at it and approve or deny it and edit it as I see fit.

Pay close attention to the text in between the angle brackets ($<$ and $>$) as that is the text that you need to edit. Do not leave any arrows in the private message. When quoted posts are required, feel free to press the quote button next to the removed post and paste the output in the template, replacing the already existing quote tags, so that you do not have two sets of quote tags.

Thank you.

Copyright Infringement: Text

Hello <USERNAME>,

Thank you for visiting <**YOUR SITE'S NAME**>.

Unfortunately, I have had to remove your post quoted below as it violated our [url=<**LINK TO YOUR USER GUIDELINES**>]User Guidelines[/url] as copyright infringement.

<PASTE THE PORTION THAT VIOLATED OUR GUIDELINES>

When quoting an article or written work that you did not author or do not have permission to reproduce (which is our assumption in this case—if it is incorrect, please let us know and include some way for us to verify this fact), you may only quote a small portion of the article (usually no more than 1/5 or 1/6) and you must link to the source (if online) or provide the source (if offline).

Please keep this in mind to prevent further violations in the future.

Thank you for your time and cooperation.

Sincerely,

<YOUR NAME>
<**YOUR SITE'S NAME**> Moderator

Cross-Posting

Hello <USERNAME>,

Thank you for visiting <**YOUR SITE'S NAME**>.

Unfortunately, I have had to remove your post quoted below as it violated our [url=<**LINK TO YOUR USER GUIDELINES**>]User Guidelines[/url] as cross-posting.

<PASTE THE POST THAT WAS REMOVED>

Cross-posting is posting the same content in two or more locations. Please keep this in mind to prevent further violations in the future.

Thank you for your time and cooperation.

Sincerely,

<YOUR NAME>
<**YOUR SITE'S NAME**> Moderator

General

Hello <USERNAME>,

Thank you for visiting <**YOUR SITE'S NAME**>.

Unfortunately, I have had to remove your post quoted below as it violated our [url=<**LINK TO YOUR USER GUIDELINES**>]User Guidelines[/url] as <DESCRIPTION OF VIOLATION>.

<PASTE THE PORTION THAT VIOLATED OUR GUIDELINES>

Please keep this in mind to prevent further violations in the future.

Thank you for your time and cooperation.

Sincerely,

<YOUR NAME>
<**YOUR SITE'S NAME**> Moderator

Hotlinking

Hello <USERNAME>,

Thank you for visiting <**YOUR SITE'S NAME**>.

Unfortunately, I have had to remove your post quoted below as it violated our [url=<**LINK TO YOUR USER GUIDELINES**>]User Guidelines[/url] as hotlinking.

<PASTE THE PORTION THAT VIOLATED OUR GUIDELINES>

Hotlinking is when you link directly to a graphic, video, audio clip, archive (.zip, .rar, etc.) or otherwise downloadable or streamable file instead of linking to the page where that item can be found. Generally, people place this content on their websites as a means to bring people to those websites. When you link directly to the file, the person clicking the link does not visit the site, while using the site owner's bandwidth, which costs money and/or resources. Instead, you must link to the page where this content can be found, rather than directly to the content itself. This is unless you have permission to link directly to the content or the site owner has posted on their site that it's allowed. If this is the case, please provide us with information that allows us to verify it.

Please keep this in mind to prevent further violations in the future.

Thank you for your time and cooperation.

Sincerely,

<YOUR NAME>
<**YOUR SITE'S NAME**> Moderator

Inappropriate

Hello <USERNAME>,

Thank you for visiting <**YOUR SITE'S NAME**>.

Unfortunately, I have had to remove your post quoted below as it violated our [url=<**LINK TO YOUR USER GUIDELINES**>]User Guidelines[/url] as inappropriate <DESCRIBE WHY IT WAS INAPPROPRIATE>.

<PASTE THE PORTION THAT VIOLATED OUR GUIDELINES>

Please keep this in mind to prevent further violations in the future.

Thank you for your time and cooperation.

Sincerely,

<YOUR NAME>
<**YOUR SITE'S NAME**> Moderator

Inflammatory

Hello <USERNAME>,

Thank you for visiting <**YOUR SITE'S NAME**>.

Unfortunately, I have had to remove your post quoted below as it violated our [url=<**LINK TO YOUR USER GUIDELINES**>]User Guidelines[/url] as inflammatory.

<PASTE THE PORTION THAT VIOLATED OUR GUIDELINES>

Generally speaking, when a post is inflammatory, it isn't adding much to the thread outside of hostility.

Please keep this in mind to prevent further violations in the future.

Thank you for your time and cooperation.

Sincerely,

<YOUR NAME>
<**YOUR SITE'S NAME**> Moderator

Report, Don't Respond: No Violation in Response

If the post they responded to was not actually a violation, please remove ''as it was in response to a post that had to be removed as it violated our [url=<**LINK TO YOUR USER GUIDELINES**>]User Guidelines[/url]''.

Hello <USERNAME>,

Thank you for visiting <**YOUR SITE'S NAME**>.

Unfortunately, I have had to remove your post quoted below as it was in response to a post that had to be removed as it violated our [url=<**LINK TO YOUR USER GUIDELINES**>]User Guidelines[/url].

<PASTE THE POST THAT WAS REMOVED>

In the future, if you feel a post may be against our User Guidelines or may otherwise require some sort of attention, you should always report it through [url=<**LINK TO YOUR CONTACT PAGE**>]e-mail[/url] or send me or another member of staff a private message. After you have done so, forget that the post exists (do not reply to it further, even to say that you have reported it). We will then handle it appropriately.

We appreciate when members inform us of violations to our User Guidelines, rather then responding to them and making the situation worse.

Thank you for your time and cooperation.

Sincerely,

<YOUR NAME>
<**YOUR SITE'S NAME**> Moderator

Report, Don't Respond: Violation in Response

If the post they responded to was not actually a violation, please remove "In this post, you were responding to a post that violated our User Guidelines."

Hello <USERNAME>,

Thank you for visiting <**YOUR SITE'S NAME**>.

Unfortunately, I have had to remove your post quoted below as it violated our [url=<**LINK TO YOUR USER GUIDELINES**>]User Guidelines[/url] as <DESCRIPTION OF VIOLATION>.

<PASTE THE PORTION THAT VIOLATED OUR GUIDELINES>

Please keep this in mind to prevent further violations in the future.

In this post, you were responding to a post that violated our User Guidelines. In the future, if you feel a post may be against our User Guidelines or may otherwise require some sort of attention, you should always report it through [url=<**LINK TO YOUR CONTACT PAGE**>]e-mail[/url] or send me or another member of staff a private message. After you have done so, forget that the post exists (do not reply to it further, even to say that you have reported it). We will then handle it appropriately.

We appreciate when members inform us of violations to our User Guidelines, rather then responding to them and making the situation worse.

Thank you for your time and cooperation.

Sincerely,

<YOUR NAME>
<**YOUR SITE'S NAME**> Moderator

Signature: General

Hello <USERNAME>,

Thank you for visiting <**YOUR SITE'S NAME**>.

Unfortunately, your signature is currently in violation of our [url=<**LINK TO YOUR USER GUIDELINES**>]User Guidelines[/url] as <DESCRIPTION OF VIOLATION>.

<PASTE THE PORTION THAT VIOLATED OUR GUIDELINES>

Please adjust your signature as soon as you can and please keep this in mind to prevent further violations in the future.

Thank you for your time and cooperation.

Sincerely,

<YOUR NAME>
<YOUR SITE'S NAME> Moderator

Signature: Too Long

Hello <USERNAME>,

Thank you for visiting **<YOUR SITE'S NAME>**.

Your signature is currently <NUMBER> lines long, which is in violation of our [url=**<LINK TO YOUR USER GUIDELINES>**]User Guidelines[/url], which only allow for **<NUMBER>** lines.

Please adjust your signature as soon as you can and please keep this in mind to prevent further violations in the future.

Thank you for your time and cooperation.

Sincerely,

<YOUR NAME>
<YOUR SITE'S NAME> Moderator

Site-Related Feedback, Problem/Error Reports, Etc. Posted in Forums

Hello <USERNAME>,

Thank you for visiting **<YOUR SITE'S NAME>**.

Unfortunately, I have had to remove your post quoted below.

<PASTE THE POST THAT WAS REMOVED>

We ask that all site-related feedback, questions, problem/error reports and the like be sent via [url=<**LINK TO YOUR CONTACT PAGE**>]e-mail[/url] or private message so that we do not miss them and can handle them in the most efficient manner possible. Please be sure to keep this in mind for the future.

<PROVIDE ANSWER TO THEIR QUESTION, IF POSSIBLE—IF YOU DO NOT KNOW THE ANSWER OR CANNOT ANSWER, LEAVE THE FOLLOWING> <**ADMINISTRATOR'S NAME**>, our administrator, will be in touch with you as soon as possible regarding your post.

Thank you for your time and cooperation.

Sincerely,

<YOUR NAME>
<**YOUR SITE'S NAME**> Moderator

Vulgar

Hello <USERNAME>,

Thank you for visiting <**YOUR SITE'S NAME**>.

Unfortunately, I have had to remove your post quoted below as it violated our [url=<**LINK TO YOUR USER GUIDELINES**>]User Guidelines[/url] as vulgar.

<PASTE THE PORTION THAT VIOLATED OUR GUIDELINES>

Please note that if we do not allow a word or term, we do not allow a word or term—it doesn't matter if it is abbreviated or self-censored.

Please keep this in mind to prevent further violations in the future.

Thank you for your time and cooperation.

Sincerely,

<YOUR NAME>
<**YOUR SITE'S NAME**> Moderator

Glossary

Here is a list of commonly used terms mentioned in this book that you are likely to come across in the management of your community.

.htaccess: On Apache servers, this a directory configuration file, allowing you to define how requests to that directory (or folder) are handled. Without getting technical, it can do things like require a username and password to access the directory and customize error messages.

Administrator: Generally, the person in charge of a community. It can also refer to administrator powers, as in being denoted as an administrator by the community software.

Affiliate link: A link that leads to an affiliate (someone associated with a program) earning cash, points or some sort of credit for clicks on or actions made through the link.

Avatar: A picture or graphic that a member uploads to their account that is displayed on the community, frequently next to their posts and on their profile, in addition to other places. What is depicted in the image varies wildly by member. It can be a picture of them, something that reflects an interest they have (music group, sports team, TV show, hobby, etc.) or something that has just struck their fancy for whatever reason.

Ban: Banning is the act of blocking something or (more commonly) someone from your community. When someone disregards your guidelines and/or warnings, you have no choice but to prevent them from doing so in the future—hence, banning them.

BBCode: Formatting code that is used on your community, usually in posts and signatures. This code can be used to change the look of text (size, color, style, place it in a special box to offset it, etc.), create a hyperlink, display an image in line and more.

Bot: Something that interacts with your community in an automated fashion. These can be used for good (automatically posting articles from your content section to your forums) and for bad (the mass creation of posts or posting of advertisements).

Bumping: The act of posting a reply onto an existing thread (usually one that has not been active recently or in the past few days, at least) for the explicit purpose of placing the thread back on the active topics list once again so that more people see it, hence bumping it back up to the top of the list of topics in forums and searches. Posts that bump threads are generally posts that add nothing new to the thread outside of a pointless reply. Sometimes these are acceptable and sometimes they are not.

Closed thread: A thread that is no longer open to reply.

Content thief: Someone who steals content from your community, usually posting it at another website without permission.

Crontab: Without getting technical, a means of automating commands on your server. They can be used to automatically process tedious tasks on a schedule, so you don't have to mess with them. This includes things like exporting a copy of your database, running a file that repairs a table in your database and more.

Cross-posting: Posting the same content in two or more forums or threads on your community. Sometimes this is alright, such as when one person answers the same question, posed by two different people, twice. But, other than cases like that, a post generally belongs in one place or another.

Duplicate post: An identical post made more than one time on the same thread. Often times, this is done by accident. But, other times, it's done by an attention seeker looking to get more people to look at his post.

Duplicate thread: An identical thread posted more than one time in a single forum. Similar to a duplicate post, this is commonly done as an accident, but not always.

Flaming: Personally attacking or insulting someone.

Flood controls: A method to curb flooding, generally through preventing two posts to be made by the same user within a specified period of time.

Flooding:	Posting multiple (and perhaps many, many) undesirable messages within a short period of time. They can be undesirable for any number of reasons—maybe they are all the same, they are rude and disrespectful (trolling) or they disrupt your community in general. Private messages can be flooded, as well.
Forum:	Though it can be used to mean the community as a whole, it's mostly used in this book (and perhaps more commonly) to mean a single forum within a community that features multiple forums. Forums are used to organize threads on your site. For example, on a sports site, you may have a baseball forum and a football forum. Baseball threads go in the baseball forum, football threads go in the football forum and so on.
Hack:	There are different definitions for the word hack. Of course, there is the meaning of it being some sort of unauthorized or illegal entry into a system. But, it can also have a positive meaning. Hacks are code modifications that can be made to your community software to add new functions or features, adjust the site in some way or otherwise improve it in line with the wishes of the administrator.
Hotlinking:	Also referred to as bandwidth theft, this is the act of linking directly to files (most commonly images or videos) on a website or server from your server without permission. Generally speaking, people place these files on their websites so that people will have a reason to visit them. Linking directly to them circumvents this and costs the server owner money and resources with no benefit. Instead of directly linking to files, you should link to the pages on that site that have those files (or links to those files) on them.
Internet Protocol (IP) Address:	Without getting technical, suffice to say that everyone online has an IP address associated with them or, more specifically, the network that they are connected to the Internet through. Their IP address can change and is most likely not unique to them alone. However, these addresses are valuable because they can help you to track the actions of users on your site and to identify and deal with troublemakers.
Merged thread:	When you have two topics started on the same subject that may seamlessly fit together you can combine them into one, cohesive thread.
Moved thread:	A thread that has been moved from one forum to another, so that it resides in the most appropriate forum on your community.
Permissions:	A system that controls the level of access that various types of members have on your community. This can include the ability to view forums, view posts, post new threads, post replies, edit posts, post polls, moderate, and plenty more. Permissions vary by member level. For example, a guest

might only be able to view while a member will be able to view and post and a moderator will be able to do all that, plus have access to the moderator functions.

Post: A single message posted on a thread.

Private message: A message sent directly from one member to another member or group of members, viewable only to them.

Registration: The act of creating an account on your community. During registration, users can pick their username, provide an e-mail address to be associated with their account, define their password, enter personal details and more.

Removed post: A post that has been removed from public or registered member viewing on your community and is now only viewable to members of staff or the administrator.

Reported post: A post that has been reported by a member as being a potential violation of your guidelines or in need of attention from a staff member in some way.

Scraper: For the purpose of this book (and in most cases), a scraper is someone or something that takes (scrapes) content from your community in an unauthorized fashion, placing it on another site or in another format. Scraping can be authorized, of course, assuming the copyright holder(s) give such authorization.

Shadow topic: When a topic is moved from one forum to another, a shadow topic can be left in the old forum, so that anyone looking for the thread there can find it in it's new location. A shadow topic link looks just like other topic links, except that there is some sort of text denoting that it has been moved.

Signature: An image or portion of text that appears at the bottom of a user's posts, private messages and perhaps elsewhere on your community. Common signature elements include a user's name, contact information, their job and/or title, websites, something related to their hobbies, a favorite quote, etc.

Smilie: Most commonly a graphic depicting an emotion in the form of a face. For example, a smiling face would mean that you are happy or that you smiled when you read or said something.

Spam: Spam has adopted a very wide meaning. If someone posts a bunch of unwanted messages, some people call it spam. If someone posts an advertisement, that can be called spam. If someone posts the same message many times, that is also called spam. The same goes for those things happening via private message or e-mail through your site.

Spidering:	Also known as crawling, without getting technical, spidering is the indexing of content by search engines for listing in their results. Spidering has other uses, but this is how it is used in this book and is, most likely, the most common usage that you will run into.
Split post:	A post that is split off from an existing thread in order to be removed or to create a new thread. For example, if a thread goes off topic, you may split all of the posts that took it off topic and place them in their own thread, creating two unique threads.
Sticky thread:	A thread that is always stuck to the top of a forum, displayed even before topics that have been more recently active than it.
Syndication:	As used in this book, when you make web feeds (such as the RSS file format) available so that content from your community (such as threads with new posts) can be viewed and tracked outside of your community, generally through a feed reader.
Thread:	Also referred to as a topic, this is a collection of posts (though it starts with and can contain only one post—the first one in the thread) grouped together, usually due to their common interest. The first post in the thread generally sets the subject of the thread. Unless the thread is closed, users are then able to reply to the first post (and to each other) with each post displaying on that same thread, usually divided into pages with a certain number of posts per page.
Troll:	Someone who purposely posts messages that are disrespectful, controversial or that disagree with the intent of annoying or angering other members.
User group:	A method of linking a set of people for interaction or activities related only to people in that group. On a community, it may mean a group for moderators (where permissions for people in that group are those of moderator permissions), a group of people who receive the community newsletter, a group of premium members or something else.
User profile:	A section that displays information related to a specific member. This can include things such as their instant messenger usernames, interests, occupation, signature, avatar, a link to view all of their posts and much more.
User title:	A title associated with a given member, often displayed under their username next to their posts and elsewhere. It's also called a rank title when it denotes the "rank" that someone has on your community. For example, a rank title can be dependent on the number of posts someone has or, in the case of a staff member, could display the title that you give your moderators or other members of your staff.

Username: The alias or handle that a member adopts on your community, associating them with all of their contributions.

Welcome message: A message shown to guests (or users who are not logged in) on your community, usually imploring them to register.

Word censoring: The utilization of your community software to prevent a word or term from being posted.

Index

About the Author

Patrick O'Keefe is a writer, web developer, and community administrator who has been professionally developing websites since 1998 and managing online communities since 2000. Beyond just being the administrator, however, he's spent substantial amounts of time contributing to communities from all angles, as a member, staff member, and owner.

He founded and owns the iFroggy Network (http://www.ifroggy.com), an Internet network featuring several communities, including SportsForums.net, KarateForums.com, phpBBHacks.com, DeveloperCube (http://www.developer cube.com), CommunityAdmins.com, PhotoshopForums.com, and BadBoyForums .com

Besides writing content for the entire iFroggy Network, he has actively written editorials, news pieces, and product reviews for several websites of varying interests, including SitePoint, where he is an Advisor (moderator) in the SitePoint Forums. He writes for multiple blogs, including YanksBlog.com, Managing Communities.com, and Bad Boy Blog (http://www.badboyblog.com), and he maintains a personal blog (http://www.patrickokeefe.com).

He wrote the foreword for *Building Online Communities with phpBB*, the first book ever published about phpBB, and served as a technical reviewer for the book. He was also a reviewer for *Volume I: Foundations* and *Volume II: Applications* of *PHP Anthology* and for the book *Blog Marketing*.

He presently resides in Harbinger, North Carolina.